FRIENDS

The Cultural History of Television

FRIENDS

A Cultural History

Jennifer C. Dunn

ROWMAN & LITTLEFIELD
Lanham • Boulder • New York • London

Published by Rowman & Littlefield
An imprint of The Rowman & Littlefield Publishing Group, Inc.
4501 Forbes Boulevard, Suite 200, Lanham, Maryland 20706
www.rowman.com

6 Tinworth Street, London SE11 5AL

British Library Cataloguing in Publication Information Available

Library of Congress Cataloging-in-Publication Data

Names: Dunn, Jennifer C., author.
Title: Friends : a cultural history / Jennifer Dunn.
Description: Lanham : Rowman & Littlefield, 2019. | Series: The cultural history of television |
    Includes bibliographical references and index.
Identifiers: LCCN 2019017657 (print) | LCCN 2019018434 (ebook) | ISBN 9781538112748 (Elec-
    tronic) | ISBN 9781538112731 (cloth : alk. paper)
Subjects: LCSH: Friends (Television program)
Classification: LCC PN1992.77.F76 (ebook) | LCC PN1992.77.F76 D86 2019 (print) | DDC 791.45/
    72—dc23
LC record available at https://lccn.loc.gov/2019017657

♾ ™ The paper used in this publication meets the minimum requirements of
American National Standard for Information Sciences Permanence of Paper for
Printed Library Materials, ANSI/NISO Z39.48-1992.

CONTENTS

ACKNOWLEDGMENTS

When you write a book about *Friends*, you must acknowledge your friends. First and foremost, the friends and family who share my passion for *Friends*: my husband, Anthony Cervone; my Dudette, LeeAnne Mathews; and my brother, Jeff Dunn. Thank you for being the Joey, Phoebe/ Rachel, and Chandler to my Monica/Ross and watching and rewatching every episode with me. You are the reasons that I can still find people to play *Friends* trivia games with me. Additionally, I must thank my mother-in-law, Carol Cervone, and my friends Molly and Anne Marie Loutos for being my "Way, No Way" *Friends* trivia team. We will get first place next time.

Some people have one or two good friends and others have many. I have been lucky enough to have groups of friends whom I met at particular points in my life, who have had significant impacts on me, and who have stayed with me in one way or another through my life. From the Dudettes—Kaetea, Kahele, LeeAnne, Lori, Rachel, Sabrina, and Suzanne—who shaped my high school years to my Comm-rades—Danielle, Jimmie, Kathy, Michelle, Stephanie, and Tony—who influence my work, career, and personal life today, and from my college debate teammates and opponents to my international travel cohorts in Japan, Guatemala, and Germany, you have all helped me to discover who I am, who I want to be, and what I should strive for. Thank you for being my friends and making my life better.

I also want to thank the friends and colleagues who helped bring this book to print. First, to Bob Batchelor and Kathleen Turner for introducing me to Stephen Ryan and showing me that one of the best ways to get a book published is to sit down and talk it through with an acquisitions editor. Those conversations are the ones where you learn that no one has yet written a cultural history of your favorite television series. I also want to thank Kathleen for reading early versions of chapters to give me feedback. Finally, to Stephen Ryan and Deni Remsberg, for their feedback, patience, and support through the publication process.

Finally, while this book includes the best of *Friends*, it also critiques the less-than-perfect qualities of the series. Even so, I want to thank everyone who worked on the show, from the producers and stars to the assistant directors and production assistants. You all created a series that has become a constant friend to me. Your work comforts me when I am down, brings my friends and family together, and is, as cliché as it may sound, always there for me.

INTRODUCTION

Friends and "Must-See TV"

On May 6, 2004, 52.5 million viewers—the fourth-largest audience for a television series finale—tuned in to say good-bye to a series with which they had had an enduring relationship for ten years and, probably, to see if Ross and Rachel finally got together. *Friends* starting position in the NBC Thursday "Must See TV" lineup from 1995 to 2004 alone cemented its place in television history. Its focus on the relationships between six twenty-somethings living on their own in New York City changed the sitcom genre itself.

Before *Friends* came along, most sitcoms focused on the home or work "situation" and the hijinks of the family or workmates for the "comedy." The very first sitcom, *Mary Kay and Johnny* (1947–1950), cast the mold for family sitcoms from *The Adventures of Ozzie and Harriet* (1952–1966) and *Leave It to Beaver* (1957–1963) to *Modern Family* (2009–present) and *black-ish* (2014–present). Workplace sitcoms provided opportunities for both men's and women's work outside the home to be the butt of the jokes in early series like *The Gale Storm Show* (1956–1960), well-known fare like *The Mary Tyler Moore Show* (1970–1977), and more recent mockumentary-style shows in settings like *The Office* (2005–2013) and the White House in *Veep* (2012–present).

Originally titled *Six of One*,[1] *Friends*, for the most part, takes the parents, children, and workmates out of the picture and focuses on six twenty-something friends who say they will be there for each other no matter what. The story begins in the coffee shop, Central Perk, where four friends sit drinking coffee and chatting about nothing special. Lovelorn Monica tells the others about a date she has planned that night. Sarcastic Chandler reveals his mommy issues when he tells the others about a recent dream. Phoebe shows that she is the quirky, holistic one with comments about an ex who eats chalk and her attempts to cleanse Ross's aura. When morose Ross enters, we learn that his marriage just ended because his wife realized she is a lesbian. Womanizer Joey suggests the solution to Ross's problem: strip club. A short time later, the sixth friend and final member of the ensemble, Rachel, enters in her wedding dress. She exposes her spoiled, privileged background when she explains that she left her husband-to-be at the altar because she was more excited by the gifts she was getting for the wedding than getting married to him. Unlike that other series supposedly about nothing (*Seinfeld*, 1989–1998), *Friends* is about these people, their relationships, and their support for one another. It is as simple as that. In just one episode, the stage is set to explore how they serve as each other's support system and changed television sitcoms forever.

Although its initial audience testing was less than stellar, within one year of being on air, *Friends* moved to the 8 p.m. time slot in the NBC "Must See TV" lineup, where it stayed through the rest of its run. *Friends* became one of the last "blockbuster" series. In its second year, it aired an hour episode, "The One after the Superbowl," on January 28, 1996, which drew in 52.9 million viewers. The unexpected ratings success of *Friends* inspired television producers to try to replicate it. In their attempts, NBC and other networks created shorter-lived and lower-rated shows like *Suddenly Susan* (1996–2000), *Veronica's Closet* (1997–2000), *Jesse* (1998–2000), and even the Ellen DeGeneres–led, literally named *These Friends of Mine*, which after its first season changed its name to *Ellen* (1994–1998). Despite different settings and actors, the idea was the same: groups of friends acting as each other's family and support networks. This model continues to shape television sitcoms made today, with varying degrees of success for broadcast network shows such as *Happy Endings* (2011–2013), *New Girl* (2011–2018), and *The Big Bang Theory* (2007–2019) and cable and streaming series such as *Girls* (2012–2017), *You're the Worst* (2014–2019), *Unbreakable Kimmy Schmidt* (2015–present), *The Guild* (2007–2013), and *Difficult People* (2015–2019). Family and workplace sitcoms are still developed and air, but they are joined by these shows that share the focus on groups of friends who hang out with one another, whose families are rarely if ever seen, and who turn to one another when in need.

The relationships of the *Friends* provide audiences with people and experiences to relate to. This was true when the show first aired and still is true as it continues to air in syndication (it has never been off TV) and via streaming services such as Netflix where all the episodes are still available to anyone with a subscription. When we first see that Ross's high school crush on Rachel lingers, we get it. When Ross and Rachel first kiss, we cheer them on just as we all want that kind of romance and fulfillment in our own lives. We all wish we had a quirky friend like Phoebe to make up songs about mundane activities to make our days more enjoyable (I still sing "Lather, Rinse, Repeat/As Needed" when I shower). When Joey finally falls in love, we think about all the bad boys and seemingly unobtainable womanizers and hope they, too, will find love and "settle down." While I may not want to admit that I have tried to keep my partygoers' activities organized like Monica, when they want to escape her party, I realize how sometimes I, too, can be a killjoy. And who doesn't want Chandler's wit? Seeing how Rachel or Monica fail to deliver a punchline the way he does is something any one of us unfunny people can relate to.

Tuning in to a television show week after week for ten years becomes a relatable and memorable experience. Add to those initial viewings the reruns we watched, the syndicated airings since, and continued viewings on Netflix, and it is no wonder why analyzing and understanding a show like *Friends* is important. Their relationships provide models for us to aspire to with our own friends and even lessons about what not to do. As Anne Marie Todd explains it:

> Families organize their living rooms around the television set; people arrange their schedules around favorite shows; and fans discuss and dissect what happened in last night's episode. Helping shape beliefs, attitudes and values, television has made entertainment itself the natural format for the representation of all experience.[2]

In other words, the stories the show tells, its popularity, and its enduring presence and appeal to multiple generations of fans make a series like *Friends* an important site in which to examine the cultural values, beliefs, and practices that are promoted on television. In this way, we can better understand how television reflects and constructs our culture.

As part of a series about the cultural history of television, I hope that this book will provide insights into *Friends* as an intellectual and imaginative work that both reflects and constructs human thought and experience. Whether you're a fan who has watched the show a million times or a newcomer who has just begun to stream it, there is something in this book for you. For repeat viewers, perhaps you will see details, examples, and insights that provide a deeper way of watching, just as the text may provide newcomers with a primer for how to watch a twenty-five-year-old show. I must warn frequent-viewing fans though: this book is far from comprehensive. There are just too many examples, episodes, and ideas to fit into just one volume. So I ask you to forgive me if I left out any of your favorites and to enjoy the examples and ideas that are included.

The first section develops the discussion from this introduction further to show how *Friends* impacted sitcoms and the television landscape when it came out. The first chapter discusses how the series changed the television landscape by representing an ensemble of twenty-somethings who stuck together on- and off-screen and popularized "hang-out TV." Chapter 2 explores *Friends* and the actors' places in celebrity culture. Chapter 3 indicates how the series reimagined televisual families to focus on chosen kinship relationships rather than blood ones. The second section interrogates cultural identities represented on *Friends*, including the characters' lackadaisical attitudes toward work (chapter 4), the anti-intellectual strain of humor (chapter 5), and the ways the series depicted intersectional issues of identity, such as race, ethnicity, and body image (chapter 6) and gender and sexuality (chapter 7). The final section of the book turns its attention to ongoing fan interactions with the show through the accumulation of popular-culture capital—including the music, fashions, and coffeehouse culture—in chapter 8; their creation of alternative narratives (chapter 9); and the impacts catchphrases, fan creations, products, experiences, and intertextual worlds created by the stars post-*Friends* projects still have on original and new fans of the show (chapter 10).

Finally, writing this book involved a process of sharing my own fan perspective of the show as interpreted through a critical eye. As such, I have gained a new understanding of a series I thought I knew backward and forward. I hope that in reading the book you gain new insights (whether you agree with mine or not) of a show that shaped our cultural landscape in ways we rarely recognize. I also hope that in engaging with the show in this way, you may enjoy the series anew.

I

FRIENDS CHANGES THE
SITCOM LANDSCAPE

When *Friends* premiered in 1994, traditional television viewing continued to play a dominant role in most Americans' lives: families organized
their living rooms around the TV set; people scheduled their lives around
what nights their favorite shows were on, whether they watched it live or
had to set their VCRs (later DVRs) to record it; and fans discussed what
happened on the previous night's episodes when they saw each other at
work the next day.[1] Television shapes people's attitudes, beliefs, and
values by making "entertainment itself the natural format for the representation of all experience."[2] People are attracted to what they see on
television as it communicates the familiar. Viewers see character types
and lifestyles that they identify with, or if they do not see themselves,
they are afforded a glimpse into the lives of people, places, values, and
actions that they believe to be representative of real life, or a "metaphorical real world" that "reflects, symbolically, the structure of values and
relationships beneath the surface."[3] Seeing these characters' stories on
the screen in their living rooms makes viewers feel as if they are sharing
their own private lives with the characters, which results in a merging of
experiences between the public and the private.[4] *Friends* is considered a
classic around the globe because of its "blend of perfectly timed comedy
and striking realism."[5] The series invites viewers to identify with its
ensemble of young people living on their own, without parental guidance,
just hanging out. In this way, *Friends* made one of its major cultural

impacts by challenging traditional formatting and content of the sitcom genre.

AMERICAN SITUATION COMEDIES

The situation comedy began when commercial television programming started in earnest after the end of World War II when American consumers could afford to buy their own television sets for their homes. A situation comedy, or sitcom, includes several distinctive characteristics, including its episodic narrative structure, focus on the family, and comedic tone. Sitcoms are usually a half an hour.[6] Although there may be narrative arcs that span multiple episodes and seasons, within each episode, typically, "the status quo is disrupted, and remains that way until the end of the episode where a 'reset' of the original situation is achieved."[7] This formula is reflected no matter the subgenre the series belongs to: domestic comedies (domcoms), kidcoms, couplecoms, scificoms, ethnicoms, or career coms.[8] Regardless of the subgenre, the premise in almost all sitcoms is that the family is the most important unit. The family need not be a biological one; it could be a group of people who live or work together and serve as one another's family. The "companion message to the one projected by the sitcom's structure" remains "acceptance into the group or family is part of the serenity of a changeless situation."[9]

While not the most popular genre (that honor belonged to the variety show), early sitcoms provided the comfort food of television by focusing on families and their home lives, including the bumbling father looking out of place in the home (when he would look much more at home at work), the mother trying to keep the father and children in check, and the shenanigans of the children. The most popular and long running of these early sitcoms was *I Love Lucy* (1951–1957). While *Lucy*'s primary focus was not on children, Lucy and her best friend Ethel's attempts at entering Lucy's husband Ricky's world provided enough childish hijinks for the show. *I Love Lucy* was also the first sitcom to change the genre from its origins by filming in California rather than New York and filming episodes with three cameras in front of a live audience in sequence rather than performing live;[10] and it was even first to show a pregnant woman on-screen as fictional Lucy Ricardo's pregnancy became one with Lucille Ball's real-life pregnancy.

The 1960s saw a rise in the number of sitcoms, which were focused on either the home (e.g., *The Donna Reed Show*, 1958–1966) or workplace (e.g., *The Dick Van Dyke Show*, 1961–1966), primarily the former. In the 1970s and 1980s, workplace comedies increased (e.g., *The Mary Tyler Moore Show*, 1970–1977, and *M*A*S*H*, 1972–1983) and family sitcoms continued (e.g., *All in the Family*, 1971–1979; *The Jeffersons*, 1975–1985). In the 1970s and 1980s, the tradition of building an entire show around a popular comedian exploded (e.g., *The Cosby Show*, 1984–1992, and *Seinfeld*, 1989–1998), while other series focused increasingly on young people's lives more predominantly than their parents (e.g., *The Brady Bunch*, 1969–1974; *Partridge Family*, 1970–1974; *Good Times*, 1974–1979; and *Happy Days*, 1974–1984). Even so, these series always had parents and/or adult role models readily at hand, whether two heterosexual parents or single mothers, maids, managers, or restaurant owners. These older characters served as moral compasses and mentors as the young people attempted to find their way in the world.

One of the first popular shows to focus on young people living and working together was *Laverne and Shirley* (1976–1983). Despite the title characters being two young women living on their own as roommates, Laverne's father still played a role in the show and the series focused on their home and work lives. *Cheers* (1982–1993) marked an expansion of the workplace comedy in that it also included regular characters who did little more than hang out at the bar (the workplace) even though they did not work there. Instead, characters like Norm and Cliff were part of the *Cheers* family as they found solace with the other characters who did work together.

The mid-1970s also saw the emergence of basic cable on the television landscape. No longer were there just three broadcast networks—ABC, CBS, and NBC—with programming. Where most prime-time broadcast shows were designed for an imagined audience of all families eating dinner together and then watching evening television, cable shows did not adhere to the same expectations for ratings as broadcast networks and were designed to appeal to niche markets. By the 1990s, some real effects of the emergence of basic cable and continued dominance of broadcast networks emerged: a bifurcation of programming.[11] Basic cable aired niche programming to attract particular audiences, such as black audiences, with sitcoms such as *Living Single* (FOX, 1993–1998); *Martin* (FOX, 1992–1997); *Sister, Sister* (WB, 1994–1999); *The Parent'hood* (WB, 1995–1999); *Moesha* (UPN, 1996–2001); and *Girlfriends* (UPN, 2000–2008). While broadcast networks suggested their programming appealed to "everyone," the reality was that network sitcoms used white casts they believed appealed to everyone in shows such as *Seinfeld* (NBC, 1989–1998), *Frasier* (NBC, 1993–2004), *Everybody Loves Raymond* (CBS, 1996–2005), *Home Improvement* (CBS, 1991–1999), and *Will & Grace* (NBC, 1998–2006).[12]

One particular niche audience that was defined in the early 1990s was the "slumpy" audience of "socially liberal, urban-minded professionals" ages eighteen to forty-nine.[13] While *Friends* was another sitcom intended to appeal to "everyone," it had particular appeal to its white Generation X viewers who were around the same ages as the characters and the slumpy audience. *Friends* appealed to the characteristics of Gen X in a nondisruptive way (see more in chapter 4) and used strategies, such as the inclusion of gay characters, to appeal to "the slumpy audience's investment in socially liberal politics as 'hip.' With its recurring lesbian characters and apparent ease with alternative sexual identities and family formations, *Friends* is a prime example of broadcast television's efforts to attract this demographic."[14] Beyond its appeal to this niche audience, the series also contended with a changing social and employment landscape, where young people were more often living on their own, without parental control or guidance, and were characterized as less career-driven than their parents. As such, its characters, while employed, did not spend much time at work. Rather, its primary settings were the homes the friends shared together: Monica's and Joey's apartments and the coffee shop, Central Perk. While Rachel and Joey both worked at the coffee shop for periods of time, the focus was not on work, nor was it on family, in the traditional nuclear or biological senses. Instead, one part of its cultural legacy is its ensemble of friends who stick together (on- and off-screen), who serve as each other's family, hanging out together.

FRIENDS ENSEMBLE ON-SCREEN AND OFF-SCREEN

When *Friends* started, each of the starring cast members were paid $22,500 per episode. After the 1996 season, David Schwimmer was getting movie offers and was expected to ask for a raise. Based on the advice of his divorce attorney mother and his experience working in theater, according to then NBC Entertainment president Warren Littlefield, Schwimmer organized the cast to ask for equal money for equal work. Ultimately, they were each given $100,000 per episode.[15] Lisa Kudrow explained Schwimmer's point: "Any one of us or two of us could get more than the others, but that it's more important that there's no resentment and we all make the exact same amount."[16] No cast in history had ever collectively bargained for pay raises successfully. Matt LeBlanc notes that other casts may have tried to do it in the past but did not always stick together. He said that the six made a pact to stick together, and each of them agreed to come to the others if the network or producers tried to negotiate with them individually. He even admitted that there were a couple of times when one cast member actually left the building over a particularly big issue and the others followed. The network acted quickly, and everyone was back on set the next day.[17] The *Friends* cast stuck together in their negotiations for all ten years of their tenure.

Kudrow clarified that the negotiations were not about the money per se but about seeing them as the friends they were being depicted as on-screen. If any one of them resented the others for making more money, that magic may have been lost.[18] Their negotiations became well-publicized and ultimately earned them a record-breaking one million dollars each per episode for the last two seasons of the series. The public learning about their unified negotiations had the added benefit of convincing the audience that they were truly friends, on- and off-screen. Courteney Cox explained that the castmates took turns keeping each other united in their negotiations off-screen just as the writers stayed conscious about keeping them equal on-screen. She concluded, "I think it's because of their writing that we felt strong enough to pull this off."[19] Packaging their friendships on- and off-screen became important for the premise of the series, but it was also significant for the format of this particular show, that is, being focused on all six characters.

Series creators Marta Kauffman and David Crane made the ensemble nature of the show explicit by titling the original pilot *Six of One*. Their first series, HBO's *Dream On* (1990–1996), had one actor in virtually every scene because it was told from his point of view. For this reason, they wanted to do an ensemble for their next show.[20] The creators and director James Burrows saw from the first run-through with all six actors and the audience reactions to the pilot that the cast had a chemistry that could make the show a hit.[21] As Schwimmer described it:

> There was something *really* special about the six different voices and the energy of the six of us. There are six pieces of the puzzle that happen to click *just* right because of casting and because of the particular energy of the six people. . . . To find *one* magical actor who is just right for the role is difficult enough, but to find six and then to have them actually *have chemistry* with each other is just kind of a miracle.[22]

Having James Burrows as their director for seven episodes of their first season gave the cast the opportunity to explore their chemistry as he liked to try different things and explore their characters' relationships. For example, he was not sure why the other cast members would be friends with Phoebe and encouraged the cast to discuss this relationship, and Matt LeBlanc's Joey was very flat on the page, so Burrows and LeBlanc worked on how and why Joey would be friends with these three women, for example, without hitting on them.

Courteney Cox encouraged the cast to give each other feedback and help make each of them as funny as they could be. She was probably the most experienced in the television world when the show started as she had guest starred on *Family Ties* (1982–1989) and *Seinfeld* as one of Jerry's love interests. Cox reportedly said that on *Seinfeld* the cast helped each other be funnier and suggested the *Friends* cast do the same.[23] While it seems logical to outsiders that actors working together would give one another notes, Kudrow explained that there is a "code" among actors to *not* give one another notes. So, when Cox gave them permission to do so, it set a tone within the group that brought them closer together.[24] The actors made it clear to each other, the producers, and their audience that they were friends who would work together to make the best show they could about their characters' friendships.

With a cast who sticks together telling stories of a group of friends, the writers had their work cut out for them. They now had to write a full series focused on all six characters. This took the form of not just two storylines per episode, as was typical for sitcoms, but usually three storylines. At least one of those storylines usually impacted the rest of the cast, if not the rest of the series. To do all of that in twenty-two minutes was quite a challenge, but the writers managed to balance screen time between the actors and accommodate them when they were involved in other projects, which was increasingly the case as the series went on.

How the writers and cast dealt with relationships demonstrates the ensemble nature of the show. To put it bluntly: no relationships outside the group or romantic relationships within the group were sustainable if the ensemble nature of the show was to be maintained. When Ross dates Julie in the first season, they had to break up in order to make room for Ross and Rachel to get together. When Ross and Rachel do get together, the writers turned around and broke them up too. The tricky part was then to find a way for them to remain friends so as not to disrupt the group. Even when Monica and Chandler did get together at Ross and Emily's wedding, the creators thought that they would just sleep together, not that their relationship would last. However, when they revealed themselves under the sheets in London (Episode 4.24, "The One with Ross's Wedding, Part 2"), they had to stop shooting for several minutes while the audience screamed with excitement.[25] The producers, writers, and cast had to find a way to keep the focus on the six, even with the emergence of one romantic relationship within the group. Chandler and Monica's attempts to hide their relationship from the rest of the group for the first half of season 5 fed the comedic fire of the show. (Remember when Chandler kept kissing Phoebe and Rachel too every time he accidentally kissed Monica in front of the gang in Episode 5.2, "The One with All the Kissing" or the classic game of "They don't know we know they know . . ." in Episode 5.14, "The One where Everybody Finds Out"?) It also allowed the writers and producers to test how the relationship might work while still maintaining group coherence. Ultimately, the series ended with four of its main characters paired up, suggesting not that romantic relationships would end their group, but that "friendship itself is the foundation of love" and "the best thing to do is to fall in love with your best friend, spend ten years in on-again-off-again status, and then live happily ever after."[26] LeBlanc also credits the emotional thread in the stories and characters with their appeal, while Kauffman claims it was always about the whole cast: "One crazy lesson from the show was that everything was better with the six of them. . . . What the audience wanted, we had to learn, was the six of them in a room."[27] Top-rated episodes like "The One where No One's Ready" (Episode 3.2), "The One where Ross Got High" (Episode 6.9), and "The One with the Videotape" (Episode 8.4) prove her point.

Their group coherence was built by spending so much time together on and off set, especially during the first few seasons. Burrows famously took the whole cast to Las Vegas on the Warner Bros. plane after they had been taping shows but before they had premiered. He took them out to dinner at Wolfgang Puck's restaurant and even loaned them money to gamble. He told them that this was likely the last time they would be able to go out together without being recognized. During filming, between scenes, they would all hang out together playing poker in Burrows's dressing room (because it was the largest at the time). They were all around the same age, and they were the only six who truly understood what the others were experiencing. Schwimmer describes the early years as a time when they never wanted to leave one another. They went out to dinner after work, ate lunch together on set, or just played poker. "I think we were genuinely having the time of our lives, and also there was something very bonding about how scary the whole experience was. We had the other five, like a very protective cocoon."[28]

They were lucky to have one another when the backlash came too. The cast appeared on countless magazine covers and cashed in on endorsements for everything from jeans to milk during their first two seasons on the air. Matt LeBlanc had a deal with Saks Fifth Avenue; Jennifer Aniston and Matthew Perry were hawking for Microsoft; Jennifer Aniston and Lisa Kudrow promoted milk. At the end of only their first season, the whole cast appeared on the cover of *Rolling Stone* on May 18, 1995. Who could blame them for trying to profit from what might have been their fifteen minutes of fame? But it was the Diet Coke campaign that everyone—the cast, media, producers, and audience—saw as the moment they became overexposed. The Diet Coke campaign paid an estimated $10 million (including between $250,000 and $500,000 for each cast member) to use the show's name and cast in a series of interactive ads where someone stole a Diet Coke from Monica and Rachel's apartment. Audience members were then asked to send in bottle caps to help solve the mystery and for a chance to win a trip to Los Angeles to watch a taping of *Friends*.[29] After two years of increasing presence across multiple media, the public, who were the ones who wanted more and more and more of the cast in the first place, had seemingly had enough.

Even so, ratings were still high (and remained so through the series finale), but the unadulterated adoration of the cast and show had been tarnished. What was seen as "relentless greed and overhype around the

show" seemed to be cheapening the franchise. Cashing in on a
made the cast, creators, and NBC merely look greedy. Executi
ers Kauffman, Crane, and Kevin S. Bright suggested a mora
media interviews.[30] NBC started to work with the cast to protect them
from overexposure. Littlefield contends, "We realized the cast was so
white-hot that we had to pull back, to help protect both them and their
show. To their credit, they all just kept their heads down and worked.
Worked hard."[31] All their time spent together, and the publicity it garnered, meant that the cast became each other's support system at the same
time that they became real friends to each other and their audience even
in the midst of controversies.

FRIENDS POPULARIZED HANG-OUT TV

Before landing the role of Phoebe Buffay on *Friends*, Lisa Kudrow
guested on *Mad about You* (1992–1999) as Ursula the (terrible) waitress.
When Kudrow told *Mad about You* star Paul Reiser that she had an
audition, he asked, "So it's six people sitting on a couch—how is that a
show?"[32] Cut to the start of the first episode where four friends sit in a
coffee shop, Central Perk, chatting about relationships (Monica has a date
tonight) and Oedipal issues (Chandler imagines calling his mother during
sex). In walks friend number five, Ross, depressed because his wife,
Carol, just moved out after coming out as a lesbian. Phoebe tries to help
by cleansing his aura, and Joey suggests strip joints are the answer. However, Ross declares, "I just want to be married again," just as friend
number six, Rachel, walks in wearing a wedding dress (Episode 1.1, "The
Pilot"). In this four-and-a-half-minute series opening scene, we learn that
Monica does not have a great dating track record; Chandler relieves tension with jokes; Ross's malaise comes from his impending divorce from
his lesbian wife; Phoebe represents the spacey-hippie while Joey is the
oversexed, hot guy; and Rachel, having escaped her own wedding, might
just be the one Ross ends up marrying.

We also learned that these friends are just as comfortable at Central
Perk as they are in their own homes. Monica sits with her legs tucked
under her on the orange couch in the middle of the coffee shop. Ross
walks in and goes directly to the group, knowing where they will be

sitting. Rachel finds Monica because the superintendent of her building knows where to find her: at the coffee shop.

There are fan theories that claim that *Friends* was just a huge marketing strategy by Starbucks to boost coffeehouse culture.[33] While the series' and Starbucks' popularity certainly coincided, there is little evidence of collusion in this particular case. Rather, the show represented what was occurring at the time: Generation X was coming of age and spending their time socializing daily, increasingly, at their local coffeehouses. In "The One with the Flashback" (Episode 3.6), the gang even laments that their local bar is closing and being turned into the coffee shop. While the creators wondered if fans across middle America would be able to identify with a group of New York friends just hanging out in their neighborhood coffee shop, they came to realize that *Friends* was more than a show; it was marketing a lifestyle.[34] Past sitcoms may have been focused on families in the home or work "families" at their places of employment, but *Friends* popularized the "hang-out"[35] comedy showing the group in their surrogate home,[36] Central Perk, or each other's apartments as extensions of their own homes. Generation X was known for hanging out and

Friends on the orange couch in Central Perk. *Warner Brothers / Photofest © Warner Brothers*

talking (see more on this topic in chapter 4). *Friends* capitalized on representing and popularizing this culture.

Popular culture often represents that which young people see as cool, hip, and happening at the time. Even so, *Friends* did what no sitcom had done before: these six twenty-somethings were hanging out and living together without parental guidance. Unlike a series like *Living Single*, where the young people lived together but focused on work, or *Seinfeld*, where the cast hung out together but were united around the famous comedian, this series did not focus on work and was an ensemble from start to finish. Four months before the premiere, the pilot was screened for an audience of thirty-five-plus-year-old (Baby Boomer) viewers. They suggested that audiences would not like these characters because they "did not care about one another the way that real friends would" and were "smug, superficial and self-absorbed . . . and not like people they would want to know"; and ultimately the audience believed they were "not real friends."[37] These same criticisms ultimately became reasons the show earned praise and ratings through the roof with Generation X, "slumpy," and other viewers aged eighteen to forty-nine.

Rather than just representing youth culture at the time, *Friends* suggested that we were "now living in a culture where youth rules, where the image of youth has become the dominant image of our culture."[38] The creators and NBC executives realized that they had found conceptual territory that had not been portrayed that much on network TV—young adult relationships.[39] While the cast and characters were twenty-something when the show began, they were thirty-something when it concluded. The series allowed the characters to grow somewhat (Joey gets real acting jobs, Monica and Chandler get married, Rachel and Ross have a baby, and Phoebe marries Mike). However, it also drew out this period in young people's lives when they are still trying to sort out their lives into a realistic (for Gen X) decade-long process. Unlike Baby Boomers, who entered jobs and careers in their teens and twenties that lasted much of their lives, *Friends* showed that youth culture of the 1990s and early 2000s was one where work and careers became contingent (not one character remained in their same job the entire series) and more time was spent just hanging out with friends than at work or with a biological family.

Friends was one of the first shows to focus on the lives of its young people with little to no parental guidance. Past shows that focused on young people (e.g., *The Brady Bunch*, *Happy Days*, *Good Times*, and *The Cosby Show*) still included the characters' biological parents or an older mentor figure for the young people. When Kauffman and Crane brought the show to NBC, the network suggested having an older character to give them guidance.[40] While Terry, the manager (and later owner) of Central Perk, appeared in a few episodes the first two seasons of the show, he never really panned out as a mentor. Some of the friends' parents appear on the show for a few episodes here and there, but few appear in more than one or two episodes. Instead, the six friends became one another's surrogate family, with Monica as the sometime mother figure (see more in chapter 4). Instead of Joey hitting on all the women, he hit on all the women except these three, who, for most of the series, he treated more as sisters. It became a reflection of the lives Kauffman and Crane had been living in New York before they started in television, where their friends were their family.[41]

Even as they served as one another's family, the show still reminded the audience that it was a show about single *friends* in their twenties with the ways they interacted with one another and with what they talked about while they were hanging out. While *Sex and the City* (1998–2004) is usually credited with bringing frank sexual talk to television, *Friends* did it first, did it on network TV (not pay cable), and did it in cross-sex friendships. In the first episode of the series, Monica has a date with "Paul the Wine Guy" from work. After learning that he had not had sex since his marriage broke up two years prior, Monica ends up sleeping with him on the first date. When Rachel sees her the next morning, Monica says she cannot stop smiling, to which Rachel replies, "I can see that. You look like you slept with a hanger in your mouth" (Episode 1.1, "The Pilot"). In the end though, we learn that Paul has used this line before to get women to sleep with him, and Monica ends up giving him a taste of his own medicine by breaking the watch he left behind at her apartment. The first episode of the series then has a single woman unapologetically having sex on the first date, her new roommate making a thinly veiled oral sex joke, the guy turning out to be a cad, and the woman rejecting him despite having had sex with him. After the first run-through of the episode, a studio executive, Don Ohlmeyer, expressed concerns over Monica's premarital, casual sex. According to Kauffman, Ohlmeyer said that "when Monica slept with Paul the wine guy, she got what she deserved."[42] So NBC decided to hand out a questionnaire to the audience that, again according to Kauffman, basically asked: "Do you think Monica sleeping with wine guy makes her (a) a slut, (b) a whore, (c) a trollop"; surprisingly, "even with the deck stacked that way, the audience didn't care."[43]

Overcoming this hurdle early on set the stage for the show to regularly, hilariously, and unspectacularly have the characters engage in sex as a natural act in which consenting adults participate and then hang out with one another talking frankly about it. In the first season during a blackout, all but one of the friends (Chandler) hangs out at Monica and Rachel's apartment. They go around the table sharing the most interesting places they have had sex—a pool table (Monica), women's restroom in the New York Public Library (Joey), Milwaukee (Phoebe), the foot of the bed (Rachel), and on the "It's a Small World After All" ride at Disneyland (Ross) (Episode 1.7, "The One with the Blackout"). Later in the same season, Joey's participation in an NYU fertility study is met with jokes about what he was donating (Monica: "Please tell me you're only donating your time") and the money he was going to make (Phoebe: "Wow, you're gonna be making money hand over fist"). Because Joey cannot have sex during the study, Joey takes Monica's suggestions to "be there for her" and the running joke through the episode is the fruit baskets his girlfriend, Melanie, sends him for all the time he spent pleasuring her orally (Episode, 1.24, "The One where Rachel Finds Out").

It is worth noting that both the male and female characters in the show are single and sexually active. Although the show often deals with their sexualities in gendered ways (see more in chapter 7), it also promotes the sexual pleasure of all the characters. Monica draws a diagram to teach Chandler about the seven erogenous zones he should attempt to stimulate to improve his sexual prowess, and Rachel chimes in to suggest alternate positions (upside down) and body parts (toes) to include (Episode 4.11, "The One with Phoebe's Uterus"). Phoebe regularly jokes about her penchant for sexual adventurousness, such as when Joey says that a potential suitor, Cliff, is not into anything weird sexually, to which Phoebe responds, "Enter Pheebs" (Episode 8.23, "The One where Rachel Has a Baby, Part 1") or when she suggests to the gang that she has her husband, Mike, tied to the radiator at home (Episode 10.18, "The Last One: Part 2"). Even so, Joey is the most sexually active of all the friends.[44] However, we rarely see him with any of the women he has casual sex with. When Joey and Rachel discuss her continuing to live with him after her baby is born, she suggests that having a baby around will dampen his sex life. He tells her that it is the baby that matters and adds that if he meets a hot woman, he can have sex with her at the club (Episode 8.7, "The One with the Stain"). Ross goes to Joey for advice about how to bed his date as Ross had not had sex in six months. Joey says that he had sex that day, and after their conversation he heads out for another date, where presumably he will have sex again (Episode 8.4, "The One with the Videotape"). These examples suggest that Joey frequents clubs and has frequent casual sex with random hot women, but we rarely see it.

By the end of season 2, Monica and Rachel both have significant others, Richard and Ross, respectively. But this does not slow down the sex talk. In "The One where Dr. Ramoray Dies" (Episode 2.18), the gang discusses their "number" or the number of sex partners they have each had. While Ross and Richard's numbers are low (three and two respectively), both Rachel and Monica struggle with telling the other their numbers because they are higher. While Rachel eventually tells Ross that she has been with five men, we only know that Monica has been with "a loot" of men (according to Phoebe) and that Richard, even as an older man from the Baby Boomer generation, does not find her number a problem.

Just as the characters dealt frankly and amusingly with sex, they also addressed the issue of safe sex. Later in "The One where Dr. Ramoray Dies," once Monica and Rachel have revealed their numbers to Richard and Ross, respectively, Richard tells Monica he loves her and Ross tells Rachel that he wants to show her what kind of passion they have together. But when Rachel and Monica run into each other in their apartment bathroom to get condoms, they find there is only one left. Despite trying to persuade one another that she is worthiest of the condom, Rachel wins their game of rock-paper-scissors and gets to have sex with Ross. Monica has to tell Richard that they are not going to have sex that night. Rather than object, Richard merely asks if she could show him the schedule ahead of time in the future. Later in the series, in "The One where Rachel Tells Ross" (Episode 8.3), we also learn that condoms are only 97 percent effective. We learn this when Ross asks how Rachel can be pregnant when they used a condom. When Ross tells Joey that it says so on the box, Joey pulls out a long string of condoms to confirm Ross's shocking revelation.

Some contend "The One where Dr. Ramoray Dies" is unrealistic in that a brother and sister would not have sex with their respective partners in the same apartment at the same time and because a man who has started on the path toward sex would not stop just because there was no condom.[45] However, both episodes promote the idea that safe sex is necessary, that both men and women are responsible for planning for and only carrying on with safe sex, and that even safe sex with condoms is not 100 percent effective. Given that the characters and primary audience came of age during the emergence of HIV/AIDS and saw the lackluster response from Presidents Reagan and Bush, popular culture in general and *Friends* specifically dealt with the subject in ways that allowed them to be sexually frank with one another but to also address the so-called elephant in the room. As Kaufmann concludes: "These people are in their 20s and they're sexual. . . . These two women were fighting over the last condom because whoever didn't get the condom *wasn't* going to have sex. To me that is so much more responsible than not dealing with sexuality."[46]

The characters' frank talk about sex is just one of the ongoing subjects they discussed when they hung out together. What made it so relatable was that this was the life of many a twenty-something in the mid-1990s through early 2000s. Talk about sex became increasingly acceptable, in some ways out of necessity in the aftermath of the emergence of the HIV/AIDS crisis. The absence of parental figures or older people in their everyday lives made such conversation believable. Normalizing hanging out with your group of friends and talking about a whole host of subjects, including those once considered taboo, is a significant part of *Friends'* legacy.

FRIENDS' CONTINUING LEGACY

The cultural legacy of *Friends* as a hang-out TV ensemble comedy continues with the subsequent careers of its creators, producers, and primary cast; its impact on the current sitcom landscape; and audiences' continual access to the show via multiple platforms. Neither the creators nor the actors from *Friends* ever needed to work again after the conclusion of the series. The success of the show ensured their financial futures and also provided them with the opportunity to pick and choose their subsequent projects. Creators and executive producers Kauffman, Crane, and Bright were able to capitalize on *Friends'* success while the series was still in production. They used the hang-out TV model to create and produce *Veronica's Closet* (1997–2000) and *Jesse* (1998–2000). These shows highlighted the comedy stylings of Kirstie Alley and Christina Applegate, respectively, but the hang-out concept did not work as well when supplanted into the work or family home settings of these series. They all had their names attached to Matt LeBlanc's short-lived spin-off, *Joey* (2004–2006), as creators of the character as well. While Kauffman's series *Related* only lasted from 2005 to 2006, she continued to produce television movies and documentaries until she created a contemporary Netflix hit, *Grace and Frankie* (2015–2018) starring Jane Fonda and Lily Tomlin, which Kauffman also writes and directs. Similarly, Crane's creation *The Class* (2006–2007) lasted only a year, but then he and LeBlanc (and Jeffrey Klarik) teamed up for *Episodes* (2011–2017). The combination of LeBlanc playing an exaggerated version of himself and Crane's writing (he wrote all forty-one episodes) led both to earn Emmy and Golden Globe nominations (acting for LeBlanc and writing for Crane) and LeBlanc to win the Golden Globe for Best Performance by an Actor in a Television Series—Comedy or Musical in 2012.

Friends' legacy extends beyond the wakes of its creators and stars to the sitcom landscape today. Remember that no other show had ever focused on a group of young adults outside the presence and influence of their parents or an older mentor before *Friends* and that the show popularized hang-out TV and the ensemble comedy. The logic of safety dictates that production companies will take the formula of any hit, tweak it a little, and try to replicate that success. Some of the early attempts to replicate *Friends'* success came from their creators and producers themselves, including *Veronica's Closet* (or *Friends* at a lingerie company) and *Suddenly Susan* (1998–2000) (or *Friends* at a fashion magazine). While they tried to replicate the *Friends* ensemble casts, both shows focused on a star at the center and are better categorized as workplace comedies. *These Friends of Mine* also premiered in 1994. While the friends on this show hung together, they did so at work (a bookstore) and at the lead's, comedian Ellen DeGeneres's, house. After the success of the first season of *Friends*, *These Friends of Mine* was renamed for its star, *Ellen* (1994–1998). *Ellen* certainly made the news when DeGeneres came out in real life as gay and then was the first to do so on her show. But the show did not last.

The *Friends* model continues through today with British sitcoms *Coupling* (BBC, 2000–2004) and *Two Pints of Lager and a Packet of Crisps* (BBC, 2001–2011) and American series such as *Girlfriends* (2000–2008), the U.S. version of *Coupling* (2003), *How I Met Your Mother* (2005–2014), *Cougar Town* (2009–2015), *Perfect Couples* (2010), *Happy Endings* (2011–2013), *New Girl* (2011–2018), *Friends with Better Lives* (2014), *Undateable* (2014–2016), and most recently *Friends from College* (2017–2018). The most famous series to benefit from the *Friends* formula must certainly be *The Big Bang Theory* (2007–2019). Interestingly, the show began focused on four male scientists and the dumb, sexy blonde who lived next door to two of them. However, once that sexy blonde, Penny (Kaley Cuoco), hooked up with one of the scientists, Leonard (Johnny Galecki), other love interests were introduced for the other men. Two of those love interests, Bernadette (Melissa Rauch) and Amy (Mayim Bialik of *Beaches* [1988] and *Blossom* [1990–1995] fame), who are also scientists, contributed so much laughter and balance in the scripting that they were added to the main cast.

Currently, *The Big Bang Theory* focuses on four men and three women as they take hanging out to the next level (eating take-out dinner together almost every night) and use the *Friends* formula not just for the content and format of their show but also in the cast's negotiations. Three of the series stars were offered $1 million per episode in their 2014 negotiation, but by 2017–2019, these same stars offered to take a pay cut so that the others in the ensemble would get raises.[47] CBS will do almost anything to keep *The Big Bang Theory* on the air as it garners *Friends*-like ratings in an era when those numbers are all but obsolete. However, they just announced that the 2018–2019 season will be their last.

THE END OF MUST-SEE TV

The *Friends* theme song repeats "I'll be there for you" over and over again. No one knew in 1994 that they meant they would *always* be there for us, or at least they would continue to air in syndication for another twenty-five years (so far). Today *Friends* serves as a form of comfort TV, providing what now feels like a safe, stable environment for fans, whether they were watching every Thursday night during its original run, in reruns on multiple channels since, through DVD box sets, or via stream-

The Big Bang Theory cast on their couch. CBS / Photofest © CBS

ing services like Netflix today. Television celebrities provide a sense of familiarity for audiences in that they spend time in our homes with our families and become part of our daily lives. This is especially true with long-running sitcoms that end up in syndication, where characters' images circulate in perpetuity, creating familiarity between characters, actors, and viewers.[48] Spending twenty-five years with Chandler, Joey, Monica, Phoebe, Rachel, and Ross has made them a constant presence in our homes. They have become our friends that we can spend time with whenever we flip on the TV. In the sitcom format, we also know that no matter what happens, things really will work out in the end (of the twenty-two-minute episode). A majority of the show took place pre-9/11 when the economy was booming so even domestic and international issues seemed irrelevant to many. In some ways, "*Friends* is about the last moment before everything went wrong."[49]

After 9/11, television networks were unsure about when it was appropriate to premiere new episodes of their 2001 seasons. Most series, including *Friends*, delayed their typical early September debuts given the insecure climate in the United States. When the eighth season of *Friends* premiered on September 27, 2001, the country was still reeling, but their ratings were higher than they had been since season 3. The cast and creators believe the show provided comfort at a time of uncertainty. Schwimmer notes that their post-9/11 ratings boost made them feel good about their work, as if what they were doing had meaning.[50] It was not that the show tackled political, economic, or international issues that were relevant at the time, but the show gave relief at a time when everyone else had to deal with such issues in their daily lives. Kauffman notes, "I think *Friends* was like comfort food for people at that time. . . . We *weren't* dealing with the larger issues. We were just doing comedy, and I think people wanted to laugh more than they wanted to see all the images over and over and over again of the Towers coming down."[51] The cast and the audience found solace in laughing with their *Friends*, and they won their first and only Emmy for Best Comedy for season 8.

Friends has found new audiences in recent years. In recognition of its ongoing appeal, *New York Magazine* asked in 2016, "Is *Friends* Still the Most Popular Show on TV?" They wondered why it was that "so many 20-somethings want to stream a 20-year-old sitcom about a bunch of 20-somethings sitting around in a coffee shop."[52] For one thing, coffeehouse culture has only expanded since *Friends*. The twenty-somethings today are still hanging out with their friends, working, chatting, and streaming in those coffee shops. When they were on *The Oprah Winfrey Show* back in March of 1995, Oprah showed the cast people in Internet cafés posting about their series online. It was an early indicator of what the relationship between television and the Internet might be: convergent. Now it is no surprise when television and the Internet converge when cast members live tweet during a first-time airing of a television episode, for example. But in 1995 it shocked the cast to see how fans were reacting in such an immediate way to the lifestyle they were promoting in the show. Of course, the fans were doing it in the very coffee shops *Friends* featured.

While that comfort comes from knowing the characters, relating to their trials and tribulations, and being able to turn it on nearly anytime anywhere, how it provides those relationships today has changed. We used to watch the series in chronological order each Thursday night when it was part of the "Must-See TV" lineup, along with *Seinfeld* (1989–1998) and *ER* (1994–2009), wondering each week whether Ross and Rachel would get together (they did), if everyone would find out about Monica and Chandler (they did), and whether Phoebe and Joey would ever do it (they did not). Today, with episodes airing on multiple cable channels and the entire series available on DVD, BluRay, and Netflix, we rarely watch episodes in chronological order anymore. Now we wonder if an episode is before or after Ross and Rachel and Monica and Chandler get together, if Ross is working at the museum or if he is a professor yet, or if Rachel is living with Monica, Joey, Phoebe, or Ross. "There is no doubt that twenty-first century multiplatform television programming has helped enable the continuing global reach of the series. It airs on Comedy Central in the United Kingdom and India, Netflix in the United Kingdom, United States, and Canada, and the streaming service Stan in Australia; it is also widely available on DVD."[53]

While accessing the series via these multiple platforms broadens the audiences who can enjoy the show, it also changes how everyone, including longtime fans, engage with it. For one thing, it seems as if our *Friends* are always there for us since we literally access them whenever and wherever we have access to a television and/or Internet connection or even just a smart phone. For another, we more often than not watch the series episodes out of sequence. Viewing it as a nonlinear narrative, viewers might wonder if Monica and Chandler have gotten together yet or if Phoebe and Mike have met yet. Since the nature of the sitcom is that all problems are resolved and normalcy restored within the twenty-two-minute episodes, being able to engage with "endless out-of-sequence repeats and then on-demand viewing" only "compound[s] the additive sense that everything was always OK in a world that would never change."[54] Additionally, television tends to be intertextual and self-referential. In other words, shows reference one another, making the television world seem interconnected in some ways. These characteristics "have only become more extensive as conglomeration and the number of channels and platforms for television content have expanded."[55] So when characters in *Friends* reference Rose Marie on *The Dick Van Dyke Show* (Episode 2.15, "The One where Ross and Rachel . . . You Know") or Rachel compares her potentially living with Chandler and Monica to Jack, Janet, and Chrissy on *Three's Company* (Episode 6.2, "The One where Ross Hugs Rachel"), Gen-X or Baby Boomer viewers harken back to earlier TV shows they watched growing up. Today, we also have Jay-Z recreating the *Friends* title sequence with an all-black cast for his video "Moonlight"[56] or *How I Met Your Mother*'s Ted Mosby buying his forever home in Westchester (site of Chandler and Monica's future home in the series finale). The worlds of television, music, the Internet, and its social media platforms all come together to allow us to watch this show whenever and wherever we'd like just as the convergent world of media makes it one of the essential texts that help us to know and understand others' connections and references (for more on this topic, see chapter 2).

At the same time, the ubiquity with which we can access the show brings about an end to how we used to conceive of "Must-See TV." From 1994 to 2004, "Must-See TV" referred to NBC's Thursday night lineup of shows. They were "must see" in that they were the most popular shows on television at the time and therefore missing them when they first aired on Thursday nights meant missing out on watercooler conversations about the episodes the next day at work or at the coffee shop. Today, *Friends* remains a "must see" show, but now there is less urgency in the need to view it at a particular time and place. Instead, we "must see" it in order to understand the culture of television sitcoms today, to "get" references others make from it. Watching *Friends* allows us to continue to see young people who served as one another's surrogate families whom they could talk to about anything when they hung out and to find comfort knowing that they will always be there for us in one form or another.

2

FRIENDS ON-SCREEN AND OFF

In David Wild's behind-the-scenes book, *Friends . . . 'til the End*, Matt LeBlanc suggests that having televisions in your bedroom, living room, and even bathroom makes viewers feel like the characters are part of fans' everyday lives. This presence in fans' intimate spaces creates relationships and makes viewers feel they have a connection with the stars and their characters.[1] Long-running sitcoms in particular foster such familiarity as audience members spend at least twenty-two minutes a week with their favorite characters over the course of the run of a series, not to mention additional time watching reruns in syndication, the extras on the DVD boxsets for each season, and now on streaming services such as Netflix. For a sitcom like *Friends*, that produced a total of 236 episodes over ten years, this means that since it premiered in 1994, fans have spent a minimum of eighty-seven hours with the characters (assuming they only watch each episode once) in addition to any interactions they have had with the actors' public personas in media, such as magazine features, television interviews, and/or gossip websites.

Friends premiered amid a celebrity media environment in which the overturn of the Fairness Doctrine in the United States in 1987 increasingly demanded that news be guided by the bottom line rather than fairness, equity, or even the truth. Additionally, "the year 1994 was arguably when the iteration of America's gossip machine that culminated in *Bollea v. Gawker* began in earnest . . . [and] the year the Supreme Court ruled that parodies were protected under fair use."[2] Add to these major legal decisions that the Internet became an integral part of the news, especially where celebrity reporting was concerned, and you have all the ingredients necessary to collapse distinctions between actors and their characters.

While the *Bollea v. Gawker* case was not decided until well after *Friends* ended, the issues it focused on are ones all of the friends had to deal with during and after the run of the series. Terry Bollea, aka Hulk Hogan, had been secretly recorded having sex with his best friend's wife. The celebrity gossip website *Gawker* posted a clip of the video online and refused to take it down after Bollea asked. *Gawker* founder Nick Denton justified his actions by explaining the purpose of *Gawker* in an interview in *Playboy*, "If there's a gap between your private behavior and your public status, that's what makes the story for us."[3] The crux of this case was the relationship between a character and the person playing the role. Federal judge James D. Whittemore ruled on November 14, 2012, that the "Plaintiff's public persona, including the publicity he and his family derived from a television reality show detailing their personal life, his own book describing an affair he had during his marriage, sex life, and the Video all demonstrate that the Video is a subject of general interest and concern to the community."[4] This decision was notable because the courts do not usually rule on what is or is not of concern to the people. Usually the courts leave this issue up to media outlets to decide. However, Bollea quickly appealed the decision. The appeal honed in on the issue of whether Bollea's privacy had been violated as, he argued, Hulk Hogan was his public persona and Terry Bollea was the private person who had sex with his friend's wife and who was secretly taped doing it. The appeals court determined that his privacy had been violated and awarded him $140 million.[5]

Bollea's privacy was determined to have been violated by the same type of gossip media sites that emerged online during the run of *Friends*. So it was no surprise that after the first season of the show became a hit, the friends' lives would never be the same. Director James Burrows famously took the *Friends* actors to Las Vegas before the show premiered. He advised them to enjoy the trip as after the show aired, he warned, their lives would change forever. Despite this warning, Burrows could not have known just how prescient his advice would be nor the level of celebrity they would enjoy. As Lily Loofbourow explains in "The End of the Friends Era of Gossip, Fame, and Meta-Spinoffs," "In *Friends* we were watching a sitcom, but we were also—in ways that are only becoming clear two decades after the fact—watching six actors explode into an unprecedented celebrity vortex together, and cope with a virulent appetite for gossip."[6] These forces led to superstardom for the *Friends'* actors, but it also contributed to the difficulty many fans have separating the actors from their characters.

This vortex included the *Friends* characters, the actors who played them, the endorsement deals for the cast, and the popularity of the show and all it encapsulated—from coffeehouse culture and catchphrases to New York apartment living and plots focused on twenty-somethings living on their own (discussed more in chapter 3). For example, when the *Friends* actors signed the infamous deal to appear in a series of Diet Coke ads, the writers of the show wrote the dialogue for the ads. So, while it was Jennifer Aniston, Courteney Cox, Lisa Kudrow, Matt LeBlanc, Matthew Perry, and David Schwimmer endorsing the product, it was their characters appearing in the ads. In "I'll Be There for You: *Friends* and the Fantasy of Alternative Families," Jillian Sandell notes that the *Friends*/ Diet Coke campaign was unusual for so blatantly blurring distinctions between actors and their characters, but that it was also a sign of things to come where actors endorse products and ways of life through their characters.[7]

The connections created between the series, actors, and their characters during the run of the show and continual airing of it since created a culture in which the stars had difficulty moving on due to audience perceptions of them. Alice Leppert explains in "*Friends* Forever: Sitcom Celebrity and Its Afterlives," that television has a tendency "to represent older texts in the present, and thus to flatten distinctions between past and present [which] helps circulate the images of sitcom stars frozen in time—effectively presenting the past as present into perpetuity."[8] So as long as audience members have access to *Friends* as it appeared from 1994 to 2004, the characters and actors will continually be connected with that world in our minds. Additional references to the actors'/characters' on- and off-screen lives in other television shows (from *The Big Bang Theory* to *How I Met Your Mother*) recreates an environment of intertextuality and self-referentiality that the actors have difficulty escaping even today. Self-referentiality is the idea that *Friends* episodes, in this case, refer to other media, television in particular, including actors, their characters, shows, and even celebrity gossip, and vice versa; today, series such as *The Big Bang Theory* or *New Girl* include references to older TV shows and actors, like *Friends*. Intertextuality refers to the relationships between texts, such as *The Big Bang Theory* being a newer version of the type of "hang-out TV" that *Friends* popularized (discussed in chapter 1). While this type of celebrity culture is inescapable today, the *Friends* actors' experiences with and contributions to the forces of celebrity culture that emerged with this series set a new standard for what it meant to be an actor/character in a hit show at the end of the century. This chapter will discuss how the *Friends* characters/actors' personas collapsed into one another through the series and their media representations to contribute to a new kind of celebrity culture.

JENNIFER ANISTON

Some associations between the actors and their characters were inevitable. They were twenty-somethings playing twenty-somethings, for example. As Jennifer Aniston puts it, "If *we're* experiencing these growing pains and these experiences in our real life, I'm sure all people in their mid-20s had something to watch and relate to and kind of laugh at themselves."[9] Emphasizing such similarities was to their advantage in promoting the show. Aniston also notes that as Rachel matured, more of herself went into her character, naturally, as she herself developed.[10] Even as she noted similarities between herself and Rachel, she also pointed out differences, such as not growing up rich like Rachel.[11] But fans know that her father, John Aniston, played Victor Kiriakis on *Days of Our Lives*. Even though he did not start this role until 1985, when Jennifer was around sixteen years old, for fans, it is easy to assume that Jennifer grew up much like Rachel in a house with a successful, moneyed, soap-star father. The timing of his emergence and her becoming "Jennifer Aniston," successful star, became collapsed.

In addition to the similar ages and maturity levels between the actors and their characters, the actors became associated with the traits of their characters. For Aniston, this meant emphasis on her looks and being seen as devoted to fashion like Rachel. Pictures of Aniston on red carpets being evaluated by outlets like E's *Fashion Police* and appearances on fashion magazine covers, including *Elle*, *Glamour*, *Cosmopolitan*, and *Vogue* throughout the run of the show, merely contributed to this collapse between actor and character. Add to these public appearances her endorsement deals with beauty products, such as Aveeno, L'Oréal, and

Elizabeth Arden, and it became natural for fans to assume that both Rachel and Jennifer Aniston were fashionistas concerned with appearances. [12]

Aniston became further elevated in the hierarchy of celebrity culture by her choices in male companions. Although she was photographed in shorter-term relationships during the filming of *Friends* with Counting Crows front man Adam Duritz in 1995 and Paul Rudd in 1998 (who later costarred on *Friends* as Phoebe's love interest and later husband), it was her relationships with Tate Donovan and Brad Pitt that created extra layers of meaning and referentiality between Aniston and Rachel. Alice Leppert notes that the numerous guest stars that appeared on *Friends* created a "celebrified" world where each character was involved with a celebrity, whether through romantic or blood relations. "Although these stars are rarely playing themselves, much of the comedy comes from the viewer's understanding of the star's image outside of their *Friends* role, especially in romantic pairings." [13] Fans will remember that Donovan played Rachel's love interest Joshua Bergin for five episodes in 1998. Aniston and Tate Donovan dated between 1995 and 1998, getting engaged in 1998. Donovan claims that many people who knew they were dating thought that they met on the set of *Friends*. The truth was that they had been dating for two years prior, were engaged, and had just broken up when his stint on the series began. While Donovan reports that the cast, all of whom he knew as Aniston's friends off-set, treated him really well, he also notes how tricky it was to act like Joshua and Rachel were first meeting and falling in love when Tate and Jennifer were actually in the process of breaking up. [14] Watching their scenes together, then and now, provides fans with an opportunity to examine whether any of their off-screen turmoil interfered with their on-screen chemistry (it did not!). Instead of knowing the trajectory of Aniston and Donovan's relationship off-screen, their on-screen relationship as Rachel and Joshua remains more prescient to fans.

Jennifer Aniston's stardom arguably reached its pinnacle not with Rachel or costarring with Donovan but when she started dating and later married film star Brad Pitt. Pitt dated actress Gwyneth Paltrow beginning in 1995 after the two met on the set of *Se7en*. Although they got engaged in 1997, they broke up shortly thereafter. When he subsequently started dating Aniston in 1998, comparisons in the celebrity press between Paltrow and Aniston were inevitable. Such sources "emphasized Aniston's

"The One with the Rumor" episode, guest starring Brad Pitt (seated). *Warner Brothers / Photofest © Warner Brothers*

'girl next door' ordinariness in comparison to film star Paltrow's extraordinariness even while pointing out their similarities: both born into Hollywood families."[15] Her character Rachel was the "unattainable" love interest for Ross on *Friends*. Yet "ordinary" Aniston somehow had landed the most unattainable, eligible Hollywood bachelor. This seeming oxymoron (ordinary yet unattainable) between actress and character led not to confusion or inconsistency but to creating a perception of Aniston as superior to her costars, as the unattainable one, and to film stars, as Pitt seemingly chose this "ordinary television star" over up-and-coming film star Paltrow.

Pitt and Aniston married in 2000, and he appeared in *Friends*' Thanksgiving episode (8.9, "The One with the Rumor") in 2001, which further collapsed the worlds between Jennifer and Rachel. In the episode, he plays Will Colbert, a high school friend of Monica and Ross's who hated Rachel so much in high school that he and Ross cofounded the "I Hate Rachel Green Club." Aniston claimed that when film actors, from Isabella Rossellini to Bruce Willis, appeared on the series, they were often nervous or even terrified. She says of Pitt's appearance that he was more nervous than she had ever seen him and that he worried that he would blow it. Of course, it became a self-fulfilling prophecy and he did screw up his first line.[16] Despite the nerves and initial stumble, Pitt's appearance earned him an Emmy nomination for Outstanding Guest Actor in a Comedy Series in 2002. Of course, Jennifer Aniston attended the ceremony with him, and shots of him, sitting next to Matt LeBlanc, looking lovingly and admiringly at Aniston accompanied her acceptance speech when she actually won the Emmy for Outstanding Lead Actress in a Comedy the same year. While the storyline in the episode had Ross affirming his choice to date, and later co-parent, with Rachel, her conflicts with Will/Brad provided much of the humor. Seeing the two of them on- and off-screen in the context of *Friends* mixed the worlds in which fans knew them. Her winning a lead actress award and his only being nominated for a guest Emmy suggested that they were more on par with one another than the film/television comparisons suggested. As a matter of fact, when the series was ending, many gossip sources speculated about what her post-*Friends* career might look like. Her agents offered the following scenario: "Rachel goes to Hollywood to be a movie star, wins an Oscar and never appears on television again."[17] While today's media world includes actors appearing on television and film, Aniston had her pick of film and television projects post-*Friends*. She also had her choice of male companions after she and Pitt broke up in 2005.

"Perhaps indicative of her transition from television to film star, Aniston's appearances in gossip magazines often eclipse her film appearances, and the extratextual information that circulates about Aniston's personal life is heavily shaped by her television stardom," Alice Leppert contends.[18] This point is especially salient when considering how her breakup with Brad Pitt was shaped in the post-*Friends* world. Whether he had an affair with Angelina Jolie while the two were filming *Mr. and Mrs. Smith* is not relevant. What is important is that fans believed he did and that he was with Jolie immediately following his split with Aniston. As with Paltrow, both Aniston and Jolie come from acting families as Jolie's parents are Marcheline Bertrand and Jon Voight (the latter of whom is name-checked in an argument between Ross and Monica's boyfriend, Richard, over whether Jon Voight or John Savage were in *Coming Home* or *The Deer Hunter* in Episode 2.18, "The One where Dr. Ramoray Dies"). In numerous media reports, Aniston was characterized as "America's Sweetheart" whom Pitt left for the glamourous, seductive movie actress Jolie. *OK! Magazine* characterized Jolie as effortlessly authentic, using ChapStick and wearing low-cost vintage clothing, whereas Aniston was positioned as a social climber trying too hard with her expensive makeup and designer gowns. This article attempted to characterize Aniston as desperate to be like Jolie as well as make Aniston seem superficial and fashion-obsessed like her character Rachel.[19] American gossip magazines also pitted the women against one another, but their bent was largely for "team Aniston," the all-American girl-next-door.

Casting Ron Leibman and Marlo Thomas as Rachel's parents, Dr. Leonard and Sandra Green, furthered Aniston's/Rachel's all-American girl-next-door image as well as her connections with acting and television history and culture. Ron Leibman puts it succinctly when he says that he is more recognized as Rachel's dad than he is for playing Shylock at the New York Shakespeare Festival or winning a Tony for *Angels in America*.[20] In addition to his theater credits, Leibman was married to TV's *Alice*, Linda Lavin, from 1969 to 1981 and later to actress Jessica Walter (1983–present), who is best known these days for her role as the matriarch of the Bluth family on *Arrested Development*. Leibman's connections to such well-known television stars of the past and present nearly pale in comparison to Marlo Thomas's role in television and celebrity history, as Ann Marie in *That Girl* from 1966 to 1971. Thomas says that Aniston was supportive of her casting as she was a fan of *That Girl*. Aniston even told Thomas that Ross was Rachel's Donald.[21] Connections between *Friends* and Thomas's series continued when Phoebe wears a *That Girl* T-shirt in Episode 3.9, "The One with the Football," which evokes thoughts of the single, working woman she played in comparison to her "daughter," Rachel, who seems to be following her mother's/Ann Marie's footsteps. Off-screen Thomas married longtime television talk show host Phil Donahue in 1980.[22] The two remain married, and both have always been active in liberal politics. Thomas's public presence continues in her role as spokeswoman for St. Jude's Children's Hospital, a cause that Aniston has also appeared in ads for. Add to Leibman and Thomas Rachel's sisters, who are played by Oscar winner Reese Witherspoon (Jill Green) and *Married with Children* star Christina Applegate (Amy Green), and you have "a complex lineage of television and film stardom" that set Aniston up to be a tabloid darling both during and after *Friends*.[23]

Despite *Friends* ending in 2004, Aniston remained in the gossip head-lines for her films as much as for her relationships. She costarred with and dated Vince Vaughn from 2005 to 2006. Their film, *The Break-Up*, came across as somewhat autobiographical as she broke up with Pitt at the same time. She saw filming the movie as a way of exorcising some of what came with her own breakup at the time.[24] Although there were a few years where her love life was less than front-page news, she famously dated John Mayer from 2008 to 2009[25] and later dated (from 2011–2015), married (in 2015), and then divorced (in 2018) actor Justin Theroux.[26] "The circulation of Aniston's post-*Friends* image is indebted to Rachel and television more broadly in a variety of ways."[27] First, the gossip media continued to use the same through-line in their characterization of Aniston: the girl-next-door searching for everlasting love. Just as Rachel's union with Ross was deferred for nearly eight seasons, so too has Aniston's ability to find lasting love been deferred, time and again. Gossip media articles often perpetuated the delayed gratification of Aniston's character onto her life such as when "an *Us Weekly* article from 2010 details Aniston's love interests using the episodic organization of *Friends*, labeling three men, 'The One Who Likes Younger Girls,' 'The One Who Dated Lohan,' and 'The One Who Is Getting Divorced.'"[28]

Despite such interpellation of Rachel into Aniston's life in the media, Jennifer Aniston has been able to capitalize on and also break free (in some ways) from her *Friends* stardom. She had attempted to make it before *Friends* starring in short-lived series like the *Ferris Bueller* (1990–1991) TV series and campy horror films like *Leprechaun* (1993). But once the audience saw her haircut and her comedic acting chops, they were sold on her as Rachel. Her work on independent films and in smaller roles in blockbusters while filming the series helped audiences to see her in other roles post-*Friends*. Whether playing the lead in romantic come-dies such as *Rumor Has It* (2005) and *The Break-Up* (2006) or in dramas like *Derailed* (2005) and *Cake* (2014), audiences and critics alike em-braced her. She found surprisingly positive responses even when she played a comic villain in *Horrible Bosses* (2011) and *Horrible Bosses 2* (2014) and a stripper-cum-fake mom/drug trafficker in *We're the Millers* (2013). It is not that all of her movies are hits (did anyone see *Mother's Day* [2016]?), but Aniston has had the most consistent success with com-ic and dramatic roles in films and on TV after the series ended. Even so, the intertextual world of *Friends* continues as Aniston is currently developing and executive producing a TV project with her *Friends* sister Reese Witherspoon.

COURTENEY COX AND DAVID SCHWIMMER

As they played sister and brother on the series, the intertextual and referential qualities of Courteney Cox and David Schwimmer can be considered together. As with Rachel/Jennifer, Courteney Cox and her costars see similarities between Courteney and Monica. Matthew Perry says of Cox that she realized her own comedic chops on the series by "bringing her own kind of crazy neurosis to the part."[29] That neurosis became infused into Monica's character through her neatness, overzealous organization, and basically being a "control freak." Cox describes her work as a home-decorating show producer as difficult. "Everyone needs a decision on every single thing and if you're a control freak like myself, you want to give the answers. And you don't want anyone to make decisions for you. So that can get difficult, but the truth is that I love it."[30] As much as she loves it, she is also good at it. David Schwimmer claims that Courteney is organized, can juggle multiple things, and, more importantly, knows what she wants and "she has really taken that part of her personality and infused it into Monica."[31]

In addition to characteristics shared by Courteney and Monica, Cox was also fortunate enough to marry one of her costars: David Arquette. The two met on the set of the movie *Scream* in 1995. The following year, Arquette appeared in Episode 3.3, "The One with the Jam," where he played Ursula's stalker whom Phoebe almost dates and helps get over her sister. On June 12, 1999, Cox and Arquette were married, with Jennifer Aniston standing by Cox's side as her maid of honor, just as Rachel did for Monica at the end of season 7 in 2001. The opening episode of season 6 had Courteney newly credited as Cox-Arquette. To honor the moment, the rest of the cast also took Arquette's name in the opening credits of the episode (Lisa Kudrow-Arquette, Matt LeBlanc-Arquette, etc.) and the closing credits included a congratulations to the happy couple. Cox and Arquette appeared in subsequent *Scream* movies together between 1999 and 2011 as Gale Weathers and Deputy Dewey Riley. Their characters' romantic relationship developed over the course of the first three movies, culminating in their marriage at the end of *Scream 3*. However, much like their off-screen cohorts, Gale and Dewey's relationship was on the rocks in *Scream 4*, which came out in 2011. Although Cox and Arquette did not officially divorce until 2013, they announced their amicable split in 2010. Despite not being married, Cox and Arquette continued to produce television together through their production company, Coquette, including Cox's subsequent television appearances in *Dirt* (2007–2008) and *Cougar Town* (2009–2015) as well as the game show *Celebrity Name Game* (2014–present). Cox was later reported in gossip news to have dated Brian Van Holt, who played her ex-husband Bobby on *Cougar Town*, a series often considered *Friends*-at-40-in-a-cul-de-sac-in-Florida. To add another self-referential moment, Arquette was responsible for breaking the news that Cox and Van Holt had broken up when he was drunk and called into Howard Stern's SiriusXM radio show on October 31, 2013.[32]

Schwimmer's love life, on the other hand, left gossip magazines little to write about as he was famously private about it. It was reported that he dated Australian singer Natalie Imbruglia from 1995 to 1996; that he met his wife, Zoe Buckman, in 2007; and that they were married in 2010. As of April 2017, they are reportedly separated, although it is unclear if they have divorced.[33] Unlike Aniston or Cox, stories about Schwimmer focused more on how his life compared to Ross's in other ways. Schwimmer notes that his relationship with Courteney/Monica, as brother and sister, came naturally. He speculated that it may have been because she reminded him of his own sister, Ellie, that he "immediately felt brotherly towards Courteney."[34] His brotherly feelings toward her are only one quality David and Ross share. They are both New York natives. Schwimmer was the intellectual of the group just as Ross was, as Schwimmer attended prestigious Northwestern University whereas Geller earned his PhD from Columbia University. Just as Ross dated one of his former students, who was thirteen years his junior, Schwimmer's wife, Buckman, is nineteen years younger than he is. Buckman is also London-born just as Geller's second wife, Emily, was from England. He and his wife have one daughter, Cleo, just as Ross and Rachel have daughter Emma.[35] Such intertextual connections between Ross and David contribute to fans seeing his off-screen self as an extension of his on-screen character.

In contrast to Schwimmer's private wedding ceremony that was announced months later, Ross's wedding to Emily occurred over a well-publicized, season-ending, multi-episode arc. In this storyline, British actors Jennifer Saunders and Tom Conti played Ross's soon-to-be in-laws. As well-known British actors, their appearances, along with those of other well-known Brits such as Jane Carr (*The Prime of Miss Jean Brodie*), Hugh Laurie (*House*), Olivia Williams (*Rushmore*), and June Whitfield (who played Saunders's character Eddy's mother in *Absolutely Fabulous*), in the episode extended *Friends* self-referential qualities across the pond. Best known in the United States for her role as mostly drunken Edina "Eddy" Monsoon in *Absolutely Fabulous*, Saunders's role as Geller's mother-in-law had her sparring with Phoebe and flirting with Joey and Ross. Conti (*Reuben, Reuben*), as Stephen Waltham, squared off against Elliot Gould as Jack Geller and to a lesser extent Christina Pickles as Judy Geller, Ross and Monica's parents. Integrating such famous British actors gave the *Friends* actors a new place in the world of British film and television celebrity.

Just like Thomas and Leibman, Pickles and Gould hold particular places in the history of film and television that added an intertextual dimension to their roles as Monica and Ross's parents. Christina Pickles was born in England and attended the Royal Academy of Dramatic Art in London beginning at the age of fifteen. Classmates included Albert Finney, Peter O'Toole, and Brian Bedford.[36] She moved to New York in the 1950s and starred in multiple plays on Broadway before starting on television in the 1970s on soap operas such as *Guiding Light* and *Another World*. She made her mark with the American public playing Nurse Helen Rosenthal on *St. Elsewhere* from 1982 to 1988, earning five Emmy nominations for her work. She was also nominated for an Emmy early on for playing Monica and Ross's mother in *Friends* in 1995. Pickles continues her work today in the intergenerational web series *Break a Hip*, which she also produces and for which she was finally awarded an Emmy for Outstanding Actress in a Short Form Comedy or Drama Series.[37]

Elliott Gould entered Hollywood with a splash but ended up having trouble even treading water after some well-publicized snafus. As with Pickles, Gould began acting on Broadway in the 1950s. At the age of twenty-three, he met nineteen-year-old Barbra Streisand while costarring with her in Broadway's *I Can Get It for You Wholesale*. The two wed the following year, and Barbra earned her first top ten album with her debut, *The Barbra Streisand Album*. However, by 1969, they were separated, Gould noting that he just could not take be referred to as Mr. Streisand anymore nor being married to someone who was married to her own success. During their separation but before their divorce was finalized in

1971 was when Gould's movie career hit its pinnacle with an Oscar nomination for 1969's comedy about free love, *Bob & Carol & Ted & Alice*, and his role as ladies' man "Trapper" John McIntyre in *M*A*S*H*. With these roles, he became a counterculture icon and "Time magazine put him on the cover, calling him 'the standard bearer for the Western world's hung-up generation.'"[38] Some bad choices in jobs and life left him unemployable for years after these successes though. He left the United States to work with Ingmar Bergman and ended up with a reputation for volatility possibly spurred by drug use. His reputation was also not enhanced by his gambling problems at the time. Even though he never quite earned lead roles that would bring him to the forefront again (at least so far), he continued to work consistently for decades, making him an ever-presence in Hollywood.[39] His role in Steven Soderbergh's 2001 *Ocean's Eleven* remake (and its sequels) capitalized on his 1970s counter-culture roles by showing what such a lothario might look like in his sixties, in Vegas, in the early twenty-first century and brought him back into mainstream consciousness. In contrast, his role as Jack Geller in *Friends* showed what a 1970s Elliott Gould might have become had he settled down in the New York suburbs, married, and had two children. In other words, he became not counter-culture but dad-culture. His and Pickles's Jack and Judy Geller are the parents that embarrass their kids with their parental humor and by showing that older parents can still be hot for one another even as it horrifies their adult children. These roles are consistent with Pickles's and Gould's attitudes toward their careers as they both have made efforts to work with younger generations.

MATTHEW PERRY

Matthew Perry was the person most like their character on *Friends*. Perry even says that he was really the guy who spent his early twenties "not living a life and making fun of other people"[40] just like Chandler at the start of the series. At first, he did not audition as he was already committed to another show. But when he finally decided to audition, Perry actually *knew* what the creators and producers were looking for as he had been helping fellow actor friends prepare for their auditions for the part, including Craig Bierko, who was offered the part. Perry kept thinking about Chandler, "This is *me*. This is *me*."[41] So, after Bierko turned the part down, he finally went in to audition. He did not even need to bring the script as he already knew the whole thing and producer Kevin Bright said, "He *was* Chandler."[42] Perry read for Warner Brothers on a Thursday, auditioned for the network on Friday, and then started on the show on the following Monday.[43] Even as the creators had an idea of who Chandler was, "an observer of other people's lives" who "existed to say the funny thing at the end of scenes in which other people were doing things,"[44] Perry notes that Kauffman and Crane took each of the actors out to lunch separately between the pilot and first episode to find out more about them. When they met, they asked about qualities of the actors that they could incorporate into the show. From Perry they realized that he "is just the funny. He's got a nonstop mouth and 80 to 85 percent of what comes out is funny."[45] They were able to maintain Chandler as funny but made it not just about the punchline, but about his discomfort with serious situations. Perry's quick wit still allowed his vulnerable side to come through as well.

Qualities that Matthew and Chandler did not share, but that have become part of the intertextual cultural history of the series, were Perry's drug addiction that plagued him through most of the run of the series and his high-profile dating life. Perry reported in a *People* magazine interview in 2013 that he was already abusing alcohol when he started working on *Friends*.[46] After a Jet Ski accident in 1997, he also became addicted to prescription pain medicine. Perry reported to talk show host Larry King that taking the pills was in an attempt to drink less.[47] Although Perry says that he was never drunk or high while filming *Friends*, he admits that he was sometimes "painfully hungover"[48] and that season 3 (filmed 1996–1997) "was a low point for me, a high point for my addiction. . . . But still the show went on—with me and sometimes despite me."[49] Later in 1997, he went into a twenty-eight-day rehabilitation program for Vicodin addiction.

Perry's addictions, and his attempts to combat them, played roles in the stories about the series from 1997 through the end of its run. Even without stories in the tabloids, Perry's weight fluctuation appeared front and center in each season of the series. Notable weight losses marked his appearances in season 3 and at the start of season 7, after hospitalization for pancreatitis (related to his addictions). Despite how public his struggles with addiction were, Perry reports it as a very lonely time.[50] Unfortunately, his addictions have also led to his inability to remember nearly three seasons of the series. He reported to BBC radio host Chris Evans that he did not know what his least favorite episode was as he did not remember much between seasons 3 and 6.[51] Early in 2001, he re-entered rehab to recover from his use of Vicodin, methadone, amphetamines, and alcohol. He claims that he was sober in later seasons of the series and has since become an award-winning addiction and recovery advocate. He reported that his favorite season was eight (2001–2002) as it was the first season he can say he remembers all of as he was finally sober.[52] However, he also completed another stint in rehab as recently as 2017.[53] Although Perry's struggle with addiction never became part of the story-lines of the series, seeing him on-screen in the show along with the stories in the gossip media about where he was with his addiction led fans to pay closer attention to his appearance and performances wondering whether he was high on-screen on not.

In addition to his relationships with pills and alcohol, his relationships with women also topped the gossip headlines, creating an intertextual and self-referential layering of meaning between his roles as Chandler on-screen and as Matthew Perry off-screen. During filming of *Friends*, gossip columns linked Perry with several of his film costars, including Neve Campbell (*Three to Tango*), Amanda Peet (*The Whole Nine Yards* and *The Whole Ten Yards*), and Elizabeth Hurley (*Serving Sara*). Elizabeth Hurley is referenced in Episode 3.5, "The One with Frank Jr.," as one of the women who makes Ross's laminated list of women he can sleep with even though he is dating Rachel. He was also linked with tennis star Jennifer Capriati, former tennis star and soap actress Maeve Quinlan, as well as Renee Zellweger, Heather Graham, and Lauren Graham (who later guest starred in two of Perry's post-*Friends* series, *Studio 60 on the Sunset Strip* and *Go On*, as well as Lisa Kudrow's *Web Therapy*). Whether these relationships were really a part of Perry's life or not is not particularly important to this chapter. That the gossip media attempted to create connections between Perry's on- and off-screen lives came to define his love life throughout the run of the series.

Adding to the credibility of these stories, Perry dated Julia Roberts after she appeared as a childhood classmate-cum-potential lover, Susie "Underpants" Moss, in Episode 2.13, "The One after the Superbowl," and Yasmine Bleeth, whom he and Joey obsess over in episodes of *Baywatch*. It is amazing how private Perry is able to be with his relationships given

Matthew Perry and Julia Roberts. *NBC / Photofest © NBC*

that he dated actress Lizzie Caplan while her star was on the rise from 2006 to 2012.

The casting of Morgan Fairchild and Kathleen Turner as Chandler's mother and father, respectively, provided additional layers of intertextuality and self-referentiality. Fairchild, a 1970s and 1980s sex symbol, played his successful romance novelist mother, Nora Bing. Her frank references to her own sex life make Chandler uncomfortable, in ways that the audience understands not just because of what she says and does on-screen, but particularly from our knowledge of her roles on the daytime soap opera *Search for Tomorrow* (1973–1977) and prime-time soaps *Flamingo Road* (1980–1982) and *Falcon Crest* (1985–1986). Although Chandler's father does not actually appear in the series until season 7, Matthew Perry's actor father, John Bennett Perry, appeared just as uncomfortable as Joshua's (Tate Donovan's) father in Episode 4.18, "The One with Rachel's New Dress," in 1998, when he saw Rachel in her slip-dress. Interestingly, when Billy Crystal and Robin Williams appeared in a cameo in the show, Episode 3.24, "The One with the Ultimate Fighting Champion," Crystal noted that he was excited to work with Perry as he has lost the chance to work with his father John in *Soap* when he was recast at the last minute.[54] (In 1999 and 2002, Lisa Kudrow played Crystal's wife in *Analyze This* and *Analyze That*.) His TV mother, real father, and their relationships with other actors on and off the show place Chandler/Matthew in the center of daytime and evening programming history of television.

In season 7, when Chandler and Monica are planning their wedding, Chandler's cross-dressing father first appears when Monica and Chandler go to Las Vegas and see his burlesque show, "Viva Las Gaygas," and invite him to their wedding. Casting Kathleen Turner as Chandler's father in one fell swoop evokes thoughts of the past roles the gravel-voiced actress played as sexual women (in movies such as *Body Heat*) and queers our understanding of what a father is by having her play a man who dresses as a woman in the same ways that Julie Andrews did in *Victor, Victoria*. Turner says being a woman playing a man playing a woman was irresistible in itself but getting to engage in a "bitchfest" with Morgan Fairchild and having Perry still call her "Dad" today made it even better.[55] While there may be some problems with a woman playing a gay, cross-dressing man, these are discussed further in chapter 7. For the purposes of this chapter, it is important to note that questions about Chandler's sexuality, suggested by his mannerisms, tastes in music and movies, and indefinable "qualities" pointed out in Episode 1.8, "The One where Nana Dies Twice," are expanded by actually showing his father rather than merely making joking references about his sexuality, show, and role in Chandler's life.

LISA KUDROW

Phoebe made for a "quirky foil" to spoiled Rachel and uptight Monica on the page as well as the screen. Even so, Kudrow seemed to generate less star presence outside of the *Friends*' storyline.[56] Additionally, Kudrow married French advertising executive, Michel Stern, in 1995, after the first season of *Friends* wrapped, making her personal life less headline-worthy than Jennifer Aniston and Courteney Cox, who married film stars during the run of the series. Even so, elements of her married life entered the series. Phoebe may have spent her teen years living on the street, but she somehow became fluent in French and speaks Italian. Given that her husband was French, this skill for Kudrow was no surprise. When Ku-drow got pregnant in real life, they wrote her pregnancy into the show. They were the first show to have embryos from a brother and his wife implanted into his sister's womb, so that Phoebe did not have to become a parent on-screen even as Kudrow became a mother off-screen. Unfortu-nately, one of Phoebe's most well-known skills, playing guitar, is not one that she and Kudrow had in common. Kudrow admits that it was "pretty cool" playing with Chrissie Hynde on the show but admitted that she never committed to learning guitar, which may be one reason Phoebe's songs did not play as large a role in later seasons of the show as they did at the beginning or during the "Smelly Cat" furor.[57]

Kudrow's place in the intertextual world of 1990s NBC's "Must-See TV" Thursday lineup began before *Friends*. Kudrow's Ursula first ap-peared in a recurring role on *Mad about You* (1992–1999). When *Friends* premiered, the character of Phoebe was introduced and soon thereafter Ursula appeared on the series as her twin sister, forever connecting the diegetic worlds of both series. To further this connection, Helen Hunt and Leila Kenzle cameoed as their *Mad about You* characters, Jamie Buch-man and Fran Devanow, respectively, in Episode 1.16, "The One with Two Parts: Part 1." The connections between *Friends* characters and other series and actors connected them to an extended off-screen celebrity diegesis as well. One where, as a *Los Angeles Times* reporter puts it, "[*Friends*] quickly turned itself into a self-conscious star parade that was consistently reinforcing its own status as a cultural phenomenon, and expanding on its own presence in the culture until it became a highly stylized, almost formal exercise in celebrity, star power, and self-referen-tiality."[58] The celebrity diegesis is furthered when Phoebe dates Parker, played by Alec Baldwin, in two episodes in season 8, one of which is Episode 8.18, "The One in Massapequa," placing Baldwin back in his birthplace even in his fictional role as Parker.

Having Teri Garr and Bob Balaban as Phoebe's birth parents and Audra Lindley as her grandmother further places Phoebe/Lisa in a self-referential celebrity diegetic. Although Phoebe lives with her grandmoth-er when the series first begins and she does not pass away until five seasons later, she only appears once. Audra Lindley, who appeared as Phoebe's grandmother, previously played Mrs. Helen Roper, Jack, Janet, and Chrissy's landlady, on *Three's Company* from 1976 to 1982. Despite having ended over a decade before *Friends* began, when Rachel thinks that Chandler is moving in with both her and Monica in Episode 6.2, "The One where Ross Hugs Rachel," she suggests they will be like the two female and one male roommate premise of *Three's Company*. Rachel even sings part of the theme song of the series. Although Teri Garr did not appear in *Three's Company*, she did appear in two episodes of Marlo Thomas's *That Girl* (between 1967 and 1968). Where Garr really made a name for herself was as a comedienne in her appearances in twelve episodes of *The Sonny and Cher Comedy Hour* (1972) and a variety of other guest appearances before she started appearing in career-defining roles in film, such as Inga in *Young Frankenstein* (1974), Ronnie Neary in *Close Encounters of the Third Kind* (1977), and *Tootsie* (1982). The one common thread in most of her roles was her space-cadet, "dumb blonde" qualities. Her casting as flighty Phoebe's birth mother, then, created intertextual connections between their "floopy"-ness (Episode 4.1, "The One with the Jellyfish"). Bob Balaban also appeared in *Close Encounters of the Third Kind* as well as a number of independent films leading up to his casting on *Friends*, including *Waiting for Guffman* (1996), *Conversation with the Beast* (1996), *Deconstructing Harry* (1997), and *Clockwatchers* (1997), which Lisa Kudrow also starred in. He also appeared as Russell Darlymple, an NBC television executive considering a *Seinfeld*-like series, in five episodes of *Seinfeld* two years before *Friends* premiered, providing a connection between those two New York–set, "Must-See TV" programs. Balaban further extends the self-referentiality between these worlds with his role as NBC executive Warren Littlefield in the TV movie about the late-night talk show rivalry between David Letterman and Jay Leno called *The Late Shift* (1996). Phoebe/Lisa's personal life does not play as much of a role as some of the actors on the series, but her roles in the "Must-See TV" lineup, along with the casting of her family members, created a celebrity diegetic that placed her firmly at the center of the cultural history of television.

MATT LEBLANC

Joey was the least developed character on the page. This made it extremely important for the creators and writers to find what Matt LeBlanc could bring to the character to develop it. When they found out how good he was at playing dumb, they capitalized on it for the character. Even so, as

LeBlanc grew and matured, so did Joey. At the same time, when he appeared in the *Charlie's Angels* reboot movies, David Wild noted a trend in LeBlanc working with three hot women, a trend that LeBlanc said that he would not mind keeping going. Even so, LeBlanc's love life stayed out of the gossip media for the most part. He did marry Melissa McKnight, a former model, in 2003, but they divorced in 2006. LeBlanc was then said to have dated his *Joey* costar Andrea Anders from 2006 until early 2015.

As noted in the previous chapter, Joey's parents did not play a significant role in the series. They only appeared once in the first season in Episode 1.13, "The One with the Boobies." Both were likely cast primarily for their Italian American pedigrees. While Joey Tribianni Sr., played by Robert Costanza, has a long list of acting credits, including guest roles on many series, TV movies, and films, most often as a police officer, including three episodes as Mr. Broadwater on *St. Elsewhere* (between 1982 and 1988), he was cast as the quintessential Italian father of Joey and his sisters. Whereas Brenda Vaccaro's casting as his mother, much like the casting of Rachel's, Monica and Ross's, Chandler's, and Phoebe's parents, evokes self-referentiality to her 1970s and 1980s roles. Early in her career, she was nominated for Golden Globe Awards for New Star of the Year for her performance in *Where It's At* (1969) and Best Supporting Actress as Shirley in Best Picture Winner *Midnight Cowboy* (1969). She also won the Golden Globe and was nominated for an Academy Award for Best Supporting Actress in *Once Is Not Enough* (1975). Although a short-lived series, Vaccaro was also nominated for an Emmy for Outstanding Lead Actress in a Drama Series for her performance as the lead in *Sara* (1976). She remained well-known for her frequent guest-starring roles in series as diverse as *The Love Boat* and *St. Elsewhere* (both in 1984) and earned an Emmy nomination for Outstanding Guest Actress in a Comedy Series for her role as Angela Petrillo in *The Golden Girls* in 1990.

While the careers of the actors playing his parents create moments of television referentiality for Joey/Matt, the intertextual diegetic surrounding him most often took the shape of the soap opera world in which Joey appeared as Dr. Drake Ramoray on *Days of Our Lives*. In some episodes of *Friends*, Joey appeared on-screen in his role as Drake (e.g., Episode 8.23, "The One where Rachel Has a Baby: Part 1"), at work on the set of *Days of Our Lives* (e.g., Episode 8.5, "The One with Rachel's Date"), or at events related to his work (such as attending awards shows in Episode 7.18, "The One with Joey's Award"). In all of these episodes, actors from *Days of Our Lives* appeared as themselves or their characters. Interestingly, they often did not even have lines, such as when Joey hosted a party for them all on the roof of the building in Episode 9.20, "The One with the Soap Opera Party," which resulted in them playing what amounted to extras on *Friends*. Even so, for fans of *Days* and *Friends*, these episodes wrapped the two shows into the same narrative world. As a matter of fact, Joey's role as Drake Ramoray "is itself an intertextual reference to longtime *Days* actor Drake Hogestyn, and Joey's signature 'smell the fart' eyebrow raise is characteristic of Hogestyn's portrayal of John Black."[59]

Friends even gave Joey/Drake his own fan/stalker in season 2 and cast Brooke Shields in the role. Giving Joey/Drake his own obsessive fan gave his role as Drake some credibility, and casting Shields, a well-known model and child actor who happened to be dating tennis star Andre Agassi at the time,[60] furthered *Friends* connections within the world of film and television. Shields, known previously for her roles in *Pretty Baby* (1978), *The Blue Lagoon* (1980), and *Endless Love* (1981), and as spokeswoman for Calvin Klein jeans, made a mark on Hollywood as an innocent-appearing Lolita-type. Reappearing over a decade later on *Friends* as an obsessed fan helped Shields score her own NBC show, *Suddenly Susan* (1996–2000). Shields explains that she said yes even before seeing a script because she saw the show as "incredibly hip." She also relished the opportunity to play the character in the world of television that she was mostly unfamiliar with. She never expected it to change her life so drastically.[61] Ultimately, seeing such a well-known actress appear to be a fan of Joey/Drake and express her fandom of *Friends* brought the show into the world of Hollywood celebrity early in its run.

Later, *Friends* cast Susan Sarandon as a longtime actress on *Days of Our Lives*, Cecelia Monroe. The storyline has *Days* writing Monroe off the show and putting the character's brain into Drake's brain-dead body, bringing him back to life as Cecelia. The casting of Sarandon and the storyline provide an opportunity to examine the nature of celebrity by comparing film stars with soap opera stars within the context of a successful sitcom.[62] At one point, Cecelia laments having stayed on *Days* rather than accepting earlier opportunities to star in Mexican films. While Joey is impressed, the audience laughs at this moment as it suggests that being a soap star in the United States is on par with being a foreign film star. Both being "less than" the stardom Sarandon has achieved as an Academy Award–winning star of American films provides the gap between reality and television that makes the audience laugh. At the same time, casting Oscar-winning actresses and supermodels (such as Elle Macpherson as Joey's roommate-turned-girlfriend Janine) to guest star on the show suggests the *Friends* cast is on the same plane as this A-list celebrity world.

Friends' place in the world of celebrity culture may have been cemented by its popularizing of the representation of twenty-somethings living on their own and spending so much time just "hanging out" with one another (see chapter 1). Becoming part of a broader diegetic of television and film actors—both on- and off-screen—along with the proliferation of celebrity gossip news on television, especially in the age of the emerging Internet, put the stars of the show on a new level of celebrity reporting and access. Add to their presence on the show, and the reporting about it, their roles as celebrity spokespersons and you have a vortex of celebrity presence that contributed to the collapse of actors and roles that has kept the *Friends* actors associated with the show and their roles to extent rarely seen before. Just as *Friends* has never left the air since its premiere twenty-five years ago, so too do the stories about them as Jennifer/Rachel, Courteney/Monica, Lisa/Phoebe, Matt/Joey, Matthew/Chandler, and David/Ross continue to define how fans and audiences see them. They will always be our *Friends*, but their relationships on- and off-screen also define how we see them and who we associate them with throughout television history and celebrity culture.

3

FRIENDS AS FAMILY

Does television reflect or construct reality? The answer to this question is, of course, both. Representations of families on television in the United States, for example, have changed over time to reflect, mirror, and rework larger social trends in ways that highlight public concerns or cultural tides.[1] In the 1950s, sitcoms focused primarily around family life at home or the workplace. The home in these shows provided a safe space in which characters could escape the anxieties of work, even as the home was depicted as a utopia that rarely, if ever, really existed outside the television screen.[2] By the 1970s, the focus of many comedies became the "work family," "which blurred the boundaries between work and home life, and in which the public or professional realm provided a space of solidarity, intimacy, nurturing, and emotional intensity outside of the domestic sphere."[3] Series such as *The Mary Tyler Moore Show* and *M*A*S*H* provide examples where work families substituted for the ideal biological family that never seemed achievable. As home and work sitcoms continue today (e.g., *American Housewife* and *Brooklyn 99*), the 1990s saw the emergence of the "pal-com," or series focused primarily on home life but where "families" are replaced by a "chosen kinship network made up of friends (and sometimes co-workers) rather than biological family."[4] More recently, the pal-com can be seen in *How I Met Your Mother*, *New Girl*, and, of course, *The Big Bang Theory*. Each of these shows owes a debt to *Friends* as one of its most important cultural legacies lies with its form as ensemble situation comedy that popularized the portrayal of friends as each other's primary familial unit.

Friends reflected the lives of its twenty-something characters in the mid-1990s as Generation X (those born between 1965 and 1984), also known as the Divorce Generation. The divorce rate for Gen-Xers' parents steadily rose during the 1970s and hit an all-time high in 1981,[5] leaving many without both parents under the same roof and increasing experiences of split families, where kids spent weekends with one parent and the rest of the week with the other. It is not any wonder, then, that young people began to rely on each other and often ended up privileging friends over family.[6] *Friends'* executive producers, Kevin Bright, Marta Kauffman, and David Crane, explicitly said their show was "about love, sex, careers, and a time of life when everything is possible. It's about searching for commitment and security—and a fear of commitment and security. And, most of all, it's a show about friendship—because when a person is young and single in the city, friends and family are synonymous."[7]

Such transient and uncertain day-to-day experiences with biological families became balanced by individuals' choices to create their own alternative families and kinship networks. These friends as family became the foundation upon which their alternative families were built. "Alternative families" refers to groups of people "with common social and economic needs and resources, and with a historical legacy and shared sense of future."[8] *Friends* puts its alternative family at the center of the show to demonstrate how chosen kinship networks privilege the common social needs of the group, provide economic support when needed, and, most importantly, provide the kinds of everyday support individuals often lose when they move away from their biological families. This chapter will focus on how *Friends* constructed its alternative family in such a way as to create a cultural legacy of what alternative families *should* be.

ADULT SIBLINGS AS FRIENDS: MONICA AND ROSS GELLER

Although the primary storyline for the series focuses on a group of friends, it was the biological relationship between two of the characters, sister and brother Monica and Ross Geller, that served as the centripetal force that drew this group together in the first place. Monica brought in

Phoebe (her former roommate) and Rachel (her high school best friend and new roommate from the first episode of the series) whereas Ross attracted Chandler (his college roommate) and, by default, Chandler's current roommate, Joey. Over time, the relationships among the group became intertwined in many other ways.[9] Ross and Rachel are romantically involved (sometimes), get married (in Vegas) and divorced, have a baby together, and (spoiler alert!) get together in the end. Chandler and Monica hook up at Ross's second wedding (to Emily), and after a half season of hilarious moments as they attempted to hide their relationships from their friends, they end up moving in together and ultimately get married too. Despite a couple of kisses along the way (to help Joey get over Phoebe's twin sister, Ursula, and to assist Phoebe's desire to experience a perfect kiss), Phoebe and Joey never actually get together romantically, though fans often shipped them. Their utility to the group went unquestioned as Joey's apartment serves as locale for rotating roommates, including Ross, Chandler, Rachel, and Phoebe, and Phoebe and Rachel forge an unlikely bond when Rachel lives with her for a time. Their necessity to the group is questioned a couple of times though. In "The One with the Kips" (Episode 5.5), in an attempt to get his now-wife Emily to make up with him and move to New York (after he said Rachel's name at the wedding), Ross agrees not to see Rachel anymore. When Rachel comes into Central Perk, Joey and Chandler warn her that Ross is in the bathroom. Immediately, she is reminded of Chandler's old roommate, Kip, who, after a failed attempt at a relationship with Monica, the group "phased out." While Monica rejects the notion that Rachel would be another Kip, Rachel says that Ross would not be cut out as he is her brother and Chandler's college roommate. However, she also suggests that if anyone were to be phased out, she always thought it would be Phoebe. While Phoebe objects, Rachel concludes that not being related to anyone and living far away makes it easier to lift her out. Monica consoles Phoebe, but the audience knows Rachel is correct. Even so, later Rachel makes up with Phoebe and creates a plan to start their own group together, with Joey, of course. While it is true that Phoebe could be lifted right out of the group, her quirkiness, kindness, generosity, and even her edge would be missed. Bringing Rachel and Phoebe together at a time when Rachel's place in the group is challenged shows how they had bonded after five seasons. Ultimately, Ross also steps up to say that it is his fault the group cohesion is challenged and therefore he should step out. However, he finally realizes that his friends are actually more important to him than his wife, Emily, and he opts to stay in New York, get divorced, and remain with his friends, restoring the six central *Friends'* family unit.

Ultimately, due to their biological bond, it is always assumed that Monica and Ross will remain together and that the others depend upon them for the cohesion of their alternative family. Throughout the series, there are moments that remind us of their childhood together and the enduring bonds they have. In "The One where Underdog Gets Away" (Episode 1.9), Monica tells Ross that their mother and father are going away for Thanksgiving. Ross does not believe her and pettily goes to call their mother. Even though their mother confirms what Monica told him, he does not apologize for his suspicion. Nor does Monica protest or make a big deal of his behavior as their treatment of one another has a long history and they know what to expect. Instead, she offers to make Thanksgiving dinner just like their mom's for him, including the lumpy potatoes (which irritates perfectionist chef Monica, but she does it for her brother). We see their shorthand with one another regularly, such as when they play foosball together for the first time when Chandler and Joey get the table. Monica and Ross win, give each other a high ten, grab hands, bring them down, and then kiss each other on the cheek before she leaves to go check on Rachel ("The One with the Dozen Lasagnas," Episode 1.12). No explanation of their interaction is needed as the audience understands they are brother and sister, have history, and have likely played and celebrated winning games together before.

This does not mean that their relationship goes untested. When Monica forgets that Ross is allergic to kiwi but serves him kiwi-lime pie, she has to take him to the hospital for a shot. While she apologizes for "poisoning" him, they lament other conflicts they have had in the past: when he jammed a pencil in her hand (and she still has the scar); when she hit him in the face with a pumpkin; when he stuck a broom in the spokes of her bicycle and she flew over the handlebars and hit her head on the curb (which she does not remember) (Episode 2.6, "The One with the Baby on the Bus"). Although the audience does not get to see these childhood moments, we do get to see them fight like children when Ross starts spending all of his time at Monica's apartment when he and Rachel get together. In "The One where Eddie Moves In" (Episode 2.17), Monica calls Ross a doofus while trying to get him out of her bathroom. When he comes out, he mimics her with a whiny, baby voice. Later when he is on their phone at their apartment, another call beeps in. He answers it and hands the phone to Monica telling her that it is her boyfriend, Richard. However, when Monica gets on the phone and asks if she left her diaphragm at his house, she is horrified to learn it is actually their mother. All of the tension between them comes to a head when Ross wants to watch a special about the Serengeti and Monica wants to watch *Entertainment Tonight*. She gets really angry, but he says that he thought they were just giving each other a hard time like when they were kids. Monica then reveals to Ross that she hated him when they were kids because he was mean, teased her, and always got his way. Monica then softens to explain that she does not hate him now as they have become friends, but that now he just needs to stop pissing her off before she kills him. He offers to let her watch *Entertainment Tonight*, but then Monica says he can watch his show, which, in typical Ross fashion, he takes her up on rather than being the nice older brother. Audience members with siblings get it: Monica and Ross love each other, would do anything for each other, but also drive each other nuts sometimes. *Friends* offered us the rare opportunity to see the normality of this type of adult sibling relationship on television. While their biological bond may subconsciously provide the audience with comfort that these relationships among the friends will never end, it is these moments that solidify their friendship beyond the biological bond that remind us that it is their friendship that keeps them together, not biology.

BIOLOGICAL FAMILIES' TRIALS AND TRIBULATIONS

The intertwined relationships forged among the group beyond Monica and Ross provide additional evidence that their relationships are just as strong, if not stronger, than biology. This is because *Friends* was always a show about friendship between all six of them. Their support for one another through romantic liaisons and breakups, births and deaths, being hired and fired from jobs, and all the everyday anxieties of being on your own in your twenties in New York City demonstrates their familial commitments to one another. But it is also the distance created between the friends and their biological families, both literal distance and psychological and emotional distance, that serves to validate the cohesion of the

Friends alternative family. For example, Joey has the largest biological family of the group. We meet his parents in "The One with the Boobies" (Episode 1.13) when we also learn that his father (Robert Costanzo) is having an affair. However, his mother (Brenda Vaccaro) knows all about it and pretends not to know as Joey Sr. treats her better to atone for his own guilt and she does not have to deal with him all the time when he is away with his girlfriend. We also meet all seven of his sisters (Cookie, Dina, Gina, Mary Angela, Mary Therese, Tina, and Veronica) and his grandmother in "The One where Chandler Can't Remember which Sister" (Episode 3.11). Despite such a large family, certain members of his family appear in only two other episodes, his grandmother in "The One where Ross Can't Flirt" (Episode 5.19) and his sister Dina in "The One with Monica's Boots" (Episode 8.10). When Joey stars in plays, acts on TV, gets hired and fired from these jobs, it is all of the friends who are there, not his biological family. It is not that he has a bad relationship with his family; it is just that his daily support comes from his friends. When Joey is killed off on *Days of Our Lives*, his friends watch the episode at Monica and Rachel's place while he, embarrassed, sits alone in his new apartment. As soon as the episode concludes, however, his friends rush over to his apartment. He laments having lost the job and its perks, such as being pre-approved for credit cards, when Rachel reminds him that he "will always be pre-approved with us" (Episode 2.18, "The One where Dr. Ramoray Dies").

Joey may have a good relationship with his family, even though we do not see much of them, but Chandler has a better excuse for not interacting with his parents very often. They told him that they were getting divorced on Thanksgiving when he was nine years old because his father was seeing the houseboy (Episode 5.8, "The One with All the Thanksgivings"). Chandler's hatred of Thanksgiving was born on that day. His friends are the ones who make him grilled cheese and roasted chicken and allow him to avoid most Thanksgiving traditions even as they celebrate the holiday. But it is also these friends that lead him to want to participate in the holiday with them. The friends are there for Chandler as he deals with his mother issues (his sexually assertive mother, played by Morgan Fairchild, and Ross kiss in Episode 1.11, "The One with Mrs. Bing" and she mentions the prowess of her lover at Chandler and Monica's wedding reception in Episode 8.1, "The One after I Do") and Monica helps him reunite with his father (Kathleen Turner) by taking him to see his gay burlesque show in Vegas (Episode 7.22, "The One with Chandler's Dad"). Chandler's parents play a role in who he is, how he acts, and the issues he contends with on a regular basis in the series. But their actual presence is limited to particular moments that punctuate his life. Even in flashback episodes, we see that Ross brought Chandler to the Gellers' for holidays while they were in college too (Episode 5.8, "The One with All the Thanksgivings") rather than him spending time with either of his parents. Chandler's primary support comes not from his parents but these friends.

While Rachel has a somewhat larger family—her mother (Marlo Thomas), father (Ron Leibman), and sisters, Jill (Reese Witherspoon) and Amy (Christina Applegate)—she experiences some of the same issues with divorce as Chandler. However, Rachel's split with her family plays out in the first and second seasons of the series. At the start of the pilot episode, Rachel runs into Central Perk in a wedding dress having literally run out on her wedding to Dr. Barry Farber (Mitchell Whitfield) and the life planned for her (marriage to a doctor, or dentist in her case, and kids on Long Island). By the end of the episode, we watch as the friends help Rachel cut up her credit cards (which her father pays for), symbolizing her choice to cut herself off from her biological family. Rachel's parents get divorced in season 2, and the audience is privy to the impact it has on Rachel as well. In "The One with the Lesbian Wedding" (Episode 2.11), Rachel's mother arrives at the coffee shop to check up on Rachel and ends up telling Rachel that she is getting a divorce, wants to experiment with pot, and enjoys that she has the option of experimenting sexually with women as well at Carol and Susan's wedding. Rachel struggles with this new and different mother but understands when her mother explains that she married her Barry. By Episode 2.22, "The One with the Two Parties," the impact of their divorce on Rachel becomes apparent when the gang must throw two birthday parties for Rachel: one in Monica and Rachel's apartment, which Rachel's mother attends, and one in Chandler and Joey's apartment, which Rachel's father attends. While her friends separating her parents keeps them from fighting, it does not stop each of them from complaining to Rachel about the other. Ultimately, Chandler finds Rachel in the hallway, between the parties (and her parents), trying to avoid them both. His childhood experience with divorce makes him the perfect friend to comfort her in her time of need, until, that is, Ross, her friend and at the time boyfriend, comes to take over.

The other appearances of her parents and sisters serve as comic foils, of course, but also to solidify the reasons she spends more time with her friends than her family. Her parents subsequently appear at times when Rachel seemingly needs parental guidance. For example, when Rachel and Ross are dating, Rachel asks Ross to have dinner with her and her father. Rachel desperately wants them to get along. The tension in the episode arises first between Ross and Dr. Green, but then shifts to Rachel and Ross when he bonds with her father by criticizing her (for not having renter's insurance and going to a chiropractor) (Episode 3.7, "The One with the Race Car Bed"). The tension is resolved with her father's departure and the return to normalcy between Rachel and Ross. Then when Rachel gets pregnant with Ross's baby, episodes when Rachel has to tell her father that she is pregnant but not marrying Ross (Episode 8.8, "The One with the Stripper") and when Monica and Phoebe have a baby shower for Rachel (Episode 8.20, "The One with the Baby Shower") highlight her tension-filled relationship with her parents. Her father is angry that she is pregnant but relieved when he thinks she is marrying Ross. Then he is angry with Ross and protective of Rachel when he thinks that it is Ross's fault they are not getting married. At the baby shower, Rachel's mother convinces her that she is not ready to have a baby and needs her mother to help her. In both cases, Rachel's parents try (and fail) to offer her parental guidance and protection. They are unsuccessful, however, because Rachel has her friends to help her. We see this when Phoebe is the one who helps Rachel tell her father in the first place and provides her with a distraction (going to the movies) when her father reads her the riot act in the end and when Ross acts as a friend and parental-mentor at the end of the other episode by quizzing Rachel on parenting facts. At the same time, the appearances of her sisters, Jill and Amy, merely show why Rachel would not want them in her life. Jill acts more spoiled than Rachel was at the start of the show and tries to date Ross (Episodes 6.13, "The One with Rachel's Sister" and 6.14, "The One where Chandler Can't Cry") whereas Amy cares more about her hair and married boyfriend than she does about Rachel, Ross, or her niece, Emma (Episodes 9.8, "The One with Rachel's Other Sister" and 10.5, "The One where Rachel's Sister Babysits"). While her biological family will always be her family, their presence highlights the value and support Rachel gets from her friends in her attempts to divorce herself from the life her parents expected her to lead or the ones her sisters continue to lead.

Ross and Monica's parents (Elliot Gould and Christina Pickles) have the most prominent roles on the show, having appeared in a total of twenty episodes. There are times when their parents provide comfort, such as when Jack helps Monica get over her breakup with Richard and finally sleep in "The One with the Princess Leia Fantasy" (Episode 3.1), or parental guidance, such as when Jack reminds Monica how he taught them that 10 percent of their paychecks should go into savings (Episode 2.14, "The One with the Prom Video"). Judy and Jack advise the whole gang at one time or another, such as when Judy tells them all what to do about their issues at the end of "The One where Ross Got High." Despite her straight shooting in this scene, it concludes with Judy and Jack saying that they do not know what to do about Monica and Ross. So their friend Chandler reassures the Geller parents that he should be the one to talk to them, putting him in the parental role when they are unsure how to fulfill their duties.

When Judy and Jack try to take care of their children, the tensions in their relationship with Monica and Ross come through with their favoritism of Ross, Jack's depiction as a man-child who lives in his own reality, and Judy's overbearing, hard-to-please mother to Monica. A sequence from Episode 1.2, "The One with the Sonogram at the End," shows these characteristics and relationships play out. It begins when their mother criticizes the appetizers Monica made while at the same time telling her that Martha Ludwin's daughter is going to call her for advice since she wants to do something with cooking or food because, as Judy said, Monica has a restaurant. While Monica tries to correct her, Judy says that the Ludwins do not need to know that Monica merely works at a restaurant. Meanwhile, their parents bolster Ross's ego by reminding him about all the women who were hot for him, and Monica's mother continues to criticize Monica by dismissing the entrée Monica made, spaghetti, as easy. Monica, desperate for relief, implores Ross to tell their parents about Carol's lesbian relationship and his impending parenthood to take the heat off her. Before he does though, their folks get in a few more punches when Judy reminds Monica that she's not married. When Jack tries to help, he cuts against his own compliment of her as "independent" with comments about her having been fine when she was "chubby" and "had no friends." Being in his own world, Jack ends up doubling down on the backhanded compliments when he characterizes Ross as ambitious and Monica as satisfied with her life as it is. Monica then forces Ross to reveal his news to their parents. When he does, Judy ends up blaming Monica for not telling them sooner.

In this sequence, it is clear that Judy and Jack both favor Ross for his accomplishments and have low expectations for what Monica can achieve. Additionally, Judy does not seem to value Monica's profession or accomplishments and believes her housekeeping and cooking skills could use improvement. Even when Ross tells his parents potentially upsetting news about his ex-wife, her lover, and his impending father-hood, Judy blames Monica for not telling her. These tensions between Monica, Ross, and their parents give the audience plenty of reasons for believing these siblings are better supporters of one another than their parents.

In contrast to the Geller family, Phoebe's family is the least cohesive but interestingly plays the largest role of any of the families of the friends. When the series begins, Phoebe lives with her grandmother, Frances (Audra Lindley), mother to Lily. Lily raised Phoebe and her twin sister, Ursula, while her stepfather was in prison. When they were about fourteen years old, however, Lily killed herself. Later, in Episode 3.25, "The One at the Beach," Phoebe visits an old friend of her mother's to see if she can tell Phoebe where to find her father. Instead, she learns that her mother's friend, Phoebe Sr. (Teri Garr), is really her birth mother and that Phoebe, Lily, and Frank Buffay were "in a couple" together. Phoebe only meets her birth father (Bob Balaban) once at her grandmother's funeral and learns that he did not even know that Lily had died (Episode 5.13, "The One with Joey's Bag"). But when Phoebe first starts searching for Frank, she finds that she has an half-brother, Frank Jr. (Giovanni Ribisi), who does become a significant part of her life over the course of the series as she carries he and his wife's, Alice's (Debra Jo Rupp), triplets for them. Despite living with her grandmother for the first five seasons of the show, we only see her grandmother once (Episode 2.9, "The One with Phoebe's Dad").

Phoebe's seemingly closest relative, her twin sister, Ursula (also played by Lisa Kudrow), serves as her greatest foe. Phoebe tells stories of their competition with one another, from the fact that Ursula was born first and took her first steps first (though Phoebe did both later the same day) to their fights over boys that resulted in the destruction of Phoebe's Judy Jetson lunchbox (Episode 1.16, "The One with Two Parts, Part 1"). While Phoebe tries to relate to her sister, by sharing important revelations about their mother, bringing her gifts on their birthdays, or protecting her, Ursula always acts worse than Phoebe anticipates. When Phoebe brings Ursula a Judy Jetson lunchbox and tries to get her to make up with Joey, Ursula ends up regifting the sweater Joey gave her to Phoebe and continuing to ghost Joey instead of telling him they are over (Episode 1.16, "The One with Two Parts, Part 1"). When Phoebe goes to tell Ursula that Lily was not their birth mother, she learns that Ursula already knew that from their mother's suicide note, which she never shared with Phoebe (Episode 4.1, "The One with the Jellyfish"). When Phoebe brings Ursula a Hippity Hop for what she thinks is their thirtieth birthday, Ursula informs Phoebe that they are thirty-one, not thirty, and admits that she sold Phoebe's birth certificate to a Swedish runaway (Episode 7.14, "The One where They All Turn 30"). When Phoebe learns that Ursula uses Phoebe as her stage name for low-budget pornography, Phoebe confronts Ursula rather than calling the police on her. Of course, Phoebe also gets back at Ursula when she refuses to stop using Phoebe's name by having Ursula's checks for her movies sent to her own address (Episode 6.14, "The One where Chandler Can't Cry"). Although Phoebe finds some comfort and motherly advice from Phoebe Sr., in general Phoebe's difficult life serves as a warning against trying to find comfort in those you believe you are related to or getting too close to those who are most closely related to you. Instead, Phoebe finds more support from her friends, who accept her just the way she is, and more distant relations as they enter her life as an adult.

Friends departed from the typical family or workplace sitcom by focusing on friends as family and popularizing what has become commonplace in the televisual landscape: the pal-com. Creating an alternative family out of the six friends in the series required both focus on their ever-presence in one another's lives as well as creating distance between each friend and their biological families. The ways the show used the spaces the friends occupied also served to emphasize their group as an alternative family.

OUR APARTMENT IS YOUR APARTMENT/OUR COFFEE SHOP IS OUR HOME

On *Friends*, their daily interactions as this alternative family play out not in the workplace or biological family homes, but on the couches and chairs at the local coffee shop, Central Perk, and in the living rooms of their friends' homes, which they walk into and out of as if their family had four apartments of their own. As such, *Friends* told the stories of this family of friends in the multiple spaces they called and/or treated as their homes. One of the ways the show highlighted the ensemble nature of the show and kept the primary focus on all of their relationships with one another was the use of "private" spaces. Although there is some change and movement over the course of the series, there are three primary spaces in which the friends interact: Central Perk, Monica's apartment, and Joey's apartment.[10] The centers of each of these spaces are the living rooms and kitchens. Each living room has at least one couch and multiple chairs to accommodate all six friends comfortably, and the kitchens provide additional spaces for interactions as well as for providing the domestic necessities such as food and drinks. All three spaces also have bathrooms and the apartments include bedrooms. Whether they are actually in one of their apartments or at the coffee shop, it still appears as if all the friends live in the domestic spaces they share with one another. Each of them appear to have the same rights to each other's spaces, as evidenced by their unannounced entrances and exits, ready access to food and drinks (without asking), and moving in and out of them all for different periods of time. Although each place may belong primarily to one or more of them at any given time, they all belong to the group as their alternative family's shared private spaces.

Central Perk almost always has a number of other customers lurking in the background of the main action. Centering the friends' space on the orange couch in the middle of the coffee shop with a table and chairs on the right and an armchair on the left gave all six characters places to sit together, leaving everyone else outside their semicircle.

It became so familiar to see them in this space that when other people were there, the audience was meant to see them as interlopers. When bullies take Chandler's and Ross's seats on the couch, they first turn to Gunther to help them but then end up nearly fighting the men who try to usurp their coveted space (Episode 2.21, "The One with the Bullies").

Central Perk set. *NBC / Photofest © NBC*

When they all six walked into the coffee shop to find other people sitting in their seats in the cold open of the first episode of season 3, "The One with the Princess Leia Fantasy," there was no need for the characters to say anything before they walked out of Central Perk.[11] The audience's laugh came from having their expectations violated; expectations that those seats belonged to the six friends had been firmly established in the first two seasons of the series. When some wondered how the characters always got the best seats in the house, eagle-eyed fans noticed there was a reserved sign on the table in front of the couch at Central Perk.[12] While the coffeehouse was technically a public space, the way it looked, the regular seats for the friends, and the way they treated it made it more like one of their shared homes.

The same was true of Joey's and Monica's apartments. Although more time was spent in the larger, more nicely decorated "girls' apartment," Joey's served as the first home for Joey and Chandler in the series, as a place for Ross to stay when he was evicted from Emily's cousin's apartment, and as setting for Rachel and Joey as roommates and potential romantic partners as well. The men and women walked into and out of each other's apartments without warning from early in the series. In Epi-

sode 1.13, "The One with the Boobies," Chandler walks into Monica and
Rachel's apartment without knocking. No one seems to be there. He
opens the refrigerator and then Rachel emerges from the bathroom with a
towel wrapped around her waist, drying her hair. The towel she is using
to dry her hair covers her breasts, but she drops it when she is surprised to
find Chandler in the kitchen. She yells at him for not knocking and grabs
an afghan to cover herself which Chandler points out has an open weave
through which he can still see her "nippular area." The irony, of course, is
that they have been walking in and out of each other's apartments in
every episode so far, but this is the first time an intimate moment is
interrupted. It may be the first, but it is certainly not the last as Joey, Ross,
and Phoebe all interrupt Monica and Chandler having sex at some point
later in the series. So it is perfectly natural for the guys to host a second
birthday party in their apartment when Rachel's parents both arrive for
her party and the friends are trying to keep them apart and for Joey to try
to make his apartment a home for him, Rachel, and Emma. The purchase
of the foosball table in Episode 1.12, "The One with the Dozen Lasagnas," was intended to define the space as more masculine (Monica's had a
dining table in the kitchen and Joey's had a foosball table) and provided a
place for many conflicts to emerge and be resolved. When the table first
arrived, Monica showed that she was the best player even as Joey and
Chandler kicked her out so that they could continue to play late-night
foosball without her. After Joey had moved out, Eddie became Chandler's roommate, and when Joey came back, Chandler and Joey made up
over a game of foosball. In the final episodes, when the new chick and
duck get stuck in the foosball table, Monica saves the birds by destroying
the foosball table, which symbolizes the end of the era of shared apartment spaces as well.

While the friends spent a lot of time in each of their shared spaces, it
was Monica's apartment, #20, where they spent most of their time. It was
never surprising to see Joey walk in, go straight to the refrigerator, and
get food or a drink. It became so commonplace to see this occur that at
the end of the series, when Monica offers the apartment to Ross, he turns
it down, saying that he always thought of it as her place but also that he
did not think that he could afford to feed Joey. Monica affirms his suspi-
cions when she says that it really does take two incomes to feed Joey
(Episode 10.18, "The Last One—Part 2"). While Monica's apartment
serves as the setting for many meals, including for holidays like Thanks-

giving and Christmas, it also serves as the setting for Monica and Chandler's romantic relationship. When Monica and Chandler decide to live together in her apartment, Monica gives Chandler a key to the apartment. While the giving of the key symbolized their union, Chandler said what the audience was likely thinking: that the door had never been locked in the five years the show had been on. Then when he goes out into the hall to use the key for the first time, it breaks in the lock, leaving him outside the apartment and her inside. The norm for their relationship, and that of all the friends in this family, is openness between their spaces. The typical sign of a relationship moving to the next level, the giving of the key, merely interferes with the level of physical intimacy this couple already has with one another's living spaces (Episode 6.1, "The One after Vegas").

Hosting holiday events, especially Thanksgiving dinner, became Monica's specialty. The primary setting for all of the Thanksgiving episodes on *Friends* is Monica's apartment. Even when the friends do not eat Thanksgiving dinner (such as in Episode 2.8, "The One with the List"), they still spend the holiday together. In the first season, they come together out of necessity—Jack and Judy go out of town leaving Ross and Monica with no place to go; Rachel is unable to make her flight to Vail; and Joey gets evicted from his family dinner for "being contagious" when he appears on a poster for venereal disease. So Monica, ever the hostess, makes dinner for them all, including Chandler who does not eat Thanksgiving food. When they all get locked out of the apartment, the dinner gets ruined. The gang ends up bonding over Chandler's non-Thanksgiving food, grilled cheese, instead.

By the last season, all the friends expect Monica to host the holiday. So when she says she is not going to do it in the final season, the friends play on her competitive spirit to convince her to do it anyway so that she can outdo her previous dinners. When Phoebe and Rachel go to a baby beauty pageant with Emma and Joey and Ross go to a Rangers game, they end up late for dinner, resulting in Monica and Chandler locking them out and refusing to feed them. But when Joey gets his head stuck in between the door and door jamb, they all come together to get him out. When they dislodge him and he runs into the dinner, knocking it on the floor, everyone expects Monica to freak out. However, having just received a call from the adoption agency telling her that she and Chandler may have a baby coming, she celebrates the best Thanksgiving ever with the most important people in her life, her friends. Knowing they were going to spend these holidays with their alternative family at Monica's place became an assumption of the characters and the audience. Having the season 10 Thanksgiving dinner episode gave the audience the comfort food it needed for the holiday. Having this episode be more about the friends doing separate activities and concluding with a significant event that moves Monica and Chandler closer to a new phase of their life together provided one step toward the transition to a life without the *Friends* alternative family airing weekly.

At the end of the series, Monica and Chandler buy a house in the suburbs (with a Joey apartment above the garage, of course), making the final scene of the show take place in her empty apartment. This scene allowed the cast and audience to say good-bye to the apartment (and its emptiness brought tears to the cast and audience's eyes as well). The characters pointed out that they had all lived in the apartment at one time or another and each laid their key on the counter before they left. This moment makes clear how they all considered it one of their homes. Before they all leave the apartment, however, they make plans to see each other at the coffeehouse later, suggesting that they will continue to be together in one of their domestic spaces despite not living in their primary residence anymore. Although the audience does not see them meet up at Central Perk, after ten years of seeing them on that reserved orange couch, it is easy to continue picturing them there.

ROMANTIC RELATIONSHIPS MUST NOT DISRUPT THE FAMILY

Having romantic relationships with characters outside their group of friends always had the potential to disrupt the stasis of their alternative family. Serious relationships all ended because of future goals of the friends (Monica and Richard or Rachel and Tag), departure of characters (Joey and Kate or Phoebe and David), and/or threats to relationships within the group (Ross and Julie or Emily, Chandler and Janice, Joey and Janine). Because they all recognize the difficulties they have with relationships, on the first New Year's Eve of the series, they all make a pact not to bring dates to the party. Although they all end up breaking the pact and bringing dates, at the party a series of events leaves them all without their dates and no one to kiss at midnight. Chandler suggests the solution that they kiss one another. When none of the women will kiss him, Joey ends up grabbing both sides of his face, pulling him toward him, and kissing him. Instead of a romantic partnership between the roommates, this moment serves as one that seemingly solidifies the idea that if they cannot have dates outside the group, they will not have romance in it either.

Writing in 1998, four years into the series, Jillian Sandell suggested that because of the emotional, familial support the friends offered one another in the series, "their ties must remain platonic, not sexual."[13] She went so far as to suggest that romantic relationships among the group, such as between Rachel and Ross, had incestuous overtones. There are moments that support her analysis, such as when Ross pictures Rachel as his mother in the Princess Leia costume (Episode 3.1, "The One with the Princess Leia Fantasy") or when Rachel is unable to have sex with Joey when they finally get together romantically (Episode 10.3, "The One with Ross's Tan"). However, there are many others that suggest that in this alternative family narrative, the only off-limits relationship is the truly incestuous one between Monica and Ross. Instead, romantic relationships emerge among the friends that further solidify the bonds that tie them together, such as between Rachel and Ross, Monica and Chandler, and, in theory, Phoebe and Joey.

Rachel and Ross

Rachel and Ross arguably provide the central romantic coupling in *Friends* as their relationship runs the length of the series. Interestingly, Marta Kauffman says that when they first wrote the pilot, they planned for Monica and Joey to get together. But, as Kauffman explains, the chemistry between Rachel and Ross took on a life of its own and led to their becoming central romantic figures.[14] Ross's desire for Rachel, and the fact that he has had a crush on her since high school, comes out in the very first episode of the series. When he asks if she might like to go out with him sometime, the audience is made a promise of romantic potential from them when she answers, "Maybe." Their will-they-or-won't-they get-together narrative continues through the first season up until Rachel finds out Ross has feelings for her on her birthday (Episode 1.24, "The One where Rachel Finds Out"). However, when Ross returns from China,

Friends hugging. *Warner Brothers / Photofest © Warner Brothers*

instead of them getting together, we learn he has a new girlfriend, Julie (Episode 2.1, "The One with Ross's New Girlfriend"). It takes seven more episodes for Rachel and Ross to have their first kiss (Episode 2.7, "The One where Ross Finds Out") and another seven episodes for them to get over their issues and finally admit they are one another's lobster (Episode 2.14, "The One with the Prom Video"). "*Friends* took note of the ravenous global appetite for Ross and Rachel. It gave the audience what it wanted and the resultant screams accompanying the couple's first kiss were ear-shattering. And then it broke them up."[15] Their relationship only lasts the next twenty-five episodes before "The One where Ross and Rachel Take a Break" (Episode 3.15), which means that they are only in a romantic relationship for less than 10 percent or the equivalent of one season of the entire series.

When Rachel and Ross break up in season 3, their continued animosity toward one another presents a very real threat to the cohesion of their alternative family. Instead of all six of them being able to rely on each other, the other four friends are put in positions where they seemingly have to choose between them, much like Rachel (or many Gen-X viewers) had to choose between her parents. While they tolerate one another enough to keep the group together, the contentiousness of the relationship remains present for the rest of season 3. Their desire for one another remains present as well and is apparent when each becomes jealous over the other's dating (Episodes 3.22, "The One with the Screamer"") and 3.24, "The One with the Ultimate Fighting Champion"). Their split remains contingent though. The audience wonders when they will finally get back together. In the final episode of the season, "The One at the Beach" (Episode 3.35), they flirt and kiss, and Rachel leaves open the possibility of them getting back together. When the audience sees that Ross opened Rachel's door (instead of girlfriend Bonnie's) at the beach house in the opening episode of season 4, the excitement became palpable. Over the course of "The One with the Jellyfish," however, we learn that Rachel only took Ross back because he unknowingly admitted full guilt for their breakup. Although he tries to live with this condition, he ultimately yells at her his famous line: "WE WERE ON A BREAK!" and they are once again apart.

Even so, the will-they-or-won't-they story continued throughout the rest of the series. Rachel pines for Ross and threatens to disrupt his wedding to Emily at the end of season 4; they get drunk and married in Vegas at the end of season 5; Ross continues to hold a flame for Rachel even as they work to get divorced during season 6; Rachel has Ross's baby in season 8; and Rachel hints she wants some "ill-advised sympathy sex" with Ross by the middle of season 10 (Episode 10.13, "The One where Joey Speaks French"). By the end of the series, the writers had nowhere else to go but to have them get together in the final episodes.

The only real threat to their relationship came from another one of the friends: Joey. Joey falls in love with Rachel when she is living with him during her pregnancy. Although this news disturbs Ross, he puts aside his past feelings for Rachel, recognizing they have been broken up for five years, and privileges his friendship with Joey. Ross has rarely if ever seen Joey, the womanizer, in love. Ross advises Joey to tell Rachel. Unfortunately, Rachel does not feel the same way about Joey—at least not yet. Toward the end of season 9 (Episode 9.20, "The One with the Soap Opera Party"), Rachel realizes she has feelings for Joey just as Ross meets fellow paleontologist Charlie (Aisha Tyler). Before she or Ross can tell their love interests about their feelings, however, Charlie and Joey get together. Their short-lived romance ends in Barbados when Charlie realizes she should be with Ross and Rachel finally tells Joey about her feelings for him. Although Ross has a difficult time telling Joey about his getting together with Charlie, in true friend fashion, he does. Joey understands and fully supports them getting together. Rachel and Joey have a harder time telling Ross about their impending relationship. Once he learns of their relationship, rather than admit it bothers him, Ross insists that he is "fine."

In one of the greatest episodes for David Schwimmer, "The One where Ross Is Fine" (Episode 10.2), Ross invites Charlie, Rachel, and Joey over for dinner at his house. While Ross continually affirms that he is "fine," the drunken, uncomfortable dinner party that follows suggests otherwise. He anxiously waits for the timer to indicate that each course is finished, drinks all of the first pitcher of margaritas himself, and suggests they all take a trip together. At the end of the dinner party, Charlie and Rachel leave, but Joey stays to make sure Ross is okay. The next morning, we learn that Ross stripped and danced to the soundtrack of *Chicago* for Joey before passing out. But more importantly, Ross realizes that if Rachel and Joey are going to be together, he needs to get over it, as their friend and as a past, not present, beau of Rachel's. Although they have Ross's blessing, ultimately Rachel and Joey realize that they are not necessarily comfortable being together either when Rachel is unable to have sex with him. They reason that their friendship must be more important to them than a romantic relationship between them. Early in the final season of the show, this outcome also paves the way for Rachel and Ross to be together in the end.

Monica and Chandler

Some say that Monica and Chandler, and not Rachel and Ross, ultimately became the central romantic pairing in the show. Their partnership surprised fans, helped Chandler get over his fear of commitment, slowed down but ultimately fulfilled Monica's long-term desires for a husband and kids, and solidified the stability of their alternative family rather than threatening it. The primary reason they should be considered the real romantic heroes of *Friends* is that, as Andrea So contends, they built their romantic relationship on the "communication and common ground" of their friendship instead of grand romantic gestures.[16] Before Monica appeared from under the sheets of Chandler's hotel room bed in London to reveal their initial sexual coupling in Episode 4.24, "The One with Ross's

Wedding, Part 2," it was always clear that they loved and cared about one another. When Monica gets stung by a jellyfish, Chandler pees on her to help with the pain (Episode 4.1, "The One with the Jellyfish"). In "The One with the Flashback" (Episode 3.6), we see Chandler hug Monica in her towel lovingly, thinking they might be the ones who almost slept together, but then learn he agrees with her about how soft and comfortable her towels are. Just watching them together in scenes, you often see them hugging, cuddling, and/or sitting with one another. Chandler even tries to make a deal with Monica that if they are both still single when they are forty, they would get together (Episode 1.23, "The One with the Birth") and again asked if she would date him if he were the last man on Earth (Episode 3.25, "The One at the Beach"). They both knew all of each other's relationship stories and supported one another through past breakups and still ended up together.

The time they had together before the rest of the friends learned about their relationship helped them grow into a couple. The writers deftly used the ploy of hiding their relationship from the others to mine comedy gold during season 5, when both their relationship and their hiding it could have disrupted their alternative family. When they all first get back from London, Monica and Chandler cannot help but continue to sleep together. But, because it is still casual, they do not want to tell anyone. In Episode 5.2, "The One with All the Kissing," Chandler ends up kissing Monica, Rachel, and an extremely pregnant Phoebe every time he leaves the apartment because he accidentally keeps kissing Monica and has to cover. When Phoebe and Rachel finally call him on his actions and tell him to stop, Monica covers by saying how sick it makes her. Neither Chandler nor Monica is offended by the other's actions as they are trying to cover for one another. Working together to keep their relationship to themselves at the beginning helped them to get closer and helped the audience to see how they were as a couple.

Keeping their relationship secret for the first half of the fifth season allowed the producers time to gauge fan interest in them as a couple as well as for storylines to progressively invite each other friend into the secret. Once he got over the shock of learning about their relationship, Joey also helped them keep it secret, going so far as to take the blame for men's underwear in the couch at Monica and Rachel's apartment, having set up a video camera to seemingly record sex with a first date, and having a naked picture of Monica (Episode 5.9, "The One with Ross's

Sandwich"). Later Rachel overhears them talking about Chandler's nickname ("Mr. Big . . .") and realizes something is going on between them. Having made a resolution not to gossip, when Rachel tries to tell Joey their secret, he will not let her. Their exchange, however, makes them both realize that they both know about Monica and Chandler. When Rachel hears how happy they both are, she avoids telling them she knows and instead congratulates and hugs Monica without telling her the real reason (Episode 5.11, "The One with All the Resolutions"). Phoebe came into the fold later in "The One where Everybody Finds Out" (Episode 5.14) when touring Ugly Naked Guy's apartment with Rachel and Ross. She sees Monica and Chandler having sex up against the window in Monica's apartment. Rachel and Phoebe then decide to mess with Monica and Chandler in a hilarious game of chicken with Rachel giving Monica her laundry to do (as Monica and Chandler's code for sex is "doing laundry") and Phoebe hitting on Chandler. Once Chandler gives up rather than have sex with Phoebe, Monica and Chandler declare their love for one another, making their relationship not just about sex but about friendship and love too. Ross also finds out by seeing Monica and Chandler having sex through the window of what is now the apartment he is subletting from Ugly Naked Guy, and it contributes to his nervous breakdown until he learns that they are in love and that they did not tell him because they were worried about him. Introducing the relationship to each friend in this way maintained the secret for half a season, allowed each one to have their own unique reaction, and gave them and the audience time to get used to the fact that two of the friends were in a romantic relationship with one another.

When they got together they became a couple, but their relationship did not disrupt the familial group as they retained the essential qualities of their characters. Monica always wanted to get married and have children; wanting children was the reason she broke up with the most important man in her life before Chandler, Richard. At the same time, Chandler always feared commitment, given what he saw his parents go through. Coming together helped Monica realize that having Chandler in her life was more important than an immediate family. Scenes between their wedding and later attempts to have children show her clearly articulating her continued desire for children, while at the same time waiting for Chandler to be ready. At the same time, they loved one another for who they were without trying to make them into someone else. For instance, right after the wedding, absentminded Chandler, having realized he forgot the disposable cameras at the reception, goes to another wedding reception with Ross and tries to recreate the pictures for Monica, including one of him kissing that bride. Meanwhile, obsessive Monica starts opening the wedding presents without Chandler. Before she realizes it, she has opened them all. When Chandler returns, he sees all the unwrapped presents, she confronts him about his kissing this other bride, and they decide to call it even and give one another a high five (Episode 8.2, "The One with the Red Sweater"). They feel secure in their relationship, recognize each other's faults, and love one another *because* of all of those characteristics, not in spite of them. Feeling so comfortable in their relationship with one another and in their relationships with the rest of their friends at the same time allows for this romantic couple to exist within the familial unit without changing their roles significantly in it.

Phoebe and Joey

No, Phoebe and Joey were never actually in a romantic relationship. Some contend they should have been though, and Matt LeBlanc even said, in an interview with *People* magazine, "Toward the end we actually pitched the idea that Joey and Phoebe had been having casual sex the entire time."[17] In the end, the idea was nixed, most likely because producers had to set up LeBlanc's short-lived spin-off, *Joey* (2004–2006). That does not mean that they did not have a special relationship within the group that suggested they might get together over the course of the series though. The first hint emerged in Episodes 1.16 and 1.17, "The One with Two Parts," parts 1 and 2, when Joey meets Phoebe's twin sister, Ursula. Although he asks Phoebe if he can ask her out before he does so, Phoebe only begrudgingly says yes. In her heart, however, she wishes she had said no as she is afraid she will lose her friend Joey to her sister, who always steals her things and breaks them. Ursula ends up using Joey, just as Phoebe predicted, and then blows him off. Instead of telling him that she told him so, Phoebe passes herself off as Ursula to help Joey get over her. When Joey thinks she is Ursula, he tells her that he would not give up Phoebe for her and then kisses her good-bye. As he starts to walk away, with her kiss still on his lips, Joey realizes it is Phoebe and shows how touched he is by bringing his hand to his heart. This is not the only kiss between Phoebe and Joey. She kisses him when he doubts his abilities after being told he is not a good kisser by Warren Beatty (Episode 2.24, "The One with Barry and Mindy's Wedding"). He also kisses her on what she thought was her thirtieth birthday. When she learns from Ursula that they are actually thirty-one, Phoebe laments not having completed the bucket list of items she hoped to by her thirtieth birthday, let alone her thirty-first, such as having the perfect kiss and meeting Portuguese people. So Joey gives her a perfect kiss and reveals that he is 1/16 Portuguese.

Their special kisses are not the only hints of a connection between them that made fans ship them. They also have odd shared interests, help each frequently, and have a special bond even within the group. Phoebe poses as Joey's agent twice to help him first get jobs (Episode 3.4, "The One with the Metaphorical Tunnel") and later to soften the blow of the death of his actual longtime agent, Estelle (June Gable) (Episode 10.15 "The One where Estelle Dies"). Joey poses as Dr. Drake Ramoray, his *Days of Our Lives* character, in a hospital to do reconnaissance for Phoebe with a potential love interest for her (Episode 8.23, "The One where Rachel Has a Baby"). When vegetarian Phoebe craves meat during her pregnancy, Joey gives up eating meat to offset the number of cows that would suffer as a result of them both eating meat (Episode 4.16, "The One with the Fake Party"). Phoebe tries to show Joey that there is such a thing as a selfless good deed but ends up donating to PBS, which she hates, and gets Joey on TV for taking her pledge (Episode 5.4, "The One where Phoebe Hates PBS"). Phoebe teaches Joey how to play guitar (Episode 5.11, "The One with All the Resolutions") and, unsuccessfully, how to speak French (Episode 10.13 "The One where Joey Speaks French"). They both enjoy eating Emma's baby food together (Episode 9.14, "The One with the Blind Dates") and have fake names (Regina Phalange and Ken Adams) they use with dates they might not want to call them later (Episode 8.4, "The One with the Videotape"). While not everyone else understands them, they always seems to understand one another. Even when Joey tries to convince a blackjack dealer (Thomas Lennon) that they could make money from being hand twins, Phoebe helps him by posing as, in this case, a businesswoman named Regina Phalange (Episodes 5.23 and 5.24, "The One in Vegas: Parts 1 and 2"). In Episode 6.1, "The One after Vegas," Phoebe lends Joey her grandmother's cab to drive out to his movie set in Vegas. When Joey does not want to drive it back after his movie gets shut down, Joey suggests he and Phoebe drive back together, which she dubs their "frienaissance," even as she reassures him that they do not really need a renewal of their relationship as she never stopped loving him.

Their relationship took place primarily in the moments between or integrated within the main storylines. Even so, in Episode 7.11, "The One with All the Cheesecakes," their "secret" relationship within the group takes center stage when we learn that Phoebe and Joey have dinner once a month to discuss the rest of the group. Rather than questioning this fact or objecting, Ross merely tries to flatter Phoebe so that what they say about him will be positive. However, when "Big Daddy" (a nickname Joey and Phoebe were trying out for him) leaves a note canceling their dinner plans, Phoebe furiously reads him the riot act. Although the guys agree with Joey that it is acceptable to cancel plans with friends if there's a chance for sex with a date, Phoebe proclaims to Joey that romantic relationships may come and go but that their relationship is for life. Although they make up and plan to go to dinner the next night, Phoebe ends up running into her first love, David, who is only in town for four hours. Having made such a big deal with Joey about canceling plans with friends for dates, she does not feel like she can cancel with him. So she tries to have dinner with Joey and then meet up with David. However, Joey finds out and attempts to keep Phoebe at dinner as long as possible, forcing her to leave him behind regardless of how he feels about it. After David leaves, Joey runs into Phoebe, near tears, and tells her that he understands and comforts her.

Although their friendship remained platonic throughout the series, their interactions, even in later seasons, still suggested the potential remained for a relationship between Phoebe and Joey. With Monica and Chandler's engagement pending, Rachel and Phoebe discuss their future relationship plans, including having a backup, in case they never find "the one." When Rachel learns that Phoebe has secured both Ross and Joey as hers, they argue and ultimately draw names to see who gets whom. When Rachel draws Joey and Phoebe draws Ross, they pause and then exchange names as Rachel and Ross and Phoebe and Joey in relationships makes more sense. When Monica and Chandler return from their honeymoon, Phoebe and Joey suggest that Monica and Chandler are missing an opportunity to hang out with a couple (two people) right in front of them and express their jealousy when Monica and Chandler opt to pursue their honeymoon friends, Greg and Jenny (Episode 8.4, "The One with the

Videotape"). When Monica and Chandler mistakenly think that Joey has a crush on Phoebe, she is offended to learn that he really has feelings for Rachel (Episode 8.13, "The One where Chandler Takes a Bath"). In Episode 8.3, "The One where Rachel Tells . . . ," Joey asks Phoebe if they should do something together given that Monica and Chandler are married and Rachel and Ross are about to have a baby. Phoebe replies, "All in good time, my love. All in good time."

Given their long-term flirting, shared odd interests, and the audience's desire for them to end up together, the producers and writers had to decide how to end their story and suggest future lives for both their characters. They chose to have Phoebe marry Mike (Paul Rudd), the former lawyer, current piano player, from a wealthy family, who accepts Phoebe for who she is. As Phoebe's stepfather is in prison, she asks Joey to give her away at the wedding. He not only agrees but also acts as surrogate father by making sure Mike will not hurt her. Joey pulls Mike aside at the rehearsal dinner and asks him what his intentions are with "my Phoebe" and wonders if he will be able to support his wife by playing piano as it is an unstable profession. Mike says that it is no more unstable than acting, which offends Joey. While his initial attempts at warning Mike are not very effective, Joey later pulls Mike aside and, despite quoting a terrible mafia movie to him, says that he wants to make sure Mike is going to take care of Phoebe. Mike assures him that he would die before he would let anything happen to her. Joey then welcomes him to the family (Episode 10.12, "The One with Phoebe's Wedding"). When Joey ends up officiating their wedding, and Phoebe tells Mike, as part of her vows, that he is her family, we see Joey bless their relationship. This moment solidifies the addition of a member to the *Friends* family, rather than a threat to it.

While Monica and Chandler's romantic relationship does not disrupt the ensemble nature of the *Friends* alternative family, Rachel and Ross's relationship might have. For this reason, they did not end up together until the final episode of the series. By the end of the series, Monica and Chandler, Rachel and Ross, and Phoebe and Mike are all partnered off. In the finale, Monica and Chandler and Rachel and Ross already have children, and Mike suggests he and Phoebe should have children as well. A series about six single twenty-somethings supporting one another as they try to find their way in the world suggested that by their mid-thirties, they were all where they should be: married with children (or children on the way)—that is, for everyone but Joey, as the series set up his move to California to begin his spin-off show.

CONCLUSION

The alternative family created by the ensemble of six in *Friends* served as a cultural moment on television, a moment when parents became secondary in these young people's lives and they became primary to one another. As one of the first such shows on television, *Friends* provided a model for twenty-somethings in the late twentieth and early twenty-first centuries. The network of relationships created around siblings Monica and Ross, the spaces they inhabited together, and even the romantic liaisons within their circle all served to define the boundaries of their family. These boundaries also included factors of identity, including race, class, and sexuality. As Jillian Sandell argues, "Even though the show foregrounds and celebrates kinship networks which challenge the mythical nuclear heterosexual family . . . the visibility of these 'alternative families' is made possible only by simultaneously rendering invisible other kinds of 'difference.'"[18] While these factors are not discussed in this chapter, I would be remiss not to discuss the cultural implications of representations of race, class, and sexuality in this series. Chapters 6 and 7 focus on these factors of difference that are sublimated by the ensemble of their alternative family. Even so, writer/director/producer Kevin Bright notes that the foundation of the series is the relationship between the characters.[19] Seeing the six friends in one another's apartments or on the couch at Central Perk, we believe in their group and its longevity. So when the gang sits on that couch in Central Perk looking at old photos of Monica and Ross's Nana and her friends hanging out in Java Joe's (Episode 1.8, "The One where Nana Dies Twice"), the audience is assured that our friends will always be there for us at the coffee shop too.

4

FRIENDS HAPPY NOT DOING TOO MUCH

In 1994, Bill Clinton was president of the United States, unemployment rates dropped to their lowest levels since the early 1990s recession, and nuclear tensions between the United States and Russia were decreasing. Jackie Kennedy Onassis and Richard Nixon died, and we learned that Ronald Reagan had Alzheimer's. At the same time, 1994 saw Michael Jackson marry Lisa Marie Presley and Nelson Mandela become president of South Africa even as Tonya Harding and her ex-husband, Jeff Gillooly, went to jail for the very public clubbing of rival ice skater Nancy Kerrigan's leg, Kurt Cobain committed suicide, Nicole Brown Simpson and Ronald Goldman were murdered, and Nicole's ex-husband, O. J. Simpson, went on his famous slow speed chase on the freeways of Los Angeles before being arrested for the crime. Summer and fall of that year saw the twenty-fifth anniversary concert commemorating Woodstock, the first conference devoted to commercial potential of the World Wide Web,[1] and the *Friends* premiere on NBC.

In this political, economic, and popular-culture context, *Friends* represents a Clinton-era "boom text" or a show that is relaxed and uncritical of a dominant "liberal-democratic capitalist hegemony" as it depicts a "fantasy version of early adulthood."[2] Neil Ewen contends that *Friends* created a safe space "circumscribed by the conventions of the sitcom genre, whereby daily concerns about work and careers provide humor rather than (overt) stress, and are framed within broader (conservative) happy-ever-after life narratives."[3] The space created in the show allowed its primary fan base at the time—white, middle-class Generation X-ers—to see a life they wanted to lead in upscaled Manhattan apartments and coffee shops safe from the pressures of work, politics, economics, and, well, reality. Continuing to watch the show in reruns and streaming platforms today allows Gen X-ers and new Millennial fans to reflect back to a time when politics and economic stress may have been present on the evening news, but it was not a part of our everyday social-media-saturated lives. *Friends'* enduring appeal can be understood "as a document of a key historical moment of change, at the turn of the century when Generation X [was] surpassed by . . . the Millennial generation."[4]

FRIENDS GENERATION

Douglas Coupland popularized the term "Generation X" in his 1991 book, *Generation X: Tales for an Accelerated Culture*. This novel focused on three twenty-something friends working dead-end jobs, consciously choosing to reject the aspirational goals of their Baby Boomer parents. These friends spent their free time talking. And talking. And talking. All their talk demonstrated what came to define the Gen-X lifestyle in media: all talk, no (political) action. This "slacker" persona dominated popular-culture representations of Gen X for the decade and "created a youth culture anchored in irony, apathy and disenfranchisement."[5]

As with many initial countercultural challenges (such as Punk in the early 1980s), such attitudes and behaviors became coopted into mainstream culture through their repeated portrayals in the books of Bret Easton Ellis, Elizabeth Wurtzel, and Chuck Palahniuk; the music of Nirvana, L7, and Pearl Jam; and movies such as *Reality Bites* (1994), *Clerks* (1994), and *The Virgin Suicides* (1999). As such, refusing to take responsibility for your life became a kind of narcissistic heroism. While David Schwimmer explicitly disavowed any claims that *Friends* meant to represent Generation X in a March 1995 appearance on *The Oprah Winfrey Show*, Helene Shugart explains that the show was a commercial attempt at representing X-ers.[6] *Friends'* creators David Crane and Marta Kauffman's design of the series allowed it to absorb these characteristics and present them in a palatable, prime-time form.[7] The show became "an explanation and exploration of what it meant to come of age in the 1990s"[8] and the characters were people you might know and be able to relate to.

Even the theme song for the show, "I'll Be There for You" by the Rembrandts, pointed toward generational ties,[9] including low expectations about what life has to offer, selfishness and self-absorption of the characters, and their personal devotion to each other, regardless of the circumstances. The opening verse of the song[10] played every time the show aired over a montage of the six main characters wearing black and white dancing around and splashing in a fountain with primary-colored umbrellas and clips from the previous half season of the show introducing the actors. This seemingly upbeat moment of enjoyment among friends was accompanied by the lyrics that suggested that their Baby Boomer parents had prepared their kids for a different kind of life than they were experiencing; a life where they got married, had kids, and were financially secure because they got jobs right out of high school or college and worked until they retired. As the subsequent lines of the song indicate, the friends have jobs that are jokes, no money, and therefore no security. In addition to not being married, they do not actually have much of a love life at all. However, regardless of what was happening in their lives, they would be there for one another. Today we might talk about their focus on themselves as more revealing of their white, class-based privilege (see more in chapter 6), but in 1994, white, middle-class Gen-Xers were invited to relate to them as representatives of Gen X who "got" that life was not going to be like it was for their parents' generation.

FRIENDS GENERATION AT WORK

Occasionally, the friends appear at their jobs engaging in the everyday practices their work involved: Chandler inputting numbers, Monica cooking, Ross teaching a class, Rachel putting in clothing buy orders, Joey auditioning, and Phoebe massaging clients. More often than not, however, they are hanging out in one of their apartments or at the coffee shop, Central Perk. All the time they spent together lounging about echoes the Generation-X characters in Coupland's book. But for viewers, then and now, the friends hanging out represents a time when work was less stressful and competitive and did not define one's identity. Their lives suggested there was time to be reflective and just do nothing. Even so, *Friends* serves "as a document of the particularities of the changes to middle-class work culture at a distinct juncture in the history of American capitalism."[11]

One of the defining characteristics of work on *Friends* remains its distinction from Baby Boomers' career expectations. Baby Boomers were expected to get a job after high school or college that became what they did their entire lives and defined who they were. In contrast, not one of the friends stayed at the same job the entire show. Phoebe's and Joey's jobs were always contingent. Phoebe worked as a freelance masseuse (until the last season of the show), but the uncertainty of her income was always supplemented by odd jobs along the way, such as catering with Monica part of season 4, being an extra on *Days of Our Lives* (Episode 9.11, "The One where Rachel Goes Back to Work"), and a toner salesperson (Episode 7.13, "The One where Rosita Dies"). While her uncertain work life might be dismissed as related to her difficult childhood (the woman she thought was her mother killed herself, her stepfather was in prison, her father abandoned the family, and she lived on the streets at one time), she rarely seems to have much anxiety about where her next paycheck will come from or whether it will be enough to keep a roof over her head. Despite such a trying life, Lisa Kudrow contends that her character only works in a sitcom if Phoebe really is okay about it: "For me, that completely defined her—how amazing things come out of her mouth like it's not a big deal. It's not that noteworthy—just something that happened to her."[12] Even her mainstay job as a masseuse included multiple times when her license was suspended due to inappropriate touching (and biting) of clients (Episode 4.4, "The One with the Ballroom Dancing"); all of which she seemed to take in stride as she continued to lounge on the couches next to her friends.

What Phoebe really seems to get fulfillment from is writing and singing her own songs at Central Perk, which she does as a hobby. When another singer, Stephanie (played by Chrissie Hynde of The Pretenders), is hired to sing at the coffeehouse, Phoebe sings loudly outside in protest. However, when she realizes that passersby threw more money in her guitar case for one song, "Su-Su-Suicide," than for another, "Smelly Cat," she feels bad for the latter song. Ultimately, she decides that she needs to continue singing her songs for herself and not make it just about making money (Episode 2.6, "The One with the Baby on the Bus"). To further emphasize the value of her choice and her lifestyle, the end of the episode shows Phoebe teaching Chrissie Hynde's character to play

"Smelly Cat" on the couch in the friends' safe space of the coffee shop. What Kudrow sees as Phoebe's defining characteristic is her ability to reinvent herself and embrace who she is at any given moment. [13]

Joey's work as an actor also reflects this contingent lifestyle. He was often auditioning for jobs he did not get. When he was working, his sexual dalliances with his female coworkers frequently took center stage in the narrative plot lines, upstaging any possible questions about whether he could afford his lifestyle on an actor's occasional salary. Of course, Joey had Chandler as his roommate (for five seasons) and best friend who often took care of the bills and loaned him money. With such a safety net in place, Joey's foray into odd jobs to pay the bills, such as a model for a VD poster (Episode 1.9, "The One where Underdog Gets Away") and department store perfume sample cowboy (Episode 1.2, "The One with the Sonogram"), help garner laughs more than necessary paychecks. When Joey did have more stable jobs working on *Days of Our Lives* and his short-lived TV series, *Mac and C.H.E.E.S.E.*, he spent his money on upgraded furniture, TVs (Episode 2.15, "The One where Ross and Rachel . . . You Know"), and gifts for Chandler (Episode 2.14, "The One with the Prom Video"). Rare was a time when Joey stressed over his financial situation. Rather, he focused more on the next job as fulfillment of his desire to be an actor and enjoy the company of his female coworkers.

Ross and Monica's attitudes toward work reflected tensions between the expectations of their Boomer parents and their emerging independence as Gen-X adults. When Monica gets a promotion early in the show and is subsequently fired in the same episode for taking kickbacks, she fears telling her parents and asking them for money (Episode 2.5, "The One with the Five Steaks and an Eggplant"). When she does actually tell them, her mother frets but her father assures them all that Monica will be fine because she learned the lesson he taught her about saving 10 percent of every paycheck. However, it is clear from Monica's reaction, and the subsequent loan she accepts from Ross, that she either has not been doing this or that the money has been spent elsewhere. When Ross is put on leave at his job at the museum due to his "rage," he is sent to a doctor who medicates him. Instead of worrying about his precarious financial situation, he instead meets up with his friends at the coffeehouse (Episode 5.9, "The One with Ross's Sandwich"). He also does not tell his parents, and when they find out a year later, they wonder if his smoking marijuana

Singer/songwriter Phoebe Buffay. *Warner Brothers / Photofest © Warner Brothers*

in college led to his decline (Episode 6.9, "The One where Ross Got High"). Both Monica and Ross bounce back quickly even as Monica has to take a short-term job at a theme diner (that requires her to wear a 1950s costume and dance when songs are played by customers on the jukebox) (Episode 2.21, "The One with the Bullies") and Ross has to move in with Chandler and Joey when he loses his apartment (Episode 5.7, "The One where Ross Moves in"). Monica ultimately gets hired as a restaurant reviewer, which leads to a job as a head chef (Episode 4.9, "The One where They are Going to Party!"), and Ross starts working as a university professor (season 6). *Friends* depicts the tensions between Ross and Monica and their parents and uses their job losses for narrative progression and big laughs, but despite temporary, minor stress, their attitudes toward their jobs more often reflect tensions between the Gen-X and Baby Boomer generations.

Chandler, on the other hand, truly reflects the Gen-X attitudes toward work prevalent in popular culture in the 1990s. Chandler's career for most of the series reflects what anthropologist David Graeber has termed "bullshit jobs," or a job doing something totally unnecessary.[14] Chandler reveals his discontentment with his job in the pilot episode of the show when he gets up to leave his friends and says that it is time to go to work, even though it makes no difference if he does it or not. Chandler's attitude toward his job and his snarky comments about, well, everything, embody two characteristics of Gen X commonly represented in media, "the cynical cool of rejecting ambition and popularity, and the mopey, tortured Gen X man-child who embodied that cool."[15] We see him smoke in his cubicle (Episode 1.3, "The One with the Thumb"), date a coworker whom he is supposed to fire (Episode 1.16, "The One with Two Parts, Part 1"), fall asleep and get transferred to Tulsa (Episode 9.2, "The One where Emma Cries"), and suggest to his boss that he shred documents rather than do his work (Episode 8.5, "The One with Rachel's Date"). Later in the first season, he actually quits when offered a promotion. Despite his belief that his job should merely have been a temporary position, when he takes a job aptitude test, it sadly reveals he is best suited for just the kind of job he just quit in data processing for a large multinational company. So when his boss calls back and offers him a raise, bonuses, and his own office, he goes back to the job with a shrug even though he hates it (Episode 1.15, "The One with the Stoner"). When he starts his new job, he is more enamored with using the intercom to contact his new secretary than with actually doing work (Episode 1.16, "The One with Two Parts, Part 1").

Chandler's disenchantment with his job is clear to his friends too. When Phoebe works temporarily as Chandler's secretary, she becomes friends with his coworkers and he finds out that they do not like him. He tries to relate to them by singing with them at karaoke, but Phoebe reports that they still do not like him because he is now the boss (Episode 1.22, "The One with the Ick Factor"). Later, when Phoebe is working as a toner saleswoman, a potential customer (played by Jason Alexander) says, "I've been working for ten years now at this meaningless, dead-end job and nobody even knows that I exist," to which Phoebe responds, "Chandler?" and the audience explodes in laughter (Episode 7.13, "The One where Rosita Dies"). Neil Ewen suggests this moment signifies the despondency, inertia, and suicidal thoughts associated with corporate office work.[16] To emphasize the lack of importance his job holds, none of the friends actually knows what his job really is until he quits. In "The One with the Embryos" (Episode 4.12), Monica and Rachel lose their apartment in a bet over whether the gals or guys know each other better because neither of them can name Chandler's job. In later seasons, Chandler's alternate reality shows his hidden desire to write for comics (Episode 6.15 and 6.16, "The One That Could Have Been: Parts 1 and 2"), and eventually in the last season of the show, he starts what the series suggests is his newfound dream job in advertising (Episode 9.15, "The One with the Mugging"). Despite this shift in Chandler's attitude, one of the most pervasive defining factors of Chandler's character throughout the series is his despondency with his work, which reflects the Gen-X attitudes toward late-stage capitalism.

Rachel also reflects these laissez-faire attitudes toward work, especially in the early seasons of the show when she works as a waitress at Central Perk. In the pilot episode, after running out on her wedding, we see her on the phone trying to explain to her father why she ran out. She tries to tell him that she does not want what was expected of her for her entire life: to marry a rich doctor. When she was at the church, she realized that she was more excited by a gravy boat than her fiancé, Barry (Mitchell Whitfield). In that moment, Rachel distinguishes herself from the expectations of her Boomer parents and reveals that the image of the happily married rich doctor's wife did not hold the promise of fulfillment as much as the gifts.

Despite taking a step toward independence, Rachel struggles with her first job as a waitress at Central Perk. She doesn't get paid enough and wonders who FICA is and why he is taking all her money (Episode 1.4, "The One with George Stephanopoulos"); brings customers the wrong orders or no orders at all; drinks some of Joey's coffee and tells him now there's room for his milk (Episode 1.10, "The One with the Monkey"); serves Monica hot cider with her pencil instead of a cinnamon stick in it (Episode 1.15, "The One with the Stoned Guy"); drops pie in a customer's hood (and makes Ross get it out for her) (Episode 2.17, "The One where Eddie Moves In"); and serves her friends dirty dishes instead of their orders (Episode 2.11, "The One with the Lesbian Wedding"). Even though her boss (Terry) tells her early on that she is a terrible waitress and therefore does not deserve an advance to go on vacation to Vail (Episode 1.9, "The One where Underdog Gets Away"), it is surprising that she is never fired. Instead her mishaps create many hilarious moments and suggest that this college graduate just does not care about improving herself in this dead-end job. It does ultimately motivate her to apply for jobs in fashion and put her college education to good use though. Even so, on her first day at Fortuna Fashion, the first thing she is asked to do is make coffee. Just as Chandler is able to pay the bills with his unnecessary job, Rachel too enters into more unnecessary work.

But her evolution from spoiled, rich daddy's girl to waitress and then from fashion professional to single working mother reflects the evolution of Gen-X adults living in a postmodern world. In the *Friends* generation, the logic of going from waitress at a coffee shop to fashion professional is not questioned. It is the college job to the post-college job, or in Rachel's case, going from the post-running-out-on-your-wedding-and-father's-money job to the post-college job. While most of the other friends have some desire to improve their job status, Rachel truly represents the post-feminist single working mother. Postfeminist in this case refers to women who have benefited from the achievements of second-wave feminists, but who do not necessarily claim the controversial moniker of being feminist and women who embrace choice and seeming contradictions of being empowered women (e.g., a woman wearing makeup and tight-fitting clothing to feel good about herself and not to invite men's gazes).[17] She harbors ambitions to be independent (from her father, fiancé, and even Ross, when they get together in season 2), but she also desires a man to support her lifestyle and choices. When she finally finds a job in fashion that she enjoys, Ross gets jealous of one of her coworkers, Mark (Steven Eckholdt). His jealousy leads Rachel to ask to take a break from their relationship (Episode 3.15, "The One where Ross and Rachel Take a Break"). Despite his infidelity, she tries to get back together with him, only to find out that he will still not take responsibility for his actions because (and it is true) "they were on a break!" (Episode 3.25, "The One at the Beach"). Even so, she continues to try to find "the one" and even, desperately, begs Joey not to get married before her (Episode 7.14, "The One where They All Turn 30"). She excitedly fights for and earns promotions, such as from assistant to assistant buyer, while demonstrating an extreme lack of professional behavior at the workplace by hiring and then dating a hot coworker, Tag (Episode 7.14, "The One with Rachel's Assistant"); staying home from work because of kissing her coworker Gavin (Episode 9.11, "The One where Rachel Goes Back to Work"); and kissing and inappropriately touching her future boss (Episode 5.17, "The One with Rachel's Inadvertent Kiss"). Ultimately, she is the second-wave feminist dream of the single working mother. But her stereotypical Gen-X characteristics are displayed in her lack of commitment to doing her work well. In true postfeminist form, she chooses to give up her dream job with Gucci in Paris to live with Ross in New York.

FRIENDS AS PARENTS

The impact the friends' Baby Boomer parents had on their own desires and abilities to have and raise children is clear. *Friends* depiction of parenthood (of the friends themselves) reflect Gen-X fears surrounding divorce or abandonment, the loss of independence, and the stereotypical expectations related to gender. Ross and Monica are the only two friends whose parents are still happily married. While Ross may not be the perfect father, he serves well as a secondary caregiver to both Ben (through season 7) and Emma. Monica had always wanted children. It was what ended up breaking up her relationship with Richard (Episode 2.24, "The One with Barry and Mindy's Wedding") and drove her to consider being artificially inseminated in "The One with the Jam" (Episode 3.3). The four remaining friends (Chandler, Joey, Phoebe, and Rachel), whose own parents were having affairs, divorced, or abandoned them, demonstrated fear, surprise, and lack of motivation to have children. Additionally,

Friends reified the idea that most men were children themselves and therefore not ready to be parents, while at the same time assuming the women would have children even as the narratives created hurdles for the female characters to overcome to achieve parenthood.

Before Ross and Rachel's baby was even a glimmer in the writers' eyes, Ross became a parent. In "The One with the Sonogram" (Episode 1.2), Ross's ex-wife Carol tells him she is pregnant and he can be as involved as he wants to be. He has doubts about how their parenting team of the lesbian couple and the baby's father is going to work and wonders if he has it in him to be a father. He reveals his anxieties when he tells Chandler and Joey that he dreamed he was playing football with his kid and the child *was* the football. In the dream, Ross describes how he threw the baby down the field and then realized that he was also supposed to catch him, but that he did not think he could get down the field in time. Then he woke up. Chandler reassures him that he is one of the most responsible men he knows and will make a great dad. Joey suggests he just needs better blocking (Episode 1.17, "The One with the Two Parts: Part 2").

Later in the episode, Ross asks his father, Jack, if he ever freaked out or panicked before Ross was born. Jack says that Ross's mother took care of "all that" as he was always busy with the business. The Baby Boomer/ Gen-X tension surrounding parenthood emerges as Jack wonders if Ross is going to blame him for not being around. Instead, Ross brushes that difference aside and asks when he started to feel like a father. Jack says he knew the moment that Ross put his little baby hand around his finger. Fittingly, when Ross is at the hospital later in the episode with Marcel, the monkey wakes up from sedation and puts his little hand around Ross's finger. In this moment, Ross and the audience are reassured that he will be a good father.

However, Ross's interactions with his son, Ben (Cole Sprouse), are limited since Susan and Carol are his primary parents and Ross is his secondary caregiver, which he actually hopes might be Ben's first word (Episode 2.20, "The One where Old Yeller Dies"). When they are together, there are true tender moments between Ross and Ben, such as when Ross wants to spend a weekend with him so as not to miss out on first-time events like his first word or when he tries to teach Ben about Hanukkah (Episode 7.10, "The One with the Holiday Armadillo"). Even so, Ross's parenting is often limited to times the show wants to use Susan and Carol, as Ben's two mommies, as comic fodder. While the representation of sexualities and Susan and Carol's roles are discussed in chapter 6, Ross's role as a parent reflects Gen X as the "divorce generation" just as much as Rachel's interactions with her parents when they split up and the gang has to throw her two birthday parties so they won't see one another (Episode 2.22, "The One with the Two Parties") or Chandler's anxieties about his sexually frank mother or cross-dressing father do. After Ross and Rachel's baby, Emma, is born in the season 8 finale, Ben never appears on the show again. [18]

Despite already having Ben, when Ross learns that Rachel is pregnant, his first reaction is denial. He claims that she cannot be pregnant because they used a condom. When she points out that condoms are only 97 percent effective and that it says this on the box, Ross decides that instead of dealing with the matter at hand, Rachel's pregnancy, he will instead call the condom company to complain. Later when he tells the rest of the gang about being the father and the failure of the 97-percent-effective condom, Joey pulls out a long strip of condoms from his pocket to check to see if this effectiveness standard is actually on the package (Episode 8.3, "The One where Rachel Tells . . . "). These scenes put Ross in a reluctant father role and cement Joey as fearful of fatherhood as well.

While Ross ultimately has children on the show, he is always depicted as the secondary caregiver whereas Joey and Chandler are both portrayed as commitment phobic—a forever-bachelor and fearful of children—and children themselves. When Rachel asks Joey what he would do if someone he slept with told him she was pregnant, Joey defensively wonders who called. Rachel reassures him that he did not get anyone pregnant. While Joey is relieved, he also wonders why Rachel wanted to scare him like that (Episode 8.2, "The One with the Red Sweater").

Chandler, on the other hand, does not want children until nearly the end of the show because he fears he does not know what it is to be a good parent, given his experiences with his divorced parents. After Ben is born, Rachel says she cannot believe that one of them has a child, to which Chandler replies that he is still a child (Episode 1.23, "The One with the Birth"). Chandler's and Joey's status as immature is often used as an excuse for their not being ready for children. Even after he marries Monica, Chandler is still not ready for children. In the Thanksgiving episode, "The One with the Rumor" (Episode 8.9), Monica says that by that time next year there will be a baby with them. Chandler looks aghast at her as she reassures him that Rachel's baby, not theirs, would be there the following Thanksgiving.

Later in season 8 in "The One where Rachel Has a Baby: Part 1," when the whole gang is at the hospital, it is surprising when Monica tries to freak Chandler out by telling him she is ready to have a baby and he calmly responds, "Okay." He says that he believes they are ready. Instead of him flipping out, Joey compliments him for being grown up, but Monica gets spooked. She defensively says that she is ready but wants Joey to be the father. When Joey freaks out, Monica says that his reaction was all that she was looking for. In this moment, Joey affirms his fear of having children and Monica assumes, based on past reactions from him, that Chandler still does not want kids. Joey's comments also suggest that a measure of adulthood is being ready to have kids. Therefore, he is not yet grown up, but Chandler is.

Unlike with the male characters, the show represents the desire to have children as innate in the female leads. From the first season on, Monica explicitly states her desires to have children, even by, as previously noted, considering artificial insemination and single motherhood after she breaks up with Richard because he does not want to have any more children at his age. Despite her desires for parenthood, the show never makes it easy for her, whether it is dating men who do not want kids, having her realize that being a single mother is not her dream, or making her womb "hostile" (Episode 9.21, "The One with the Fertility Test").

Seeing Monica with a child does not make accepting her as a mother any easier though. When she holds Ben in "The One with the Baby on the Bus," he only cries. He does not cry when any of the male characters, even Chandler, holds him, but he does with Monica (Episode 2.6). Giving Monica and Chandler the chance to adopt, twins nonetheless, at the end of the series allowed Monica the fulfillment of her lifelong, and serieslong for fans, dream.

When Lisa Kudrow got pregnant in real life, the writers included a pregnancy in her storyline. But instead of saddling her character with a child that they would have to write into the remainder of the show, they used her quirky character to tell a different story of her serving as surrogate for her half-brother, Frank Jr. (Giovanni Ribisi), and his wife, Alice (Debra Jo Rupp). Other than using the fact that she had her brother's babies as a punchline, however, Phoebe does not discuss children much over the course of the series. In "The One with the Worst Best Man Ever"

Monica, Rachel, and Chandler uncomfortably watch a birthing video. *NBC / Photofest © NBC*

(Episode 4.22), Monica and Rachel throw Phoebe a baby shower to try to cheer her up when her pregnancy hormones are running wild. Since she will not be keeping the babies after she delivers them, they give her gifts she could use after the births, such as leather pants and tequila. Ultimately, their attempts just depress Phoebe more. While she is in labor with Frank and Alice's babies, she does suggest to Rachel that she wants to keep one but ultimately realizes that she must give them all to their rightful parents (Episode 5.3, "The One Hundredth").

Phoebe does show her mothering instincts when she and Mike try to take care of baby rats after one of Mike's traps kills their mother, Bob. But ultimately, they have to give the rats away (just like she had to give away the triplets) when they realize just how much work they are going to be as they continue to breed (Episode 9.12, "The One with Phoebe's Rats"). Even when she gets to spend time with Frank and Alice's triplets, she cannot handle it herself. She enlists Chandler and Monica to help, but in the middle of their time together, Monica has to take Chandler to the hospital when he swallows a toy he was warned a baby could choke on (again infantilizing a male lead to confirm he is not ready for children because he is one). Phoebe is then left to watch the children alone. She ends up losing one baby while trying to change another. While she does succeed in getting all the babies to bed, she does so only by virtually destroying Monica and Chandler's apartment and, once again, the babies go back to their parents at the end of the episode (Episode 6.5, "The One with Joey's Porsche").

Her commitment to parenthood endures as a point of humor in the final episode of the series even as her desire for kids remains unclear. While trying to suggest that Phoebe and her new husband, Mike (Paul Rudd), will go on to have children after the show is over, their characters' discussion of impending parenthood makes it seem like it is still just a joke to her. When Monica and Chandler come home from the hospital with twins, Mike says that he wants one. Phoebe suggests she slip one of the twins in her coat. When Mike tries to get her to take him seriously about having a baby, she suggests they have a whole bunch and be like the von Trapp family (without the Nazis). The show suggests the possibility that they will become parents, but Phoebe's closing line on the topic keeps the reality unclear.

Although Rachel's commitment to marriage is clear through the series, her desire for children is not always articulated. As a matter of fact, the first time the issue of children comes up for Rachel's character is when Ross hands her Ben to hold. She holds him with two hands, away from her body, awkwardly until Ross suggests she hold him like a football. Rachel replies that this is how she would hold a football. Rachel quickly hands the baby back and runs up to her apartment. When Ross asks for an explanation, she makes it clear that the problem is not children per se, but that Ross has their entire future planned, including where they will live (because Westchester has good schools) and their children's names (Episode 2.20, "The One where Old Yeller Dies"). Rachel left Barry at the altar because she did not want her whole life planned for her and she does not want Ross to do so too.

When Rachel does become pregnant, it is a surprise to the friends and the audience. The series told the story of who the father of her child was and how she got pregnant in retrospect after Chandler and Monica returned from their honeymoon. In "The One with Monica and Chandler's Wedding: Part 1" (Episode 7.23), we learn about Rachel's pregnancy. She does not want to tell anyone because she does not want to steal Monica's thunder (again). However, when Phoebe finds a positive pregnancy test in the trash can, the audience and the other friends are led to believe it is Monica who is pregnant. Chandler shows growth as a man in his reaction as it is the thought of Monica having a baby alone that prompts him not to leave her at the altar. When Phoebe figures out that it is Rachel who is pregnant, they still hide the truth from Monica and Chandler and Phoebe says it is she who is pregnant. Her "pregnancy" prompts Joey to propose to her so that she will not be alone and pregnant. When he discovers it is Rachel who is pregnant, he asks Phoebe for the ring back so that he can propose to Rachel (Episode 8.1, "The One after I Do"). With the first two moves, the show reifies the idea that pregnancy requires marriage, even if it is not to the father of the baby. However, Rachel takes the time during the wedding and her discussions with Phoebe and Monica to decide what to do (though she never explicitly mentions the words "abortion" or "adoption") and realizes that she wants to have the baby. Over the course of the next two episodes, we learn the father is Ross.

Once Rachel actually has the baby, the focus of her storyline oscillates between Rachel as mother and her possible rekindled romance with Ross. As Rachel is the first friend with a live-in child, one would expect story-lines such as trying to get the child to sleep (Episode 9.2, "The One where Emma Cries"), getting let go by the pediatrician for calling him too much (Episode 9.3, "The One with the Pediatrician"), and even singing "Baby Got Back" to make her laugh (Episode 9.7, "The One with Ross's Inap-propriate Song"). Hannah Hamad suggests that in each of these types of stories motherhood seems unnatural to the female characters.[19] It is more likely that the series needed to find balance between these new kinds of storylines and their commitment to the friends' relationships with each other. Additionally, these episodes reflect Rachel's attempts to find work-life balance, a condition familiar to many adult Gen-Xers.

A LIFE NOT BETTER?

Today, in view of the 2008 financial crisis, attempts at financial recovery, rising unemployment and personal debt, pension crises, the 2016 election of the forty-fifth president, divisive debates about identities, and unend-ing social media access to information about all of these global problems, lies the appeal of *Friends* for its original Generation-X American audience and for contemporary Millennial viewers. As Neil Ewen notes, *Friends* acts as "a source of comfort in an era of ever-increasing social stratification as brought to bear by neoliberal capitalism and the abhorrent policies of austerity carried out in the name of individual responsibility and economic efficiency following the 2008 crash."[20]

The series deals with tensions between Baby Boomer parents and their Gen-X adult children, anxieties surrounding work culture, impending parenthood, and gender expectations. Some may argue that the way they dealt with these issues revealed their self-absorption, neuroses, and lack of understanding about the political, social, and economic issues impacting their generation.[21] However, the humor with which this sitcom contends with these issues provides a safe space for the friends themselves to escape many of their realities and provides a nostalgic look at a time when work was seemingly less demanding and allowed for more reflection and just plain fun.

5

FRIENDS HAPPY NOT THINKING TOO MUCH

Although Generation-Xers lackadaisical attitudes toward work, commitment, and even parenthood seemingly came from graduating college and not having anything to fight for (or against), these same attitudes led to a need to identify with the populace and not become "the man." One way to do this was to laud qualities of "the people" by, for example, distancing ourselves from our intellectualism developed in college, not developing ourselves intellectually at all, and/or denigrating those who did. Since the publication of Richard Hofstadter's Pulitzer Prize–winning nonfiction tome *Anti-Intellectualism in American Life*, anti-intellectualism has become prominent in American life and a lens through which to understand trends such as Generation X's attitudes toward thinking too much. [1]

While early twentieth-century conceptions of anti-intellectualism focused on conflicts between blue-collar workers and white-collar intellectuals, common usage of the term has become politicized in twenty-first-century America as a signifier for "refusal to give a whiff for the lofty claims of book learnin'." [2] As *Friends* ended in 2004, other signals of the rise of anti-intellectualism included the re-election of George W. Bush as president, the rise of reality television (*American Idol, The Apprentice, Survivor*), and with it the explosion of celebrity culture. Additionally Matt LeBlanc's spin-off, *Joey*, premiered, and Green Day's critique of it all, *American Idiot*, was released. In his article, "How a TV Sitcom Triggered the Downfall of Western Civilization," David Hopkins concludes that "2004 was when we completely gave up and embraced stupidity as a value" and "much of America groaned, mid-sentence at the voice of reason."[3]

In contemporary American culture, "anti-intellectualism represents a form of populism."[4] If nothing else, *Friends* began as and continues to have populist appeal. Despite being nominated for 211 awards (and winning 69), they won the Emmy for Outstanding Comedy Series only once, in 2002.[5] Even so, they were in the top five of the Nielsen ratings for nine out of ten seasons,[6] and their final episode had the fourth-largest series finale audience with 52.5 million viewers in 2004.[7] While *Friends* reflected a Generation-X perspective of the time, such as its attitudes toward work and parenthood discussed in chapter 4, as a comedy, it did so with a light touch and penchant toward getting the laugh rather than interrogating issues at hand. In keeping with this approach, *Friends* quietly promoted attitudes of anti-intellectualism by lauding its most popular characters' dumb but lovable and spacey characteristics and denigrating its one intellectual friend: Ross.

POPULARITY VS. INTELLECTUALISM

In polls, the most liked characters on *Friends* were consistently Chandler, Joey, Phoebe, and Rachel and the least liked were nearly always Monica and Ross.[8] What is one thing that all of the most popular characters have in common? Either flat-out dimness and/or a disdain for the intellectual. Rachel, Joey, and Phoebe serve as quality exemplars to demonstrate this culture of anti-intellectualism on *Friends*. Rachel is beautiful, comes from an upper-class background with a doctor for a father, and has a college degree. But the show suggests that she does not always use her smarts and is definitely not very interested in learning. In the pilot episode, she tries to come up with a metaphor to explain her life choices to her father. Her attempts at comparing herself to either a shoe or purse fail to convey her meaning to her father or the audience. We then see her struggle in the first few seasons with the tasks expected of a waitress, such as remembering who ordered what and knowing that you must clean the equipment (see also chapter 4). Her limited knowledge of the work world becomes clear when she gets her first paycheck and is surprised at how little money is there, leading her to wonder who "FICA" is and why "he" is taking all her money (Episode 1.4, "The One with George Stephanopoulos").

Rachel does get better at her job once she enters the world she cares about: fashion. But when she interviews for a job at Ralph Lauren, she ends up inadvertently kissing her boss-to-be and has trouble finding any better way of defending herself other than repeating that she is courageous and not litigious. She also forgets his name, and even though he gives her a chance at the job, she ends up brushing his crotch when trying to shake his hand on her way out (Episode 5.17, "The One with Rachel's Inadvertent Kiss").

Rachel also engages in silly actions outside the work world like buying a hairless cat for $1,000 (Episode 5.21, "The One with the Ball"); losing Ross's monkey, Marcel, when distracted by a soap opera (Episode 1.19, "The One where the Monkey Gets Away"); and trying to woo potential love interest Joshua (Tate Donovan) by throwing a spontaneous going away party for Ross's girlfriend, Emily (Helen Baxendale). During the party, she initiates a game of spin the bottle and later puts on her high school cheerleading uniform and hurls herself into an ill-advised cartwheel, ending up with a fat lip (Episode 4.16, "The One with the Fake Party"). One of her most famous snafus was making half an English trifle and half a shepherd's pie without realizing that a dessert with custard, jam, and beef sautéed with peas and onions was a mistake (Episode 6.9, "The One where Ross Got High"). While it could be argued that her antics merely reflect the comedy genre, seeing Rachel participate in such activities suggests that her degree does not reflect the intellectual status typically associated with college graduates.

More than being dumb herself, though, Rachel's anti-intellectualism emerges in her regular disdain for education. While Rachel has a crush on Ross (and ends up with him), it certainly is not because of his intelligence. In a flashback in "The One with All the Thanksgivings" (Episode 5.8), Rachel says that she changed her major from psychology because of the lack of parking near the psychology department building. Despite Ross's inherently intellectual job, she still has a crush on him after finding out that he once liked her. Before Rachel can reveal her feelings, Ross meets fellow paleontologist Julie on a dig in China. In an early conversation with the gang, Julie assured Chandler that having a third nipple in some cultures is a sign of virility. Julie's sharing of knowledge is met with a behind-her-back sarcastic response from Rachel, "Oh, Julie's so smart, Julie's so special" (Episode 2.4, "The One with Phoebe's Husband"). This resistance to education continues after Ross and Rachel have their daughter, Emma, as well. When Ross tells Rachel that Emma's first word cannot be "gleba" because it is not a word, Rachel looks it up. Although she is excited to learn that it is a word meaning "the fleshy, spore-bearing inner mass of a certain fungi" (Episode 9.18, "The One with the Lottery"), she is also deflated that Ross takes this knowledge to mean that Emma will become a scientist. Even Rachel's parenting advice comes not from the contents of a book but from its back cover, which we learn on Emma's first birthday. Later in that episode when Emma says how old she is, Ross's excitement over his daughter being a genius is quickly quashed when Rachel emphatically interrupts his dream by emphasizing that Emma will not be going to science camp (Episode 10.4, "The One with the Cake"). Becoming a scientist would require that Emma be smart, go to college, and ultimately resemble her father, but Rachel rejects this possible future for her daughter. Rachel's intellectual level resembles Joey's more than Ross's. Ross gives a keynote address at a paleontology conference while she and Joey laugh at Ross's use of "homo erectus" as double entendre rather than understanding or giving credit for his scholarly insights (Episode 9.24, "The One in Barbados— Part 2").

Joey serves as the series' continual lovable dimwit though. He and Phoebe are the only friends who did not go to college, and his reading usually consists of an occasional magazine and the back of cereal boxes. Although he is open to learning new things, he demonstrates his absolute inability to learn French despite Phoebe's earnest attempts to teach him (Episode 10.13, "The One where Joey Speaks French") and struggles with guitar training as well (Episode 5.11, "The One with All the Resolutions"). Speaking French and playing guitar are skills Joey attempts to learn to bolster his acting résumé. Joey's work as an actor provides endless examples of his limited knowledge of the world. When he plays Kevin in an infomercial for a milk spout, his character has trouble opening a carton of milk, but it is Joey who inadvertently chokes on a cookie in the ad. When he first joins the cast of *Days of Our Lives* (which he abbreviates "DOOL"), he tells the gang about his new acting technique, "smell the fart acting" (Episode 2.11, "The One with the Lesbian Wedding") even as we learn that he does not think (or know) that acting requires study (Episode 9.12, "The One with Phoebe's Rats"), does not know basic stage directions (Episode 8.21, "The One with the Cooking Class"), and has so much trouble remembering and delivering lines that his parts sometimes get cut (e.g., Episode 2.13, "The One after the Superbowl: Part 2" and Episode 5.19, "The One where Ross Can't Flirt") or he is not hired in the first place (e.g., Episode 5.18, "The One where Rachel Smokes").

Joey's friends continually support him through his challenges as well as his triumphs. They comfort him when his theater reviews suggest he has reached new levels of sucking (Episode 2.10, "The One with Russ") just as they celebrate with him when he tells them that it is "just his character that is not brain dead" (Episode 7.11, "The One with All the Cheesecakes").

Seeing Joey appear on the Donny Osmond–hosted *$25,000 Pyramid* shows the limits of his acting ability as well as his intelligence. To try to get him to guess "cream," Joey's partner gives him clues, such as asking what you might put in your coffee. Joey guesses that it might be a spoon, your hands, or your face. When his partner clarifies that what you put in your coffee is white, Joey starts another trajectory with guesses of paper, snow, and a ghost. Despite his partner's best efforts, Joey cannot seem to

Joey plays *Pyramid. Warner Brothers / Photofest © Warner Brothers*

see beyond each individual clue (Episode 10.11, "The One where the Stripper Cries"). Joey's answers on *Pyramid* provide some insights into how he sees the world, one small segment at a time. His answers show that, much like Phoebe, sometimes Joey lives in a world of his own creation. Early on, we learn that Joey does not know that tailors should not be "cupping" anything when measuring pants (Episode 2.1, "The One with Ross's New Girlfriend"), just as later he learns the hard way that silent auctions are for buying items and not just guessing how much they cost when he ends up having to buy a $20,000 boat (Episode 6.24, "The One with the Proposal: Part 1"). He also believes that an Adam's apple is named after each individual, making his the Joey's apple (Episode 7.14, "The One where They All Turn 30"), and that Ross's job is "dinosaurs" (Episode 9.2, "The One where Emma Cries").

Despite his ignorance, Joey does try to be prepared for any situation and to learn more. Because he, Chandler, Monica, and Phoebe were locked in Monica's room all night without food or entertainment while Ross and Rachel were breaking up (Episode 3.16, "The One with the Morning After"), he later put a just-in-case box under her bed in case it ever happened again. When it actually does happen again, they have snacks, Mad Libs, and condoms. The condoms, Joey explains, are in case they are the last people left on Earth and have to repopulate it (Episode 5.5, "The One with the Kips"). His limited knowledge of reproduction led him to once ask Ross if homo sapiens were extinct because they were "homo." When Ross reminds him that Homo sapiens are people, Joey still does not get it but instead defensively states that he is not judging (Episode 3.8, "The One with the Giant Poking Device").

In Joey's world, food and sex are primary motivators. So it is no surprise that Joey's punchlines often come from sexualizing situations, including the intellectual. In the first season of the show, all of the friends are comparing the strangest places they have had sex. Joey's is in the women's restroom in the New York Public Library. When he tells the gang, Monica responds by wondering why he was in a library (Episode 1.7, "The One with the Blackout"). So it is strange to later learn that Joey is volunteering at the New York University Medical School to help science. Of course, it puts it in perspective when he reveals that it is for a fertility study. Instead of taking the time to investigate how Joey is actually helping scientific discovery, Monica hopes that he is only donating his time. Joey defends his actions by saying that the research is serious and that he is going to make \$700. But Phoebe brings the point back to the sexual jokes we expect from Joey when she suggests he is going to be making money "hand over fist" (Episode 1.24, "The One where Rachel Finds Out"). Typically, we do not see Joey involved in intellectual pursuits, even in his near-constant pursuit of the ladies. Ross asks Joey if he read *Lord of the Rings* in high school, and Joey reminds Ross that he had sex in high school instead (Episode 4.9, "The One where They're Going to Party"). When Ross says that he is confused by a book that the gals are reading, *Be Your Own Windkeeper*, it is not surprising that Joey reveals that this is the reason he does not date women who read (Episode 2.19, "The One where Eddie Won't Go"). Joey plays the lovable dimwit, and the likability of his character provides additional support for the idea that if the audience likes Joey, then we laugh with him. Despite their jokes, in all of these instances, the friends support and defend Joey from potential detractors. His populist appeal helps us love him despite his faults.

Audience members also love Phoebe, often because she creates her own world too. In Phoebe's world, she spells her name for reporters by sounding it out in her own unique way: "P as in 'Phoebe,' H as in 'hoebe,' O as in 'oebe,' E as in 'ebe,' B as in 'be be' and E as in ''ello there, mate!" (Episode 8.19, "The One with Joey's Interview"). She also ends up changing her name after getting married, not to Phoebe Hannigan, but to Princess Consuela Banana Hammock (Episode 10.14, "The One with Princess Consuela"). She is the only one who really gets Ross's "sound" when he plays the keyboard (Episode 4.7, "The One where Chandler Crosses the Line"), and she has her own unique way of singing along with Ross's bagpipe rendition of Kool and the Gang's "Celebration," which relies heavily on the vowel "eeeeeeee" (Episode 7.15, "The One with Joey's New Brain"). Of course, we get the most insights into Phoebe's world through the lyrics of her self-authored songs (which you can read more about in chapter 8), whose titles include "Pervert Parade," "Ode to a Pubic Hair," and "Smelly Cat" (Episode 9.7, "The One with Ross' Inappropriate Song"). As she sings songs about what she sees in everyday life ("Lather, Rinse, Repeat"), Phoebe shows us how she sees the world and sometimes puts others in the uncomfortable position of having to face their own realities, such as when she wrote and sang, "Two of Them Kissed Last Night," about "Neil" having to decide between "Betty" and "Lulie." Even though the song began with the reminder that it was not real, it makes Ross and Rachel, who kissed the night before, very uncomfortable in front of Julie (Episode 2.8, "The One with the List"). Phoebe is the creative, at times insightful, one.

Phoebe may not be intellectual, but she is not stupid nor anti-learning. Although she did not get to go to high school, as she was living on the streets after her mother killed herself, she says that she and some other street kids taught themselves French behind a dumpster and somehow (she does not even know how) she learned Italian along the way as well (revealed in Episodes 5.19, "The One where Ross Can't Flirt" and 10.13, "The One where Joey Speaks French"). She also tries to improve herself by taking a literature class at the New School. Of course, her rationale for doing so still seems consistent with Phoebe's unique worldview: she really liked the Lamaze class she took there before. When contrasted with her classmate Rachel, who does not read the books before coming to class, Phoebe seems like a motivated and insightful student. But when Monica comes to class with her, Phoebe seems downright average by comparison. Overzealous and ultra-competitive Monica asks and answers her own questions and requests tests from the teacher (Episode 5.9, "The One with Ross's Sandwich").

Along with revealing her smarts at times, Phoebe makes it clear that she does not suffer fools or zealots. These seemingly complicated characteristics—being flighty but smart, wanting to learn but calling out others for doing so—come out in the way her anti-intellectualism does. The debate Phoebe and Ross have about evolution in "The One where Heckles Dies" (Episode 2.3) demonstrates her edge, her intelligence, and also her anti-intellectual perspective. The debate begins when Phoebe says she does not believe in either crop circles or evolution, equating the validity of the two. When Ross questions her, she says that it all seems too easy to buy. Ross indicates that evolution is scientific fact, like gravity, and not something to be bought or sold. Phoebe replies by suggesting that her feeling pushed down rather than pulled puts the theory of gravity into question. This exchange establishes Ross's resistance to Phoebe's perspective, his acceptance of scientific facts as legitimate evidence, and Phoebe not believing in evolution as well as questioning other scientific theories. Chandler tries to break the tension at the end of their exchange by suggesting that Isaac Newton must be mad and provides a moment for the audience to laugh. However, they are not laughing at Phoebe, but at the idea of a scientist being mad and coming back from the dead for being criticized.

Ross and Phoebe's conversation continues later in the episode while the gang is cleaning out Mr. Heckles's apartment when he tries to help her visualize evolution by telling her about fossils you can see that prove the theory. While Ross believes he made progress in getting Phoebe to believe in evolution, her final response in this exchange says otherwise. Phoebe finishes by asking who put the fossils there to be found and why. Ironically, Phoebe engaged Ross in an intellectual pursuit: questioning the foundation of knowledge and science itself. However, dismissing the observable facts upon which Ross bases his knowledge, not having an alternative theory, and getting the laugh for making fun of Ross results in a dismissal of the foundation upon which he is trying to base the debate and more love for playful Phoebe for putting intellectual Ross in his place.

Ross makes his frustration with Phoebe clear throughout the episode by asking her how humans developed opposable thumbs without evolution. When she responds that the overlords may have created them to steer their space crafts, he asks if there is blood coming out of his ears while she suggests that he put himself "under the microscope" to examine why he has an obsessive need to make everybody agree with him. The final straw in this anti-intellectual episode is when Ross enters and Phoebe introduces him as "scary scientist man." Instead of responding directly, Ross begins what he believes is his final lesson to convince Phoebe that evolution exists using evidence from the museum. Before he can even open the suitcase of fossils, Phoebe says that she is not denying evolution, only pointing out that it is *one* of the possibilities to explain the world. When Ross insists it is the *only* possibility, Phoebe pressures him more to open his mind that there may be other explanations. When she points out that past beliefs that the world was flat and that the atom was the smallest thing on Earth were both disproven, he gives in and admits that she may be right. She concludes their exchange by expressing her disappointment in him for caving. Before, she says, she may not have agreed with him, but she did respect him. Now that she got him to agree with her, she has lost that respect for him. Ross then closes the briefcase and leaves. After Ross leaves, Phoebe turns to Monica and Rachel and tells them how much fun it was.

When challenged to open his mind, a common request of doctors of philosophy, whether in their research or teaching, Ross does it. However, Phoebe then shifts her criticism of him from a challenge of his scientific beliefs to a challenge of his more fundamental practices, that is, the intellectual pursuit of knowledge itself. She uses philosophical perspectives of education that require open minds and questions about knowledge itself to make him seem as if he has no beliefs at all. In that moment, rather than allowing Ross to go back to the evidence at hand, the audience instead joins in Phoebe's folly: making fun of the intellectual. Even if audience members see Ross's point, the laughter in response from the studio audience affirms that it is correct to laugh *at* Ross in his defeat and *with* Phoebe in her triumph.[9]

THE INTELLECTUAL'S ANTI-INTELLECTUALISM

David Hopkins describes *Friends* as "the story of a family man, a man of science, a genius who fell in with the wrong crowd. He slowly descends into madness and desperation, lead [*sic*] by his own egotism. With one mishap after another, he becomes a monster. I'm talking, of course, about *Friends* and its tragic hero, Ross Geller."[10] The tragedy Hopkins describes is Ross's constant denigration by the other friends for his education and wanting to be recognized for being smart. Despite his PhD, the show makes fun of Ross for wanting to be considered and called a real doctor, for wanting to have his education and profession valued, and, in a seeming contradiction, for not living up to the expectations for those at his level of education.

From an early age, Ross wanted to be a scientist, which we learn from seeing his childhood toys, including a rock polisher and T-shirt that says, "Geology Rocks" (Episode 7.13, "The One where Rosita Dies"), and his self-authored comic book, "Science Boy," where his superpower is a "superhuman thirst for knowledge" (Episode 9.15, "The One with the Mugging"). After Ross accomplishes his goal of earning a PhD, he enjoys when people recognize his status by calling him doctor. In Episode 8.18, "The One in Massapequa," for example, he introduces himself as Ross Geller before giving a toast for his parents' anniversary party. His father interrupts and shouts, "Dr. Ross Geller." While Ross feigns embarrassment, he then re-introduces himself as "*Dr.* Ross Geller."

Ross's insistence that others recognize his status annoys everyone though. Another time, Ross went for a spray tan and the employee complimented Ross for quickly recounting the instructions. Ross's response

Ross works on his keynote speech. *Warner Brothers / Photofest © Warner Brothers*

was to point out that he had a PhD. The employee rolled his eyes in response. To add insult to injury, Ross then was unable to implement the instructions correctly and ended up with all the tanning spray on just the front of his body (Episode 10.3, "The One with Ross's Tan").[11] Punishing him for acting intellectually superior to the spray tan employee provides the audience with the opportunity to laugh at this seemingly smart man's ridiculous inability to follow simple directions to spray tan properly.

Despite his academic dreams and achievements, Ross's insistence that others recognize his status as a doctor is one thing that irritates his friends so much that they think he should not continually say it. In the hospital after Rachel has the baby, Phoebe asks if Ross is lying about proposing to Rachel just like the time he tried to convince them that he was a doctor. Ross responds by shouting at her that he is a doctor (Episode 9.1, "The One where No One Proposes"). He is told not to call himself a doctor in a hospital again when he accompanies Rachel to visit her father after his heart attack. When he introduces himself as a doctor, she insists he should not say that in a hospital (Episode 10.13, "The One where Joey Speaks French"). Her response implies that he should not say he is a doctor in the presence of medical doctors.

Ross also annoys his friends with his intellectual prowess when he corrects people's spelling and grammar or suggests intellectual pursuits. In Episode 4.1, "The One with the Jellyfish," he angrily points out Rachel's mistaken use of "you're" instead of "your" in her eighteen-page (front and back) letter to him spelling out her conditions for them getting back together. He later admits that he does not know why he corrects people's grammar just after correcting someone for mistakenly using "who" instead of "whom" (Episode 4.8, "The One with Chandler in a Box"). Whereas Joey gets a laugh for doing the same in Episode 8.4, "The One with the Videotape," Ross must apologize for doing it when he sees the disdain in the friends' reactions. They react similarly when he suggests they engage in intellectual activities, such as watching a documentary on the Serengeti instead of *Entertainment Tonight* (Episode 2.17, "The One where Eddie Moves In"). When Ross suggests going to a Ukrainian film, Joey immediately says no but that he would go see "a normal person movie" with him, whereas potential love interest Mona laughs, thinking he was joking, before agreeing to go with him (Episode 8.5, "The One with Rachel's Date").

Such disdain for Ross's intellectual pursuits outside of academia might seem understandable. However, when Ross is shown at work and doing his job, he never seems very good at it either. For the first four seasons of the show, he works at a museum. We see him more than once working in a display case with mannequins of early people at this museum. He and Rachel actually wake up in post-coital bliss under animal skin blankets in this window box after their first night together (Episode 2.15, "The One where Ross and Rachel . . . You Know"). This is odd though since Ross is a paleontologist (who studies dinosaurs) and not an anthropologist (who studies people) and, of course, since it is unacceptable for most people to have sex at work. Despite his not knowing anything about natural history, Ross also gets Joey a job at the museum as a guide (Episode 4.11, "The One with Phoebe's Uterus"). Ross is later put on leave after yelling at his boss for eating his sandwich and fired when his boss believes he has failed to get his anger issues under control (Episode 5.9, "The One with Ross's Sandwich").

Ross is later hired, and even earns tenure, as a college professor. Unlike the hiring and tenure process for most real college professors, Ross's journey begins when he is hired to teach one class, which would typically be considered part-time or adjunct faculty work. Somehow, as it is never depicted on-screen, he goes from teaching one class to being offered an advanced class, a position usually reserved for full-time faculty. We learn this in an episode where Ross's storyline has him making repeated attempts to go from one of the school's campuses to the other across the city in time for his second class to begin. Watching him arrive once as the class ends, arrive the next time so sweaty and out of breath from running that he passes out, and ultimately try to teach in Rollerblades makes his role as teacher seem ridiculous (Episode 8.12, "The One where Joey Dates Rachel"). The absurdity of Ross as a professor is bolstered by scenes of him teaching with a fake English accent (which he later tries to phase out) (Episode 6.4, "The One where Joey Loses His Insurance"); dating a student for a five-episode run; seemingly giving male students who are in love with him higher grades (Episode 7.18, "The One with Joey's Award"); and making out with a woman in the library in front of his own dissertation (Episode 7.7, "The One with Ross's Library Book"). Despite having his papers widely discredited (Episode 9.20, "The One with the Soap Opera Party"), Ross is chosen to give a keynote address at a conference in Barbados. Of course, he gets the part by accident. During his presentation, the interviewer fell asleep. While trying to wake him, Ross falls into his lap and covers by pretending he was hugging him to thank him for offering him the gig (Episode 9.22, "The One with the Donor"). While Ross is treated like a rock star of the intellectual world by his colleagues in Barbados, his friends are disappointed that the only time the sun is out during their trip, they have to attend his speech. Instead of supporting Ross for the honor of being keynote speaker, they would rather be at the beach.

Even when others recognize his intellectual prowess, his friends, who should be the most supportive of him, continue to denigrate his status and accomplishments. In Episode 8.21, "The One with the Cooking Class," Ross gets hit on by the clerk at a baby store because he is a paleontologist. She even compares him to Indiana Jones. But Rachel, who he is shopping with for their unborn child, points out that he is not a real doctor and complains that their conversation is so dull that even she, a woman who was born shopping, is bored doing it. While this clerk's interest in Ross is rooted in his intellectual appeal, Ross ends up not dating her because Rachel does not want him to date anyone while she is pregnant. Setting Ross up with women who are perfect for him and then making fun of them (or him) for the relationship is a common way that the series put down Ross's intellectualism. When Phoebe and Joey try to set Rachel and Ross up on bad dates (in an attempt to make them realize they belong together), Joey sets Ross up with a woman who likes puzzles and reading for pleasure. Phoebe points out that Joey has just set Ross up with his perfect woman. Joey's rejection of her for these qualities cues the audience that she is not worth dating. The punchline for Ross's storyline, though, is that Joey cancels his date without telling Ross so that he ends up stood up instead. This suggests that intellectual Ross is not worth dating in the first place.

Rachel's life also interferes with Ross's ability to celebrate his intellectual accomplishment for earning tenure. The series never explains how someone who has not been a good teacher, had papers discredited, dated students, and even gotten bad teaching evaluations can earn tenure, which gives him job security for life. Ross even focuses not on the accomplishment but on how in academic circles, tenure will supposedly get him laid. But when Ross announces that he has earned this coveted status, his popping a bottle of champagne and touting his accomplishment to his friends merely looks insensitive as he does not know that Rachel just got fired by Ralph Lauren and not hired for a new job with Gucci (Episode 10.14, "The One with Princess Consuela").

Ross's job and relationships both provide contexts in which his intellect becomes the butt of the joke, beginning with storylines that suggest that Ross is better with Rachel than he is with seemingly more appropriate partners, such as fellow paleontologists Julie and Charlie. Despite his crush on Rachel, Ross does not think he has a chance with such a beautiful, popular young woman. But he holds other women he dates to higher intellectual standards than he does Rachel. When Ross says that he does not want to go out with a woman again, Chandler asks if this is because she thinks that *The Flintstones* could've really happened (Episode 1.18, "The One with All the Poker"). Dismissing her as a legitimate date due to her lack of understanding of history does not make his intellect any more attractive.

Both of the women who Ross dates on a longer-term basis and who are more appropriate for him also earned PhDs and are women of color: Julie is Asian American and Charlie is African American. Shelley Cobb notes, "As women of color, Charlie and Julie must be significantly better than Rachel to be good enough for Ross" and "must be better than even Ross to be good enough for him and the group."[12] I discuss the issues of race and representation in *Friends* in chapter 6. Here, the important issue is the intellectual challenges that Julie and Charlie pose for Ross that seemingly make them excellent potential romantic partners for him. Julie met Ross while they were both on a dig in China. Although she is beautiful, in many other ways she represents the anti-Rachel. Julie is Asian American, smart, interested in learning, supports herself financially, and has a well-established career whereas Rachel is white, not bright (or motivated) enough to be a good waitress, not interested in learning, financially insecure, and not sure what she wants to do with her life. Most importantly for Ross, Julie wants to have a long-term romantic relationship with him (as indicated by their ultimately unfulfilled desire to get a cat together) (Episode 2.7, "The One where Ross Finds Out"). She seems to be the perfect person for Ross to fulfill Ross's wish from the first episode "to be married again" (Episode 1.1, "Pilot"). Even so, when Ross finds out that Rachel has feelings for him, he quickly breaks up with Julie.

Ross does not meet Charlie until well into season 9 and immediately has the hots for her. Why shouldn't he? She is beautiful and a paleontologist. However, their relationship is delayed when she and Joey hook up. Being the good friend that he is, Ross even helps Joey navigate the Metropolitan Museum of Art for his first date with Charlie. Unfortunately, Joey ends up going the wrong way in the museum so everything Ross helped him memorize made no sense, making what Ross taught him useless (Episode 9.21, "The One with the Fertility Test"). Ultimately, when the whole gang goes to Barbados, Charlie and Joey break up, which facilitates both Charlie and Ross getting together as well as Joey and Rachel finally kissing. Charlie and Joey break up because she is smart and he is not and therefore they do not have much in common. She enjoys museums and he enjoys sports, for example, and when they are in Barbados, she wants to go to conference sessions and he wants to go to the beach. The point at which they grasp that they do not belong together is when they realize how much fun they are having in Barbados, but not with one another. In contrast, when Charlie and Ross first make out, she calls him Dr. Geller without him even having to ask her to do so (Episode 9.24, "The One in Barbados: Part 2").

However, Charlie seems to have higher intellectual desires than Ross too. These are signaled when she chats with Ross at Joey's soap opera cast party and tells him that she has only dated men who have won Nobel prizes (Episode 9.20, "The One with the Soap Opera Party"). This point is solidified when she ultimately leaves Ross for her ex-boyfriend, Dr. Benjamin Hobart (Greg Kinnear), whose two Nobel prizes and ability to deny Ross a grant indicate his intellectual superiority to Ross (Episode 10.6, "The One with Ross's Grant"). Ultimately, Ross appears to be too intellectual to be respected by his friends but not intellectual enough to be accepted (and loved) by those who are intellectually equal or superior to him. But the series suggests to viewers that the only way Ross can be happy is to tolerate his friends' denigration of his intellectualism so that he can be with Rachel.

CONCLUSION

Yes, this is a comedy. Yes, it is supposed to be funny. But it is also important to consider the impacts of the type of humor employed. In *Friends*, making intellectualism the butt of the joke and seeing the audience think less of a character because of it suggests that denigrating intellectualism in general and Ross in particular promotes a kind of anti-intellectualism reflective of late twentieth- and early twenty-first-century culture. While the theme song warns of an inherently deceptive life, laughable careers, lack of love lives, and potential poverty,[13] it suggests the remedy is your friends. For Rachel, Phoebe, and Joey, this means being accepted regardless of how intelligent they are or how little sense their worldviews sometimes make. In contrast, for Ross, this means accepting being the butt of their jokes for being smart and pursuing knowledge.

6

THIN, WHITE, UPPER-MIDDLE-CLASS *FRIENDS*

Friends contributed significantly to television culture by popularizing "hang-out" TV, focusing on the entire ensemble, solidifying the friends-as-family narrative as a television trope, and even representing Generation-X characteristics of anti-intellectualism and not doing much. What *Friends* included also served to erase or sublimate other important issues, especially those of intersectional identities. Specifically, privileging thin, white, upper-middle-class bodies as ideal in the series functioned to denigrate fat bodies and pushed people of color and those not in the same social or economic class as the friends outside the closed circle created by their alternate family. The positive contributions *Friends* made to TV history also expose the limitations of these representations in the show. Examining how the series represented fat[1] people, people of color, and other intersecting issues of identity reveals much about where American society was in the mid-1990s through the early 2010s and allows us to see how they might have done better.

THIN = GOOD / FAT = BAD

Friends, like most television programs, represents thin bodies as the norm. Showing the slender bodies of its six main characters—and everyone they have relationships with—in contrast to the fat bodies they denigrate suggests the desirability of the skinny. The few times that male characters' weight is discussed, it is in passing reference in circumstances that only temporarily exist. For example, Chandler's seeming weight gain provides Monica with the opportunity to become his trainer to help him lose weight in Episode 2.7, "The One where Ross Finds Out." His weight is never mentioned again, despite the fact that Matthew Perry's weight markedly fluctuated during the run of the show. While there are a few other characters of size in the series, including Mr. Treeger (Mike Hagerty) and Jack Geller (Elliot Gould), their bodies are usually not the focus of their storylines. In contrast, the representation of Ugly Naked Guy and "Fat Monica" suggests fat bodies are to be made fun of and women's fat bodies must be changed to be accepted.

Ugly Naked Guy actually only appeared (uncredited)[2] in two episodes of the series. Yet he was mentioned in episodes throughout the first five seasons as the friends peered at him in his apartment across the street through the window of Monica's apartment. The friends saw when he got a Thighmaster (Episode 1.2, "The One with the Sonogram at the End"), laid tile (Episode 1.5, "The One with the East German Laundry Detergent"), lit candles (Episode 1.7, "The One with the Blackout"), got gravity boots (Episode 1.20, "The One with the Evil Orthodontist"), decorated his Christmas tree (Episode 2.9, "The One with Phoebe's Dad"), and even played cello (Episode 2.11, "The One with the Lesbian Wedding"). As they peered at him, they made comments policing his body and activities with well-timed, disgusted "ewww"s at his attempts to do naked exercise and do naked household activities. Even if the friends did not include their judgments in their reactions, we see Phoebe call him "cute naked guy" when she sees him in 1992 (two years before the series began) in Episode 3.6, "The One with the Flashback." But she laments that he appears to be putting on weight. Two years later, when the cast first refers to him in Episode 1.2, "The One with the Sonogram at the End," they now call him "Ugly Naked Guy." This shift suggests that being thin equates with being cute and being fat means being ugly.

They further feed into stereotypes of fat people by suggesting he is lazy and does not take care of his things. In Episode 3.8, "The One with the Giant Poking Device," Phoebe fears her curse of going to the dentist will result in someone's death. Once she confirms that all the friends are alive, they notice that Ugly Naked Guy has not moved in quite some time and fear he has died. Given the assumption that he is fat, and therefore unhealthy, it is a seemingly logical conclusion that he could be the one who died (regardless of Phoebe's curse). In his final appearance (and mention) in Episode 5.14, "The One where Everybody Finds Out," the gang tries to come up with what they know about Ugly Naked Guy to help Ross find out how he can relate to him. They remind Ross not to bring up his trampoline or gravity boots because he broke them nor should he mention his cat as they saw him sit on it. While his owning a trampoline and gravity boots could have been signs that he was trying to exercise, the friends focus on his breaking the exercise equipment instead. Using Ugly Naked Guy as a comic foil certainly invites people to laugh at the humor of the situations the friends see him in, but that they direct their comments at the "fat guy" does not bode well for their representations of men of size.

The creation of Fat Monica brings with her all of the stereotypes associated with fat people as well as a gendered dimension that makes clear that women should definitely be thin. *Friends* depicts Fat Monica as eating all the time, sloppy, and naïve[3] about sex, as well as unhealthy, loud, and funny. We learn early that Monica was "a total cow" in high school when Chandler compares her to "an Alp" in a picture because she was so large (Episode 1.17, "The One with Two Parts: Part 2"), and we discover that the home economics class had to make her a special band uniform just to fit her large frame (Episode 4.2, "The One with the Cat"). When Monica is going through a box of her stuff her parents brought her and pulls out her old bathing suit, Chandler says that it was "what they used to cover Connecticut when it rains." The audience first sees "Fat Monica" in Episode 2.14, "The One with the Prom Video." When Monica appears, Joey wonders if the girl he sees ate Monica. She defends herself by noting that the camera adds ten pounds, so Chandler inquires about how many cameras were on her. When Monica first emerges in her prom dress, she is also eating a sandwich. She actually ends up getting mayonnaise on Rachel's shoulder when she hugs her. Given how ultra-fastidious Thin Monica is, providing this contrast makes it easy to accept that being fat made Monica sloppy.

While Ugly Naked Guy always seemed to have exercise equipment (that he broke) that may have suggested he was trying to lose weight, Monica, on the other hand, never had intentions to exercise and was almost always shown eating and/or being possessive about food. In Episodes 6.15 and 6.16, "The One That Could Have Been: Parts 1 and 2," Joey fears Monica's reaction when he does not get her three giant Rice

Chandler, Rachel, Ross, and Monica in the 1980s. *Warner Brothers / Photofest ©*
Warner Brothers

Krispie treats to her fast enough. Later in the episode, she worries more about whether her Kit Kat got smashed than that Phoebe, the stock broker, lost $13 million. When she recovers her Kit Kat, she offers it to Chandler to celebrate his selling a story to Archie comics, but then she cannot seem to let it go until he agrees to share it with her. In yet another scene, she is in the background of the main action just eating a pint of ice cream by herself at the kitchen table and complaining about how light mayonnaise is not real mayonnaise. Finally, one of the plot points in the episodes is Monica trying to have a romantic dinner with her then boyfriend, Dr. Roger. This plot point sets up scenes that nearly always show her either eating, preparing food, and/or protecting it in some way.

In addition to the focus on his exercise equipment, in contrast to Monica's food, Ugly Naked Guy also has an Ugly Naked Gal, with whom he shared Thanksgiving dinner and naked dancing (Episode 1.9, "The One where Underdog Gets Away"). However, being fat led Monica to rejection from potential suitors. When we see Monica interact with Rachel's high school boyfriend, Chip, and with Chandler approximately ten years after high school, it is clear that when she was fat, she would not have been able to land either one of them. Now that she is thin, she has her pick. While Chip would not have had anything to do with Monica in high school, now that she is thin, he not only notices her but asks her out. When they go out, Monica discovers that the "cool guy" from high school may have peaked then as he still hangs out with the same crowd and does the same things he did in high school. In contrast, we are meant to see how far Monica has come based mostly on her weight loss. Now that she is thin, we get the same satisfaction as she does when she rejects Chip (Episode 4.2, "The One with the Cat").

Aside from a flashback that revises their relationship (Episode 5.8, "The One with All the Thanksgivings"), the same is true of Chandler and Monica. Chandler makes his feeling about fat women clear in what could be considered throwaway comments, but instead there are pauses for laughs after nearly every one of his lines as he is the funny one. When Ross criticizes his ex-wife, Carol (Jane Sibbet), and her wife, Susan (Jessica Hecht), for arriving later than him to the hospital when Carol is in labor, Carol explains that Susan wanted a Chunky candy bar. Ross insists they should not have stopped for Chunkys, to which Chandler responds, "I used to have that bumper sticker" (Episode 1.23, "The One with the Birth"). After Chandler and Monica get engaged, Monica learns that Chandler broke up with his camp girlfriend because she gained weight over the year between camp visits. While Monica asks Chandler if he would break up with her if she gained weight again, he insists he would love her no matter her size. However, we also learn that his camp girlfriend gained 140 pounds (Episode 7.6, "The One with the Nap Partners"). That he broke up with her over such a large amount of weight gain is supposed to suggest Chandler's actions were justified, especially since Monica is shocked by this number as well. But it also implies that there may be a weight limit to Chandler's love. In Episode 5.8, "The One with All the Thanksgivings," Chandler begs Ross not to leave him with his fat sister and Monica overhears it. His comment is framed as that which *finally* (according to her parents) gets her to feel full and stop eating so much. The next year Monica is shown to have lost more than one hundred pounds. Now that she is thin, Chandler hits on her.

Fat Monica's troubles with men interfere with her ability to reach sexual milestones as well, such as first kisses and loss of virginity. In a flashback during Episode 10.11, "The One where the Stripper Cries," Rachel and Monica visit Chandler and Ross at college. Monica is fat so

Chandler ends up making out with Rachel instead. Later that night, Monica's girth leads Ross to mistake her for a pile of coats and he ends up kissing her (thinking she is Rachel). The fact that her brother was her first kiss *ever* suggests a fat woman cannot get any action unless it is from her brother when he cannot see her in the dark. Her lack of sexual experience feeds into the idea that fat women are naïve about sexual matters. This aspect of Fat Monica's depiction comes through explicitly when she refers to her virginity as her "flower" and a man's penis as his "tenderness" (Episode 5.8, "The One with All the Thanksgivings" and Episodes 6.15 and 6.16, "The One That Could Have Been: Parts 1 and 2"). When the series shows Monica as fat for nearly two whole episodes, without any intent to lose weight, they show her dating Dr. Roger. Her friends criticize him for being boring. Even so, Monica says that she is tired of waiting for the perfect guy and as a thirty-year old virgin she will settle for a guy who is not horrible.

Even after Monica loses the weight, the familiar tropes in depictions of fat women continue. Monica tries to get revenge on Chandler for calling her fat but finds it unsatisfactory. She states that she is now thin and therefore her heart is not in trouble anymore, which automatically equates being fat with being unhealthy. Losing weight, then, would seem to be the solution. On two instances when Fat Monica appears, Rachel notes or asks if she has lost weight. When Monica thanks her for noticing, she says she has lost three pounds (Episode 5.8, "The One with All the Thanksgivings" and Episode 10.11, "The One where the Stripper Cries"). The humor is supposed to lie with the fact that she is so fat that losing three pounds cannot be noticed by others. So she seems damned if she does and damned if she does not lose weight. The others do not compliment her appearance unless it is in relation to her having lost significant amounts of weight, as when she first re-meets Dr. Richard Burke and he is at a loss for words at how great she looks *now* (Episode 2.15, "The One where Ross and Rachel . . . You Know"). The fact that thin actress Courteney Cox plays Monica further suggests that Fat Monica's fatness was always temporary, as if it would merely take criticism from one man to make a fat woman lose weight and meet his standards. The fact that most episodes of the show depict a formerly fat Thin Monica provides additional evidence that fat people can successfully lose the weight and be accepted by society for doing it. Even so, she still gets made fun of for being formerly fat.

Friends also created opportunities to complicate depictions of fat men and fat women. For example, Joey also has a great affinity for food. Most of the time, no one comments on his weight, regardless of whether he is eating two pizzas or a whole turkey. But when Rachel's sister Amy (Christina Applegate) visits, she asks him if he really wants to eat some leftover pizza. Joey defensively responds that he likes being curvy (Episode 10.5, "The One where Rachel's Sister Baby-Sits"). Later, when Monica and Ross's friend Will (Brad Pitt) visits, he reveals that he has also lost more than a hundred pounds. But he seems very unhappy not being able to eat carbs, dairy, or fat. When Will comments on Joey's eating habits, Joey calls him out for being an outsider, suggesting that his opinion of Joey is unwarranted.

Similarly, Ugly Naked Guy remains unapologetic about his looks and weight for five seasons. Given that he does not have to hear the friends' comments about him, we only see their point of view and not his. When the friends see that he is moving in Episode 5.14, "The One where Everybody Finds Out," Rachel notes how she is going to miss "that big ol' squishy butt." We could take that comment as positive toward his body, except that it is followed by Chandler's saying that he is done eating the chicken fried rice, seemingly to avoid looking like Ugly Naked Guy. Capping off the moment with such a jab suggests we should avoid eating fatty foods so that we do not end up like Ugly Naked Guy. However, the episode ends with Ross realizing that he knows the most important fact about Ugly Naked Guy that might help him convince Ugly Naked Guy to sublet his apartment to him: he likes to be naked. The end of the episode shows the ultimate validation of his lifestyle: Ross becomes "Naked Ross." He hangs out naked, eating muffins with Ugly Naked Guy. While his actions may be self-serving, and we do not see a Fat Ross, his becoming Naked Ross, even for the moment, validates Ugly Naked Guy's lifestyle.

Having fat male characters cast with thin female costars is typical in American television, from *The Honeymooners* (1955–1956) through *The King of Queens* (1998–2007). But having fat female leads remains limited to a select few shows, even in recent years, including *Mike and Molly* (2010–2016) with Melissa McCarthy. This makes any representations of fat women important to those of us who can identify with them. Despite how negatively *Friends* portrays women of size, there are also messages to suggest fat people are happy being fat when they are not being criticized by others. As a matter of fact, Mathilda Gregory suggests that Fat Monica could be considered a joke at the expense of fat people, merely a thin actor in fat suit, *or* a way "to elicit cheap laughs and to humiliate uptight present-day Thin Monica."[4] In multiple episodes, we get to see Fat Monica dancing. While the visual joke suggests "ha, ha, a fat woman dancing," the fact is she dances with abandon, like no one is watching. In Episode 10.11, "The One where the Stripper Cries," she dances with donuts in both hands, and in Episode 6.15, "The One That Could Have Been," she only stops dancing when her pizza arrives. The main problem, of course, is the assumption that she would be eating all the time. Additionally, the fact that she is a thin actress dancing with such lack of self-consciousness seems to take away the effect of a fat person being so free. But the unexpected positive part of this depiction is how unapologetically *happy* she appears *in her fat body* as she both dances and eats. The joke of Fat Monica is that she supposedly did not even realize how "grotesque" she was until someone else pointed it out.[5] But Monica knew she was fat. The problem, when she overheard Chandler call her fat, was not that she was learning about her weight for the first time. Rather, it was that a man she liked was shaming her for something that she believed she could not (or did not want to) do anything about it. She wanted to be accepted for who she was.[6]

While Monica is portrayed as naïve sexually, she is also depicted as desirous and lustful about food and sex too.[7] When Monica's date is putting her corsage on her in Episode 2.14, "The One with the Prom Video," she leans over to Rachel to tell her that his hand grazed her breast. She may not have lost her "flower" yet, but she certainly enjoys that moment. Her thwarted attempts to flirt with Chandler show she wants him even before he wants her. Despite suggesting that her weight is what is stopping him from returning her affection, Episodes 6.15 and 6.16, "The One That Could Have Been: Parts 1 and 2" insinuate that she and Chandler would have ended up together no matter what. He agrees to have sex with her to help her get over her nervousness about losing her virginity with Dr. Roger. After they have sex the first time, she unapologetically screams that they are going to do it again! Her desires for him are returned not only when he agrees to have sex again, but also when he diverts Dr. Roger so that he can express his desires for more than just sex with Monica, not in spite of her being fat but for all that she is. In this way, Fat Monica served as a role model. If *Friends* could have avoided the easy fat jokes, she could have potentially pushed these boundaries further for portrayals of fat white women.

PRIVILEGING WHITENESS TO CREATE RACIAL AND ETHNIC "OTHERS"

Friends has also been criticized for its unrealistic portrayal of class and privileging whiteness. Its unrealistic upscaling of the lives of these twenty-somethings just after college starts in the first episode of the series. Monica notes that her apartment is rent-controlled in the pilot episode. The intent of this one comment is to explain how she can afford such a place. Even if we were to assume that she gets away with living in the apartment in her grandmother's name, with rotating roommates, for ten years without a rent hike, her comment does not explain how Chandler, and often jobless Joey, can pay for their place, nor how Ross or Phoebe can afford their rents on an academic's and freelance masseuse's salary, respectively. Even so, *Friends* does address the economic class of its main characters explicitly in one (of its 236) episodes. In Episode 2.5, "The One with Five Steaks and an Eggplant," the gang is split down the middle between those with money and those without. While Chandler, Ross, and Monica can afford to pay for a night out to celebrate Monica's promotion *and* for dinner, a cake, and Hootie & the Blowfish concert tickets for Ross's birthday, Phoebe, Rachel, and Joey cannot. The crux of the problem, though, is that none of them know how to talk about their monetary differentials. Instead, Phoebe, Rachel, and Joey complain just to one another. Once the friends with money are made aware of the problem, they try to "solve" it by providing dinner for them all and treating them to the concert. Not wanting their "charity," Phoebe, Rachel, and Joey send Monica, Ross, and Chandler to the concert without them. At the concert, Monica, Ross, and Chandler end up getting to meet the band, and Monica even makes out with one of the Blowfish. Meanwhile, the friends without money sit home and play made-up games. It is clear the concertgoers had the better time. Just when the episode starts to get good, with all of the gang arguing over who works harder for their money and whether they should feel guilty about wanting to go and do "nice" things, Monica learns that she lost her job for taking kickbacks from distributors (the erstwhile five steaks and an eggplant that supplied the birthday dinner). Instead of resolving their arguments, they all come together to comfort Monica in her time of need. Joey even offers to pay the Central Perk bill (for $4.12) when it comes, but then has to get money from Chandler to pay it. Other than occasional times when each of the friends individually faces economic hardships (Joey needs head shots, Monica has to work at a diner, Phoebe loses her massage license), their economic disparities, with one another and with people outside their group, are rarely addressed.

Similarly, *Friends* approaches race through color blindness, as if it were an invisible, irrelevant issue. Basically, it lauds white bodies as if being white were not related to race and denigrates, explicitly and implicitly, racial and ethnic "others." The series uses "codes and signifying practices that celebrate racial invisibility and color blindness."[8] One example that demonstrates these codes is related to the issue of Ross, Monica, and Rachel being Jewish. While a menorah makes an appearance in Episodes 1.7, "The One with the Blackout" and 2.9, "The One with Phoebe's Dad," and Ross tries to teach his son, Ben, about Hanukkah in Episode 7.10, "The One with the Holiday Armadillo," Jewish religious traditions do not play much of a role in the show. That said, the series does depict Ross especially and Monica somewhat as cultural Jews, meaning that their beliefs, values, and everyday practices are influenced by Judaism. When asked about the characters' ethnic backgrounds, Jewish co-creators Marta Kauffman and David Crane told the Boston newspaper *The Phoenix* that fans can assume that Ross and Monica are half Jewish because their father, played by Elliot Gould, is, but their mother, played by Christina Pickles, is markedly not. In 1996, when this interview was published, they had not yet cast Rachel Green's father, but they noted that she might also be half-Jewish depending on who they cast as her father, as her mother, played by Marlo Thomas, was not Jewish.[9] As they ended up casting Ron Leibman, and in Episode 9.9, "The One with Rachel's Phone Number," she referred to her grandmother as "Bubbe," which is Yiddish for grandma, Rachel also became half-Jewish.

Having Jewish main characters in a sitcom set in New York seems only logical given the large Jewish population that lives in the area. However, the creators did little more than pay lip service to their religious traditions and merely used their cultural attachment to their heritage as a plot point once. Had they capitalized on their heritage more, they may have been able to claim Rachel and Ross as the hottest Jewish couple on television.[10] Instead, they used cues to suggest Rachel's stereotypical Jewish qualities, like having a large nose and getting it "fixed" while she was in college, and made comments about how Ross and Rachel's daughter, Emma, might need to get hers fixed later in life (Episode 10.5, "The One with Rachel's Sister"). Coupled with the show's stereotypical portrayal of Janice Litman Goralnik (née Hosenstein) as a loud, finicky, bighaired Jewish woman, the view of Jewish women on the show was fairly stereotypical.

They also took every opportunity to emphasize that Ross was cheap. When he earned tenure, he celebrated with the friends by bringing a bottle of "Israel's finest" champagne and had him point out that he got tenure but did not win the lottery (Episode 10.14, "The One with Princess Consuela"). Or when he had trouble getting from one of his school's campuses to the other in time for a class, they explained away the option of taking a cab by Ross pointing out that he was not a Rockefeller (Episode 8.12, "The One where Rachel Dates Joey"). When Rachel was trying to hide her Pottery Barn shopping habit from Phoebe, she told Phoebe that Ross bought his sheets at a flea market. While she was not surprised, Phoebe did advise Ross to spend a little for new sheets (Episode 6.11, "The One with the Apothecary Table"). Finally, when Ross stayed in hotels, the friends said that he would not leave until check-out time so as to get his money's worth. Rachel even said that they had the best sex they had ever had when they got a late check-out, except that Ross shouted out "Radisson" at the end (Episode 8.2, "The One with the Red Sweater"). In a later episode, Ross teaches Chandler another way to capitalize on hotel stays: taking everything that is not nailed down, including light bulbs and salt from the room service shakers (Episode 9.19, "The One with Rachel's Dream"). The series could have chosen to make a non-Jewish character thrifty, but instead their use of the stereotypical cue of cheapness served to emphasize Ross's Jewish heritage. Even so, they did not use the same types of cues to code Monica or Rachel as Jewish. As such, Monica is largely assumed to be Jewish by the transitive property, though she does complain in Episode 7.15, "The One with Joey's New Brain," about how embarrassed she was when Ross rapped at her Bat Mitzvah. Fans were also left to wonder most of the time whether Rachel is Jewish or not.[11]

Ross, Monica, and Rachel's Judaism may not play a large role in the series, but the visual whiteness of the characters does. Given the friends-as-family ensemble at the center of the show (see more in Chapter 3), "the premise and popularity of the show is predicated on its closed circle of whiteness"[12] that depends upon the exclusion of racial and ethnic "others."[13] Analysis of extras and other minor characters serves to reveal this type of exclusion, but when Rachel's Italian love interest, Paolo (Cosimo Fusco), initially appears, it takes front and center this time. The narrative frames Paolo as a womanizing lothario who threatens Ross's chances at dating Rachel. This results in the audience rooting for Ross and against Paolo. However, Ross denigrates him before anything happens between Paolo and Rachel, in order to try to keep Rachel for himself. When Ross first meets him, and knows that Rachel is hot for him, Ross calls Paolo a "crap weasel" to his face (Episode 1.7, "The One with the Blackout"). As Paolo's English language skills are limited, he does not understand Ross. After Rachel and Paolo break up, Ross gets the privilege of slamming the door in his face (Episode 1.12, "The One with the Dozen Lasagnas"). At once Ross appears xenophobic against Paolo as an English-as-second-language foreigner and sexist in trying to control Rachel, a woman who has not expressed any romantic interest in Ross.

In its limited depictions of racially diverse characters, *Friends* could have done much better. Interestingly, when the cast appeared on *The Oprah Winfrey Show* in 1995 and Oprah asked them if they would consider getting a black friend, *Friends* was number three in the overall Nielsen ratings but only 111th with black households (out of 140 prime-time network series).[14] Given that New York City is less than half white, the point is that the nearly all-white *Friends* cast alters that reality and the black audience noticed.[15] Unfortunately, like many shows that "happen to have" all white characters, most of the characters of color are usually depicted as subordinate or superior to the main characters. Docfuture1 posted a creative critique of the show on YouTube with a video of many of the black actors who had speaking roles on the series.[16] Most of them were in service roles, including waiters, cashiers, and office workers. Those who were not in service roles played main characters' bosses or potential bosses. For example, Chandler works for three different bosses who are black. The first boss, Mr. Douglas (Dorien Wilson), asks Chandler to fire another employee, Nina (Jennifer Grant). Instead of doing it, he lies to both Nina and Mr. Douglas so that he can date her. Of course, he does so by telling Mr. Douglas that she is crazy. When Nina finds out, she slams a staple through Chandler's hand, but he suffers no conse-quences from his boss (Episode 1.16, "The One with Two Parts: Part 1").

The second boss is a black woman, Ms. McKenna (Janet Huber-Whit-ten). Chandler ends up falling asleep during one of her presentations and unwittingly agrees to move to Tulsa. Despite admitting to her that he fell asleep, the only consequence he endures is having to work in Oklahoma. He even secures company support for flying back and forth between Oklahoma and New York every week so that Monica does not have to move with him (Episode 9.2, "The One where Emma Cries"). The third black person that Chandler wants to work for is Mr. Tyler (Tucker Small-wood). We meet him when he interviews Chandler for a job in advertis-ing. Despite Chandler equating "duties" with "doodies," or as he and the boss both say, "poop," at the conclusion of his interview, Chandler is still hired (Episode 8.21, "The One with the Cooking Class"). "These minor characters . . . highlight how the privileges of whiteness engender the ironic humor of the show and depend on the exclusion."[17] At the same time, these examples demonstrate the ridiculousness of the main charac-ters. The stoic, incredulous responses of the minor African American characters operate to critique the whiteness of the main characters. Chan-dler's interactions with Ms. McKenna end with his still having to move and work in Tulsa, Oklahoma. While Mr. Tyler still hires Chandler, the way he looks at him makes it clear that he is going to have his eye on him. Even so, the lack of consequences for the white characters demonstrates their privilege in relation to these black secondary characters.

Rob Fishman uses the example of when Joey takes a part-time job at the museum where Ross works in "*Friends*: Discrimination and Mediated Communication" to demonstrate further how the portrayal of these inferi-or/superior roles of black characters works.[18] Although Joey knows noth-ing about art or history, he is hired. When he and Ross are on their lunch break, Ross sits with the other scientists and academics (marked by their white lab coats) while Joey is expected to sit with the other nonscientist tour guides (indicated by their blue blazers). Fishman claims that these scenes substitute the different color coats in place of different races of people as "an ironic performance of Jim Crow segregation."[19] Rhonda (Sherri Shepherd), one of the blue blazers, uses "black diction" and is critical of social mobility. She observes that the white coat/blue blazer separation is just the way it has always been, whereas the educated black scientist does not speak at all and the Asian male scientist only speaks about his own personal behavior (having stolen a pear) (Episode 4.11, "The One with Phoebe's Uterus"). Of course, in the end Ross, the white scientist, is credited with breaking the jacket (race) line, by giving a rousing speech and throwing his coat on the ground so that he can eat with Joey. But the focus of the series of revelations that follow, by Asian and black characters, are all personal, not political, making any statement on race supposedly irrelevant to the moment.

The portrayal of love interests for the main characters furthers this racial and ethnic othering. None of the female main characters date men of color at all. This allows the series to avoid any political or social implications of white women dating men of color. Joey and Ross both, on the other hand, date the same two black women at different times. Chandler finds great amusement in learning that both Joey and Ross have asked out the same woman, Kristen (Gabrielle Union). They both meet her when she moves into their neighborhood and help her, to varying degrees, move in. After they both have gone out with her, they learn that the other has also gone out with her. They seemingly try to handle the situation like adults by allowing her to make a choice. However, they both end up trying to compete with one another to impress her. When they both show up on one of their dates, they end up childishly taking swipes at one another's character in order to influence her decision. The camera shot becomes tighter and tighter on them as they argue until only the two of them appear. When their argument becomes much more about their issues with one another than her, she leaves. They only notice that she is gone when the camera pulls back to show her empty chair between them. While *Friends* can be given credit for casting a woman of color in the role of potential love interest for the main characters, her race is considered irrelevant to the storyline. Treating her as less important than Joey and Ross's relationship with one another from beginning to end makes her black female character less important than the white male characters with whom she appears.

Secondary characters and storylines limited to one episode certainly provide insights into the portrayal of race and ethnicity on *Friends*. Its depiction of love interests and extended storylines for its few characters of color reveal more. At the end of season 1, Rachel learns that Ross has had feelings for her for years. She takes this new information and goes to meet him at the airport when he returns from a work trip to China to tell him she wants to give their relationship a try. Her efforts are thwarted when Ross comes off the plane with his arm around another woman, Julie (Lauren Tom). When Ross introduces Rachel to Julie, Rachel assumes from her outward appearance that Julie is Chinese. Rachel greets her by slowly articulating every syllable of her welcome to America, to which Julie replies loudly by overarticulating her thank you and admission that she is from New York (Episode 2.1, "The One with Ross's New Girlfriend"). Julie's clapback merely exacerbates Rachel's embarrassment and she is left having to get them both back to the city. While the audience laughs at the moment, they also feel for Rachel. She is bleeding from hitting her head after falling over trying to get away from them before they saw her, is shocked to see Ross with another woman, and has just been called out for her race-based assumption. "The intended butt of the joke here . . . is Rachel's stupidity and embarrassment, but it is a joke on her that relies on the privileges of her whiteness that means Julie can only tolerate her racism with bemusement and gently mock her."[20]

Most of the other jealousy-motivated comments Rachel makes about Julie are behind her back. Rachel mocks her intelligence in Episode 2.4, "The One with Phoebe's Husband." When Rachel learns that Monica went shopping with Julie, she tells her that she feels like she is now losing Ross and Monica to Julie. Julie tries to create a relationship with Rachel too and admits that she finds her intimidating. To her face, Rachel acts kind, but when she leaves, Rachel mocks her by saying what a manipulative bitch she is (Episode 2.2, "The One with the Breast Milk"). Despite the fact that Julie is on the same educational level as Ross, is in the same field, and they care about one another, Rachel's comments about her serve to code her as an interloper trying to take up an already occupied space in Ross's life and in the group. As such her "difference is therefore not merely ignored or erased, but explicitly coded as a form of disruption."[21] When Ross makes a choice and breaks up with Julie, we do not see it, making his only rationale that he wants to be with Rachel over Julie regardless of the fact that Julie is a more appropriate partner than Rachel is. Julie's exit is capped off though by her meeting Russ, a periodontist who looks just like Ross. Thus, Julie is good enough for a Ross knock-off, but not for Ross.

Shelley Cobb contends in "'I'd Like Y'all to Get a Black Friend': The Politics of Race in *Friends*" that the racially othered characters who appear in the series function as foils to create the "hip," ironic humor in the series and appeal to its Gen-X, slumpy audience. Julie provides an opportunity for Rachel to see Ross as a romantic partner but also suggests that Rachel and Ross are fated to be with one another. Julie and Ross may have similar educational and work backgrounds, but her racial difference dominates as the primary visible difference they have with one another, which suggests she is less appropriate as a partner than Rachel.

Similarly, Charlie appears to be a more appropriate partner for Ross as well. Instead of having them get together right away, however, the series first puts Charlie with her most unlikely male partner, Joey. As she has only dated Nobel prize and MacArthur Genius Grant winners, her dating Joey is meant to suggest that she wants a simple sexual relationship. Casting Aisha Tyler as Charlie could have been seen as a way the series addressed charges against their lack of diversity. But *Friends* creators contend she was cast as she was the best actress who read for the part.[22] Just as she was part of colorblind casting, Charlie's race goes unmentioned. She ends up being coded as a "black lady," like a Condoleezza Rice or Michelle Obama. She and Joey break up and she and Ross get together in Episode 9.24, "The One in Barbados: Part 2." Her differences with Joey (she likes to go to conference sessions while he wants to go to the beach) and similarities with Ross (they collaborate on his speech and attend conference sessions together) are highlighted in these episodes and make it clear why she and Joey should break up and she and Ross should get together.

Having both Gabrielle Union's and Aisha Tyler's characters date both Joey and Ross further privileges the white male characters as individuals and suggests that the seemingly limited black female characters can be interchanged for one another and passed from one man to another.

These episodes also contrast Charlie with Monica. The running joke through both episodes for Monica is that the humidity in Barbados is wreaking havoc with her hair and making it get increasingly curly, until it resembles a Disco-era Diana Ross (or her daughter *black-ish*'s Traci Ellis Ross currently). While Charlie does not interact with Monica much in these episodes, the rest of the white cast makes comments about how unattractive Monica's ginormous hair is. But when Monica decides to do something about her hair, Charlie is there to comment. Monica gets her hair under control with cornrow braids with shells at the bottom. Monica's "cultural appropriation sets the groundwork for the key thing her braids do—give rise to an ironic joke that explicitly characterizes Charlie as inauthentically black."[23] The friends make fun of Monica by pointing

Joey, Ross, and Charlie at a conference in Barbados. *Warner Brothers / Photofest ©
Warner Brothers*

out that she has shellfish in her hair and that they can see her scalp. While
Charlie cannot think of anything other than that "it's something" at first,
she later encourages her by saying, "You go, girlfriend!" The way she
says the line reveals her discomfort, prompting Ross to ask if she has ever
said that phrase before. She admits she has not. Interestingly, in an earlier
season, Monica too tried to be supportive by yelling, "You go girl!"
before she admitted that she could not pull off the phrase (Episode 2.19,
"The One where Eddie Won't Go"). At once, "Charlie must suffer Monica's commodified consumption of blackness and the ensuing spectacle of
whiteness and racism in the episode"[24] *and* Charlie is whitewashed as her
inability to use colloquial language is on par with Monica's.

> Much like the black scientist Peter from the earlier scene who never
> speaks, Charlie cannot use the black diction that Rhonda did. The
> classism, racism, and patriarchy that Charlie is required to negotiate as
> a black character who must assimilate to keep her space among the
> friends is made explicit. It is a *white* man who makes it clear that she is
> unable to perform blackness, precisely because, for the friends, she has
> *never been* black.[25]

Charlie ends up then as "not too black" while at the same time she ends up being critiqued for "acting" black "even as she is confronted with the spectacle of a white woman who has commodified it and who is found amusing for doing so."[26] At the same time, this particular white woman has already established that she cannot get away with "acting black." So both women are established as acting white.

Having set Charlie and Ross up as perfect partners (in contrast to her relationship with Joey), the series then faced the difficulty of how to break them up in order to continue Ross's trajectory toward Rachel in the end. Just as Charlie was created as a character who was better than Ross, they ended up giving Charlie an even better partner than Ross. Dr. Benjamin Hobart (Greg Kinnear) has two Nobel prizes and a latex fetish and controls the purse strings to a grant Ross has applied for. In contrast to Julie, Charlie dumps Ross, putting her in a position of power. The fact that she breaks up with him for his intellectual superior suggests she realizes that he is her intellectual inferior. However, that she dumps him for another scholarly white man suggests Charlie's relationship choices may be driven by social class while still trying to erase the issue of race. Just as Julie "happens" to walk into the coffee shop to find her new beau, Russ, Charlie learns that Benji still has feelings for her when he tries to use Ross's grant application to get him to break up with Charlie. It seems when Charlie and Benji come back together that they were fated to do so. As Charlie and Julie both get a partner they were meant for, the path for Rachel and Ross to get what they are destined for, each other, is now clear as well. Julie and Charlie do disrupt the whiteness of the group of friends, even if only temporarily. But their challenges are neutralized by ending up with other versions of white, male Ross.[27]

The alternate family created by the friends provides the group with emotional and material support (see chapter 3). The secondary placement of most characters of color on the show, and the expulsion of any characters of color who seemingly overstay their welcome, suggests that the friends are "a closed circle of whiteness."[28] Even when characters of color enter the circle, they are either expelled or made to be more like the friends (read: white and upper middle class) and then still ejected. The privileging of whiteness serves then to erase any potential differences characters of color may present.

CONCLUSION

Despite how *Friends* depicted bodies that were not white, upper middle class, and thin, it could be argued that programming for niche audiences in the current televisual environment and the creation of multiple viewing platforms has led to an increase in actual representations of diversity. Shows like *black-ish* (ABC, 2014–), *Fresh Off the Boat* (ABC, 2015–), *Mike and Molly* (2010–2016), and *The Mindy Project* (FOX, 2012–2015, and Hulu, 2015–2018) demonstrate that networks are trying to appeal to multiple audiences. Even so, *Friends*-inspired *The Big Bang Theory* (2007–2019), a show about a mostly white group of friends in their twenties who hang out at each other's apartments, tops them all in the Nielsen ratings, suggesting that marketing whiteness continues to have powerful appeal to Baby Boomers, Gen-Xers, and Millennials alike. That *Big Bang* has one main character of color, Rajesh Koothrappali (Kunal Nayyar), signals progress. How *Big Bang* feminizes him, criticizes him for his weight fluctuations, and addresses only his class among the characters (he starts out rich and then his parents cut him off making him struggle) suggests progress may be slow in the world where *Friends* created the expectations for hang-out comedies. The fan response to *Friends* being available on Netflix today suggests that viewers continue to follow and enjoy the show as it reaches new audiences. Critics can only hope that it is for the positive contributions the show has made to popular culture and not for its insular world inhabited by "six white twentysomethings who don't seem to encounter people of any other colour or background, and though young and striving, live extraordinarily privileged lives."[29]

7

STEREOTYPES, SEXUALITY, AND *FRIEND*-LY TENSIONS

Friends' depiction of gender is more complicated than its construction of upper-middle-class whiteness and its portrayals of fat bodies and people of color. Characters are at once feminine or masculine, gay or straight, male or female, while also challenging these binaries and stereotypes. Of course, as a sitcom, any disruption that occurs to cause conflict is usually resolved by the end of the episode. Some contend that the progress/ regress format of *Friends* suggests its place in postfeminist culture of the 1990s and early 2000s.[1] Certainly there are postfeminist characteristics in the series, such as embracing the personal over the political, assuming the progress of second-wave feminists without necessarily acknowledging their efforts, and highlighting the power the female characters attain through accentuating their stereotypical femininity. This chapter articulates how *Friends'* representations of gender and sexuality more aptly demonstrated tensions between the aging Baby Boomer generation and the emerging adults of Generation X. The series at once promoted stereotypical gender divisions between men and women *and* complicated relationships between its female and male characters at the same time that it troubled (and was troubling in its) representations of queer characters.

MEN ARE FROM MARS, WOMEN ARE FROM VENUS

In large part, *Friends* was premised on the *Men Are from Mars, Women Are from Venus* version of pop psychology that suggests men and women are fundamentally different from one another.[2] The white, upper-middle-class, heterosexual guys enjoyed pornography, had a messy apartment, watched and attended sporting events together, acted like children, and knew how to play poker whereas the white, upper-middle-class, heterosexual women shopped, kept their apartment neat and clean, did not watch or attend sporting events, took care of each other (and the male characters), and did not know how to play poker. For example, Jasmine Lee suggests in "What did 'Friends' Say about '90s Dating Culture?" that *Friends* showed men enjoying pornography as normal but for women it was weird. In Episode 4.17, "The One with the Free Porn," Chandler and Joey somehow end up with a free porn channel. The female friends try to get them to turn it off, but Chandler and Joey fear losing the porn so instead leave the television on all day and night. Later in Episode 7.2, "The One with Rachel's Book," Joey finds Rachel's version of porn, an erotic novel, under her pillow in her room. Instead of owning up to her enjoyment of the genre, she instead tries to hide it and deny that it is in fact pornography. These examples indicate that men like porn and can enjoy it in shared spaces on television while women may enjoy an "erotic" book but must keep it under wraps (under a pillow, in this case).

Interestingly, the "Free Porn" episode took place when the gals lost their apartment to the guys, so the guys were watching porn in what was formerly Monica's apartment. Seeing Monica displaced from the space she created to host her friends—and play her role as stereotypically feminine homemaker—creates one moment of disruption. It is clear from many other episodes that Monica was socialized into this role, from her childhood tea parties and Easy Bake ovens to her current job as a chef and need to please her visitors.[3] So having her whole world turned upside down (or at least moved across the hall) creates cognitive dissonance for the audience just as it does for the women. The guys are comfortable in the bigger, nicer apartment. The women just want their space back. Seeing the guys watch porn sitting in Joey's Barcaloungers in Monica's apartment with the green and purple walls also challenged what audience members had come to expect in that apartment, which further supports the idea that watching porn in the women's apartment was not the norm.

The apartments were designed to further the gendered separation of the spaces as well as to define the groups as different from one another. Monica's apartment was painted multiple colors, centered around comfortable furniture, and decorated with French posters and vintage knick-knacks. Action in Joey's apartment, in contrast, took place primarily around the foosball table, which stood in place of a dining table, and the only places to sit to watch television were two Barcaloungers or the stools that sat at the kitchen counter. The "girls" apartment was designed for socializing and comfort whereas the "boys" apartment limited the number of people who could comfortably share the space when they were not playing games.

"The One with All the Poker" (Episode 1.18) further delineates the clearly defined gender lines created in the series. The episode begins with the women wondering why the men do not have any women in their poker game. The guys say it is because they do not know any women who play. While the women object to their rationale, they also admit they do not know how to play. They schedule a game in which the women do not just lose, but lose because Monica seems more worried about the snacks than the game and Phoebe and Rachel play as if they are helping one another win a game of Go Fish rather than competing in poker. Even after having a poker lesson with Monica's aunt, the gals still cannot beat the guys. When the gang plays their third and last game with each other, the outcome becomes a referendum on whether men or women are better at poker when Rachel and Ross up the stakes so high that the gals and guys pitch in to support Rachel and Ross, respectively. When Rachel wins, it could be considered a moment in which the men's statement about women not playing poker (and therefore not being good at it) is proven wrong. As the women celebrate Rachel's victory, however, Ross revels in her happiness and refuses to show the guys his cards. His refusal suggests he let Rachel win to make her happy.

BE YOUR OWN WINDKEEPER

From these examples, we could assume *Friends* merely reinforced hegemonic gender roles. However, Lauren Jade Thompson suggests in "'It's Like a Guy Never Lived Here!': Reading the Gendered Domestic Spaces of *Friends*" that restating *and* inverting gender roles can serve as one way "to address the constraints men and women in the 1990s face, but that pushing these inversions 'too far'" can "reaffirm normative femininity and masculinity."[4] Times when the women appeared together and the men had their own storylines demonstrate ways the series both complicated gendered expectations as well as affirmed them. For example, heterosexual teen and adult women too often compete with one another for seemingly limited resources, like men. In contrast, *Friends* provided opportunities to show the women supporting one another and trying to overcome such expectations. In Episode 1.4, "The One with George Stephanopoulos," the guys go to a hockey game to help take Ross's mind off the fact that it is the anniversary of his losing his virginity to his ex-wife, Carol, while the gals hang out in Monica's apartment lamenting the status of their work and love lives. Earlier in the day, Rachel's old female friends from Long Island came by the coffeehouse to see that she actually worked there. As they celebrated their impending marriages and babies and looked down their noses at Rachel, a common waitress, Rachel tried to justify her choice not to marry Barry and to work at a coffeehouse in the city instead. They made her feel so terrible about her prospects that she ended up bringing Monica and Phoebe down with her. The three of them lament their lack of plans for their future during an impromptu cocktail-filled slumber party. Being there for one another and a drunken game of Twister ends up making Rachel realize that what she has may not be a great job or romantic prospects, but she has her friends as family.

Even though they support one another, it does not mean that they do not fight or have conflicts, even over men. In Episode 2.19, "The One where Eddie Won't Leave," the women bond over reading a book about female empowerment, *Be Your Own Windkeeper*. They attempt to embody the message the book promotes: women need to see the strengths in themselves and one another and not let others, especially men, take their power away. However, when they take the quiz in the book about their own empowerment, they call each other out for their lack of self-awareness of times when they let the men take their power. Monica reminds Phoebe that she let her former boyfriend take her power, while Phoebe claps back that Monica did the same when she slept with Paul on the first date. More importantly, when Rachel tries to gloss over the question about whether she has ever betrayed another goddess, Monica reminds her of when she kissed the guy playing spin-the-bottle even though the bottle was pointing at Monica. The women all end up storming out of the room and slamming the doors on each other. But later Rachel makes the peace by reminding them that they should be better than guys and support one another. They hug and all is forgiven.

At other times, Monica and Rachel have conflicts that even result in physical confrontations, including getting into a slap fight and destroying each other's property over who should be allowed to date Jean-Claude Van Damme (Episode 2.13, "The One after the Superbowl: Part 2") and rehashing roommate conflicts as they try to pack on the last night before Rachel moves out to make room for Chandler to move in with Monica (Episode 6.6, "The One on the Last Night"). In each case, Phoebe takes control over both of the other women and forces them into submission before making them apologize to each other. These examples could be theorized as the fictional version of girl fights on reality television shows like *The Bachelor* (2002–) or *Bad Girls Club* (2006–). However, with such a long-running sitcom, just looking at what happens in one scene, episode, or even season does not provide accurate insights about the characters and what they represented. Rather, looking across the 236 episodes provides better insights. Across the ten years of *Friends*, the female characters certainly fed into stereotypes like that women like to shop, talk to one another about everything, and even fight. But they also showed the same women able to argue, even over men, but still stand by one another in the end. So when Phoebe tells Rachel that Rachel's boyfriend Paolo hit on her, for example, Rachel believes Phoebe, breaks up with Paolo, and turns to Phoebe for support and friendship (Episode 1.12, "The One with the Dozen Lasagnas"). Representations of such complicated female relationships provide better models of female behavior. Even so, viewers must be committed to the characters and their arcs to gain such understandings.

A FAMILY LIKE OURS?

Friends' creators Marta Kauffman and David Crane included a lesbian couple in the series who were based on Kauffman's daughters' godmothers, Deb and Rona.[5] Kauffman said that they were a part of their group of six friends living in New York and so they had good material to draw on for the show. They did not intend to make a point with their inclusion. However, when Deb and Rona's daughter Avery saw Carol (Jane Sibbett) and Susan (Jessica Hecht) with a baby on the show, she "looked at the TV with big eyes and said, 'A family like *ours*.'"[6] Kauffman felt proud that they were able to provide an example for other same-sex couples and especially their kids. In Episode 2.11, "The One with the Lesbian Wedding," the series depicted Carol and Susan's wedding. Because gay marriage was not yet legal in the United States in 1996, NBC worried that they may be subject to phone calls and hate mail. Kauffman reported that a mere four people called and suggested that viewers did not object as much as the studio thought they might.[7] The episode featured Candace Gingrich (Republican politician Newt Gingrich's daughter) as the minister who officiated the wedding. Gingrich stated that *Friends* understood the importance of the message and stood up for gay marriage before it was fashionable.[8] The Gay and Lesbian Alliance Against Defamation (GLAAD) recognized the series for their portrayals of Carol and Susan in 1995, 1996, and 1997.[9]

Despite their presence, *Friends* depicted this lesbian relationship primarily from Carol's ex-husband's, Ross's, point of view rather than Carol and Susan's. It is essential to understand that when the series begins is when Ross's relationship with Carol ends. She dumps him because she "realized" she was a lesbian and left him for the woman she was having an affair with, Susan. For these reasons, Ross directs his (justified) anger at being cheated on and left by someone he trusted and loved not just at Carol, but mostly at Susan as representative of the cheating. His fear of being cheated on is conveyed in Episode 4.18, "The One with Rachel's New Dress," when he fears Susan and his then girlfriend, Emily (Helen Baxendale), are going to have an affair when they hang out with one another in England and attend a poetry reading.

That Susan identifies as a lesbian provided Ross with an additional (unjustified) target for his anger: lesbians in general. Ross resisted rather than tried to understand what it meant to be a lesbian. In Episode 1.9, "The One where Underdog Gets Away," Ross arrives at Carol and Susan's apartment to find that Carol has not yet gotten home from work. He uncomfortably wanders around the apartment looking at their book collection as he waits, wondering aloud why they have so many books about being a lesbian. Susan jokes that you have to take a course or else they will not let you be a lesbian. Ross does not know how to respond. In another instance, in Episode 1.12, "The One with the Dozen Lasagnas," Ross picks up a picture in Carol and Susan's apartment and asks when they met Huey Lewis. When Carol tells him that the person in the photo is their friend Tanya, the audience laughs at Ross's mistaking a woman for a man, even as it feeds into stereotypes of masculine-looking lesbians. Immediately after, Carol asks Ross if he wants to know about the sex. She means of their baby, as she had just been to the gynecologist, but he mistakenly thinks she means sex with Tanya and cringes.

In addition to his discomfort with lesbian sex, Ross also does not know whether to treat Susan like a woman or a man. Carol and Susan hug one another excitedly sharing the news of the sex of the baby. Ross, feeling left out, merely pats Susan on the back from as far away as possible. When he takes his leave, he kisses Carol's belly and cheek and slugs Susan in the arm. In Episode 1.9, "The One where Underdog Gets Away," he and Susan both try to put their hands on Carol's pregnant belly to feel the baby kick, but they end up trying to slap one another's hands away instead. At the end of Episode 1.16, "The One with Two Parts: Part 1," Ross attempts to bond with Susan after a Lamaze class by holding the doll baby like a football and suggesting Susan go long and catch his pass. She merely stares at him. Using humor to characterize Susan and Carol's relationship, and Ross's inability to understand it, promotes the idea that gender is binary and if these women, especially Susan, violate those boundaries, it is acceptable to treat them like men.

Although he often treats her like a man, the most common strategy Ross uses to attempt to assert his dominance over Susan is to make it clear that she does not possess the characteristics needed to be a man. When he plays his man/father card, though, Susan holds her own and does not let Ross's comments or behavior solely characterize her, Carol, or their relationship. At their first OB-GYN appointment, the three argue over the baby's name. Ross asks why the baby's last name would be Willick-Bunch when he is the father. Susan replies that it is her baby too. Ross then plays the man card and says she did not donate any sperm. Rather than just taking it, Susan points out what a "challenge" making sperm must be (Episode 1.2, "The One with the Sonogram at the End"). Susan also gets the last word when Ross asks if Susan and Carol talk about him when they talk to the baby in utero. Susan jokes that they tell the baby that he is "Bobo the Sperm Guy." Although he childishly breaks one of their flowers on the way out of the apartment, he ultimately "loses" their competition when he starts singing to the baby because he learned that Susan did it first.

The whole parenting team: Ross, Susan, and (pregnant) Carol. *Warner Brothers / Photofest © Warner Brothers*

When the three of them later attend a Lamaze class in Episode 1.16, "The One with the Two Parts: Part 1," Ross's uneasiness with their parenting team comes through. He starts his introduction of the three of them to the rest of the male/female, two-parent teams by saying his name and then gesturing to Carol's belly and asserting it is his boy in there. He follows this assertion by introducing Carol and stammering over who Susan is. When the instructor asks for clarification, Ross says Susan is Carol's "friend." Susan clarifies, "Life partner," before Ross adds, "like buddies." Susan further clarifies, "Like lovers," and Ross adds, "You know how close women can get." He may get the last word in at this class, but later in the episode just he and Susan attend a second Lamaze class alone as Carol was held up in parent-teacher conferences. Ross feels humiliated when Susan makes him take Carol's place. While problematic to characterize his feminization and being a pregnant woman as demeaning, that Susan made him take Carol's place instead of his making Susan do it challenges traditional gender binaries.

Their conflict comes to a head in Episode 1.23, "The One with the Birth," while Carol is in labor when they end up locked in a closet with Phoebe. We learn that the source of Ross's anxiety is that he will be left out when Susan and Carol go home with the baby after it is born. Susan objects saying that everyone will recognize him as the father and Carol as the mother, but that there is no "Lesbian Lover's Day." Ross quips that that is every day for them. While they see this as an impasse, Phoebe expresses her joy over the prospect of a baby who has three parents arguing over who gets to love it the most. Susan and Ross make it to the birth and come together to support Carol and agree on a name for the baby. They do not, however, delve any deeper into their anxieties about their roles on the parenting team.

Ross's discomfort and inability to treat Carol and Susan as he would another heterosexual couple, like Monica and Chandler for example, makes their relationship seem different and less acceptable in some ways. These tensions were not just present in the late twentieth century but continue into the new millennium, even as gay marriage is now legal in many countries around the world. Had the series included other major or recurring lesbian characters who did not cheat on Ross or end up with his ex-wife, perhaps more variety in the portrayals of lesbian characters could have been included. As it was though, Susan represented the Baby Boomer version of the stereotypical lesbian woman who is coded as neither wholly female nor male as well as the woman who disrupted Ross's seemingly happy marriage. At the same time, she was also indicative of a Gen-X lesbian who was strong, comfortable in her own sexuality, and not afraid to stand up for herself in resistance to a man who refused to try to understand her better.

All that said, Ross also treated Carol and Susan as family, primarily motivated by his continuing love for Carol. He buys them hers and hers towels for Christmas (Episode 2.9, "The One with Phoebe's Dad"), and when the two decide to get married, they invite Ross. At first, he agrees to go to the wedding, but he also wonders to the friends about why they need to get married when they already live together. But when Carol nearly calls off the wedding because her parents refuse to come to a wedding for two women, Ross steps up. He not only convinces Carol to follow her heart regardless of what her parents say, but he also agrees to walk Carol down the aisle (Episode 2.11, "The One with the Lesbian Wedding"). He and Monica admire how the couple glow at their reception. Ultimately, he even agrees to dance with Susan when she recognizes what a good thing he did for Carol. Of course, Susan offers to let him lead.

Friends uses Carol and Susan's "queerness [as] a 'safe' form of difference, particularly when represented by two white, professional, and conventionally feminine, women."[10] Lesbians and lesbian sexuality were primarily used to further the comedy in the series. When Rachel cannot remember Carol's last name, she calls her "Carol Lesbian" (Episode 7.16, "The One with the Truth About London"), and when Phoebe pretends to be Susan in order to meet Sting, she refers to Carol as a "hot piece of ass" (Episode 8.10, "The One with Monica's Boots"). At one of the most solemn moments of their wedding, the minister says that *any* two people coming together in love makes God happy. But Phoebe's former elderly client, Mrs. Rose Edelman, who is seemingly possessing Phoebe's body, replies through Phoebe that now she's seen *everything* and then her spirit moves on. Later in the episode, when Phoebe says aloud how much she misses Rose, a butch lesbian (played by *Orange Is the New Black*'s Lea DeLaria) offers to help Phoebe get over Rose. Naïve Phoebe goes with her seemingly not knowing she is hitting on her. Rachel's mother (Marlo Thomas) also signals the seeming lack of threat being a lesbian poses when she recognizes how nice it is to know that she has sexual options now that she is divorcing Rachel's father. Seeing the intergenerational responses to Carol and Susan's marriage highlights the tensions cis-gendered people had with increasingly public and acceptable lesbian relationships. They were visible, but the Baby Boomer mother saw their sexuality as something to be "tried" and the cis-gendered Gen-X woman does not recognize queer sexuality at all.

The seemingly innocuous vision of the "lipstick lesbian," who exists for the viewing pleasure of men, was also used as a plot ploy on occasion. Chandler and Joey finally give Rachel and Monica their apartment back after the women allow the men to watch them kiss for one minute (Episode 4.19, "The One with All the Haste"). Of course, Monica and Rachel are protected from any real questions about their sexuality as their kiss is not shown on camera. Later, Winona Ryder guest starred as one of Rachel's college sorority sisters who she once made out with while drunk at a party. When Rachel reminds her of their time together, Ryder's Melissa denies it at first. When she finally admits to having participated, she also "suddenly" becomes a lesbian in love with Rachel (Episode 7.20, "The One with Rachel's Big Kiss"). Her inexplicable behavior, along with Joey's episode-long fantasizing about the two of them, cuts against any possible positive gains of the representation of Rachel as having experimented sexually.

Another example occurs in Episode 9.12, "The One with Phoebe's Rats," when Rachel and Ross have finally hired a nanny, Molly. When Joey and Chandler first meet her, they congratulate Ross on hiring a "hot nanny." In Rachel's presence, Ross denies their claim. Even so, when she leaves, Ross admits that he had trouble sleeping thinking about how hot she is. The real trouble comes when Ross and Chandler forbid Joey from hitting on her as then that is all he tries to do. Molly ends up existing just for them to look at and fantasize about. In the end, we learn that Molly is gay when her partner comes to pick her up from work at Rachel and Ross's apartment and they kiss. Rather than end his obsession, Joey then points out that his favorite fairytale has come true.

Although all of the main characters are cis-gender and all but Joey end up in heterosexual couplings at the end of the series, *Friends* never makes heterosexual coupling easy either. Monica and Chandler hide their relationship for half a season, and Rachel and Ross take ten years to finally get together! At the same time, they pushed the boundaries of the types of relationships and families that had appeared on television before them by including families like Carol, Susan, Ben, and Ross and Phoebe's brother,

Frank Jr.; his wife, Alice; and the triplets Phoebe carried for them. None-theless, their impacts were limited by how they were represented, the conventions of television situation comedies, and Carol and Susan's disappearance after season 7.

JUST LIKE BERT AND ERNIE?

The length of the series and the number of episodes filmed created an opportunity to display complicated male relationships that trouble traditional masculinity as well. Ross, Chandler, and Joey's identities are rooted in traditional masculinity, taught to them by their Baby Boomer parents, but also contain characteristics that challenged traditional masculinity that emerged in Generation X. For example, Ross watches hockey and plays football and basketball. But when he watches hockey, he gets hit in the face with the puck and ends up at the hospital (Episode 1.4, "The One with George Stephanopoulos"); football results in him losing to his sister, Monica (Episode 3.9, "The One with the Football"); and he and Chandler avoid playing basketball so as not to lose to middle-school girls again and then the two of them get run off from the coffeehouse by bullies (Episode 2.21, "The One with the Bullies").

Although they include Ross at times, the relationship between room-mates Chandler and Joey serves as the primary platonic male relationship in the series. Through the first season and a half of the series, Chandler supports Joey, monetarily and emotionally, as he auditions and does intermittent acting jobs. Midway through season 2, Joey gets hired on the soap opera *Days of Our Lives*. When he gets his first paycheck, he gives Chandler $812 to start paying him back and a gold bracelet engraved "To My Best Bud" as a thank you for his support. Chandler ends up offending Joey when he complains about how gaudy the bracelet is and then loses it. Chandler buys another bracelet so that Joey will not find out that he lost the first one. Rachel then finds the first bracelet in the lost and found at the coffeehouse and returns it to Chandler. Joey sees Chandler with two bracelets and Chandler covers by telling Joey that he bought a second bracelet for him. Joey then says that they can now be "bracelet buddies" forever (Episode 2.14, "The One with the Prom Video"). When Joey earns more money, he invests in matching Barcaloungers and a new television for their apartment. The two end up spending the whole episode in their chairs watching TV and ordering takeout (which they have delivered to Monica's apartment so they do not need to get up). The end of the episode shows them giggling like Beavis and Butthead, while watching *Beavis and Butthead* (Episode 2.15, "The One where Ross and Rachel . . . You Know").

The two have a relationship that people envy. They know each other so well that when Chandler mumbles his famous line, "I'm trapped in an ATM vestibule with Jill Goodacre," over the phone and Joey gargles a reply, only the two of them understand (Episode 1.7, "The One with the Blackout"). When Chandler begs someone to kiss him at midnight at their New Year's Eve party, Joey is the one who steps up (Episode 1.10, "The One with the Monkey"). When their kitchen table breaks, they contemplate whether they are ready to buy a table together or not. Chandler had been burned by his former roommate, Kip, who ran off and got married after he and Chandler bought a hibachi together. While the two have trouble picking out the right table, they end up buying one that makes them both happy: a foosball table (Episode 1.12, "The One with the Dozen Lasagnas"). They are there for each other through thick and thin.

Despite their commitment to one another, they still have conflicts. Chandler and Joey have a fight over Joey using utensils and putting them back in the drawer without washing them. Meanwhile, one of Joey's coworkers is subletting his apartment and Chandler does not like that Joey is considering taking it. Their conflict leads Joey to say that they did not agree to live together forever like Bert and Ernie (Episode 2.16, "The One where Joey Moves Out"). When Joey does move out, he and Chandler both miss one another terribly but are too proud to admit it. Instead, they watch *Baywatch* together over the phone, instead of in the same room. Rachel reminds Chandler that they are only friends now, not roommates. However, before they admit their feelings to one another, Chandler gets a new roommate, Eddie. When Joey first meets Eddie, he learns that Chandler likes the way Eddie makes eggs. Jealous Joey demands Chandler choose whose eggs he likes better. While the eggs stand in for the people in this argument, Joey cannot accept that Chandler might like both people/eggs equally. Normalcy takes a bit longer than usual to be restored, but three episodes later, Joey moves back in and Eddie is out (Episodes 2.17, "The One where Eddie Moves in," and 2.19, "The One where Eddie Won't Go").

Just as Bert and Ernie's lifelong cohabitation has led viewers to contemplate their sexuality, Joey and Chandler are mistaken for a gay couple more than once. In Episode 2.6, "The One with the Baby on the Bus," they are offended when two women (one of whom is Lea Thompson of *Caroline in the City*, 1995–1999) think they are a gay couple with their child (Ross's son, Ben). Their reaction really comes out when they run into another couple of women they wish to hit on while they ride the bus, and they adamantly assert that they are not a couple. But when they leave Ben on the bus and have to go get him at the depot, the attendant will only release Ben to his father. They both then assert they are the father, put their arms around one another, and pretend to be his fathers. When the two go visit Monica's ex-boyfriend Richard's apartment to see if it is right for Joey to buy, the real estate agent assumes they are a couple as well. Interestingly, Joey tries to go with it, but Chandler insists they are not a couple. When Joey tries to protest, Chandler cuts him off and reminds him they are not going to discuss it again (Episode 9.7, "The One with Ross's Inappropriate Song").

Best friends forever: Joey and Chandler. *Warner Brothers / Photofest © Warner Brothers*

Friends codes Chandler as sexually ambiguous throughout the series. They made him more feminine than Joey, which suggests an attempt to recreate stereotypical masculine/feminine relations in their relationship as roommates. In the early seasons, Chandler resists classification as gay at every turn. Episode 1.8, "The One where Nana Dies Twice," provides an extended example of Chandler's objections. At the start, a female co-worker, Shelly (Nancy Cassaro) tells him that she wants to set him up with a guy. She is surprised and embarrassed to learn that he is not interested in men. He then finds out that the female friends all thought he was gay when they first met him because he has a "quality." However, when he learns that Shelly was going to set him up with Lowell and not Brian, he is more offended that she thinks Brian is out of his league than that she thought he was gay. That said, their conversation ends with Chandler swearing he is not gay. At the end of the episode, Chandler clarifies to Lowell that he is not gay. Lowell says that he knows Chandler is not gay, and that Brian is, because he has "a kind of radar" that helps him determine if someone is gay or not. The punchline here though is that Lowell also contends that Brian would be out of Chandler's league.

Some may contend that Chandler's resistance to being thought of as gay promotes homophobia. However, examples like this one suggest that there is a level of gender play in his portrayal. This gender play allows the series in later seasons to use symbols to make jabs at Chandler's feminine qualities while at the same time allowing him to have both masculine and feminine qualities. For example, he sings "Tomorrow" as he sorts CDs after Monica points out he owns two copies of *Annie*; he can identify the Sandra Bullock rom-com *Miss Congeniality* from the first scene; and he gets pedicures. In Episode 9.8, "The One with Rachel's Other Sister," in which Monica obsesses over her china, Chandler realizes they actually own different china than they picked out together. Monica explains it is because the pretty pink plates Chandler picked out were too feminine for her. Ross even posts on their college reunion website that Chandler is gay. When curious classmates call and Monica answers, she jokes that she should have known he was gay with all the times he made her watch *Moulin Rouge* (Episode 10.11, "The One where the Stripper Cries"). Unfortunately, coding particular actions and possessions as exclusively masculine or feminine does not allow for space where a man can also be feminine. But Chandler's character comes as close as *Friends* allows to creating that type of place.

Joey may be coded as the most traditionally masculine of the guys, with his womanizing, frequent mentions of pornography, and ability to physically dominate Chandler and Ross (which he sometimes threatened to do but never actually did), but he has touches of femininity as well. When he gets a female roommate, Janine (Elle Macpherson), he complains about all her "girlie" decorations when Chandler points them out. Even as he realizes he is becoming more feminine, when he finally confronts Janine about the décor, he actually asks Janine to put all the decorations in his room instead (Episode 6.8, "The One with Ross's Teeth"). He is also the one who openly competes with infant Emma so that he can keep his Hugsy the bedtime penguin pal. He also tries to prove to Phoebe that he is man enough to wear women's underwear. While he finds it "weird" at first when he sees Phoebe's boyfriend wearing hers, he then tries it and appreciates how the lace and silk feels. However, when he starts describing to Phoebe all the different styles and fabrics he'd like to try, he starts to realize he may like them too much and she affirms his decision to take them off (Episode 7.22, "The One with Chandler's Dad").

GAY YET?

Friends spends a lot of time during the first few seasons establishing the levels of intimacy between Chandler and Joey that suggest they are more than friends; they are roommates. But they also work hard to make sure that no one believes any of the male main characters are gay. Because co-creator David Crane is gay, David Wild contends *Friends* is very tolerant and tried to feature homosexuality without the usual homophobic clichés.[11] Even so, too often *Friends* used just being gay as the punchline. For example, after Joey teaches their building superintendent how to ballroom dance, Monica asks Joey if he's gay yet (Episode 4.4, "The One with the Ballroom Dancing"). Joey also once advised one of his soap opera acting class students to play the role of a boxer super gay in order to sabotage his audition (because Joey was up for the part too). Instead, the student earned the role because the producers liked, as Joey said, "the stupid gay thing" (Episode 3.7, "The One with the Race Car Bed"). Ross once rushed in to tell the women that he Bamboozled Chandler and then felt the need to clarify it was not a sexual thing (Episode 8.20, "The One with the Baby Shower"). Neither Ross nor Chandler accepted the idea that a student on an anonymous evaluation or an online chat partner, respectively, could possibly be male (Episodes 6.18, "The One where Ross Dates a Student" and 2.24, "The One with Barry and Mindy's Wedding"). While they were both correct, their refusal to believe a guy could hit on them reveals their homophobia. Interestingly, Ross ends up getting hit on by a male student, who later blackmails him for a grade using his fear of being exposed as having male student admirers as his leverage (Episode 7.18, "The One with Joey's Award"). After Joey shows Chandler how he would graze a woman's thigh to make a move on a date, the guys pause as they look into one another's eyes and then grunt they should play more foosball and drink more beer. Using stereotypical male symbols—foosball and beer—helped the writers emphasize the point that Joey and Chandler may have a closer-than-friends relationship but they are not gay.

Therein lies the problem with most of the gender play with the male characters in *Friends*: when the male characters breach traditional gender lines, they also feel the need to affirm their masculinity so as to make it clear that they are *not gay*! Too often *Friends* made the male characters' discomfort with suggestions of homosexuality into the laugh line for jokes. The male characters', especially Joey's and Chandler's, uneasiness with touching or being naked with one another served as a comic foil too often. Best friends Joey and Chandler, for example, often hug—in celebration, to comfort one another, to apologize, and just to say thank you—as a montage in Episode 6.20, "The One with Mac and C.H.E.E.S.E.," shows us. Unfortunately, after this montage points it out, they wonder if they do it too much, and Chandler tells Joey to get off him.

Joey and Chandler are not very comfortable with one another's nudity either, despite being roommates. Early on the series, Joey's father and his mistress spend the night at the guys' apartment. As Joey does not want them to sleep together, Joey and Chandler end up giving them their rooms and sleeping on the fold-out couch together. Joey complains that he is having trouble sleeping with his pajamas on and Chandler says to stop complaining because Chandler insists Joey wear them while they are in bed together (Episode 1.13, "The One with the Boobies"). Later in season 1, Monica warns Chandler not to go into her bedroom where Joey is preparing for a role in a movie. Chandler does not listen and ends up seeing Joey moisturizing his butt to prepare to play Al Pacino's butt double. Chandler runs out screaming, "My eyes! My eyes!" (Episode 1.6, "The One with the Butt"). Another time Joey and Chandler are presented with an opportunity to potentially have a threesome. While they never do it, they contemplate what the "rules" should be if they ever should. They first decide that they should have their eyes closed the whole time so that they do not see each other's genitals. But when they realize this may result in their accidentally touching one another's family jewels, they determine that they must keep their eyes open at all times (Episode 3.15, "The One where Ross and Rachel Take a Break"). Chandler's role as Joey's roommate leads him to try to wake Joey up when he is snoring and ends up being flashed by a naked sleeping Joey (Episode 4.20, "The One with All the Wedding Dresses"). Chandler also helps Joey take a shower and get dressed when he has a hernia (Episode 6.4, "The One where Joey Loses His Insurance"). In both instances, Chandler resists. When Joey flashes him, Chandler screams and tells Joey he needs to buy pajamas, and he reminds Joey that they agreed never to talk about the shower. Chandler is just as uncomfortable with male-on-male touching as he is with male nakedness. Chandler sits on Joey's lap to try to get him out of a chair. Joey gets Chandler to get off him when he says he feels too comfortable with Chandler on his lap (Episode 3.2, "The One where No One's Ready"). Similarly, Chandler accidentally sits naked on his future father-in-law's lap when his glasses fog up when he goes for a steam after racket ball with him (Episode 7.3, "The One with Phoebe's Cookies").

Joey and Ross also breach stereotypical male-male relationships with varying results. When Ross does not know how to talk dirty to a woman, Joey helps him by asking him to close his eyes and asks him to tell him he wants to caress his butt. Ross makes Joey turn around so that Ross does not have to look at his face while he pretends he is the women he wants to seduce. As he tells Joey how he wants to feel his hot, soft skin with his lips, Chandler walks in unbeknownst to the other two. Ross continues to describe how he wants to run his tongue all over this woman's body as Chandler leans back on the desk and knocks the chair so that it makes a sound. When the other two see that Chandler is there, Ross stops talking immediately and the two look at him speechless. While Chandler says that he was always hoping they would get together, the audience sees their discomfort and understands that their intimacy is the joke (Episode 1.15, "The One with the Stoned Guy"). After Joey and Ross fall asleep lying next to one another on Ross's couch while watching *Die Hard*, they both struggle to admit that they want to nap together again. Instead, they act as if they cannot be alone with one another for fear of "turning gay." Even when they finally violate gendered expectations and actually go to take a nap on Joey's couch together, they wake to find the other friends standing over them watching and judging them. Joey concludes the episode by jumping off the couch and yelling at Ross while Ross excuses himself, head hung low (Episode 7.6, "The One with the Nap Partners").

Not just the main male characters are used in the "gay as punchline" strategy in the series either. In Episode 2.4, "The One with Phoebe's Husband," we learn that Phoebe's supposedly gay ice dancing husband is really straight. The writers invert the "coming out" talk by having him explain how he experimented in college by getting drunk and going to straight bars and the trouble he had telling parents he was straight (even though they understand because his brother is straight too). While the message that he does not have a choice as he was born straight resonates with gay audience members, its application to a heterosexual man merely reaffirms heterosexuality as the natural state for men. The joke in this particular case is based on the violation of expectations that a male ice dancer "should be" gay. This same expectation is applied on Sandy (Freddie Prinze Jr.), the male nanny Rachel wants to hire for their daughter, Emma. Because Sandy is a man and a nanny, Ross assumes he is gay. When Sandy corrects him and tells him that he is engaged to marry a woman, Ross still doubts him. After Ross learns that Sandy makes his own diaper cream, plays the recorder and with puppets, and makes the most light and airy madeleine cookies, he suggests that Sandy must at least be bisexual. Ross fires Sandy over Rachel's objections with the excuse that it is not a good fit. The end of the episode, though, shows Sandy helping Ross deal with his insecurities over being considered too sensitive and not masculine enough for his father (Episode 9.6, "The One with the Male Nanny").

There are moments in *Friends* that suggest how they could have represented such moments better (and more often). For example, in an early episode, Chandler wants someone to kiss at midnight on New Year's Eve. He begs the women to kiss him and becomes so irritating that Joey grabs his face and kisses him. While Chandler is surprised, Joey does it without complaint or fanfare and then walks away (Episode 1.10, "The One with the Monkey"). Later in Episode 2.24, "The One with Barry and Mindy's Wedding," Joey auditions for a part that requires him to kiss a man, but director Warren Beatty tells him that he is not a good kisser. He asks Chandler and Ross to kiss him so he can find out how he can improve. Neither is willing to do it, despite Joey's best efforts to corner one of them in a weak moment. At the end of the episode, Ross (finally) lets his support for Joey overcome his discomfort in kissing a man and kisses Joey. Joey thanks him, compliments his technique, but also points out that his audition was earlier and he did not get the part. Given how often the guys, Joey and Chandler in particular, are together in intimate situations, *Friends* could have capitalized by more effectively creating humor in pushing the boundaries of homosociality rather than continuing to make being gay or discomfort with male/male interactions into laughable moments.

DRAG QUEEN FATHER + ULTRA-SEXUAL MOTHER = CHANDLER MURIEL BING

Friends provides reasons for Chandler's discomfort with his own and others' sexuality: his ultra-sexual mother and drag queen father. Chandler's discomfort with sex is not limited to his adult relationship with his mother. Chandler explains that his parents told him at Thanksgiving when he was nine years old that they were getting a divorce; the reason: the houseboy. In Episode 5.8, "The One with All the Thanksgivings," we actually get to see this interaction and the effeminate houseboy's offer of "More turkey, Mr. Chandler?" which comes across as sexual innuendo. Chandler also describes in Episode 7.24, "The One with Chandler and Monica's Wedding: Part 2," having actually walked in on his parents' threesome with the pool boy. Being traumatized by your parents' sex lives and divorce is totally understandable. We see Monica's pain when she gets trapped in the bathroom while her adult parents make out (Episode 2.16, "The One where Joey Moves Out") and when she sees their sex tape (Episode 2.14, "The One with the Prom Video"). But Chandler's situation takes on another dimension as his criticisms do not merely focus on sex but on the sexual identities of his parents.

We learn in Nora's (Morgan Fairchild's) first appearance in Episode 1.11, "The One with Mrs. Bing," that she is a successful romance novelist when she guests on *The Tonight Show*. During her interview, she describes having been arrested in London for an incident involving sex and

Kung Pao chicken and reveals that she bought her son his first condoms. Chandler's reaction, that he is going to burst into flames, demonstrates his discomfort with her sexuality. Later in the same episode, she ends up kissing a drunk and disheartened Ross, much to Chandler's dismay. At Chandler and Monica's wedding reception, Nora introduces Chandler to her date, Dennis, by oversharing that he is a fantastic lover, and Chandler suggests he is going to blow his brains out (Episode 8.1, "The One after I Do").

Unfortunately, the men's relationships with one another, and Chandler's relationship with his parents, are also grounded in homophobia. This applies to jokes at the expense of both gay men as well as the trans community. Casting Kathleen Turner as Chandler's father was both a triumph and extremely problematic. Casting her as his father capitalized on her famously husky voice and inverting her 1970s female sexuality into a man playing a sexual woman. However, since she is really a woman and Chandler's father is a man performing as a woman, her presence takes away any real challenge to constructions of gender. Despite his wearing woman's clothing in all of his appearances, however, Charles is referred to as a "transvestite," gay, and a drag queen. He is also referred to as "Dad," "Daddy," and "Ma'am" by Chandler. The trouble with referents used in the show suggests troubles during the 1990s with language used in mainstream media with naming queer identities.

Chandler's father actually appears for the first time when Monica takes Chandler to Las Vegas to make up with him before their wedding. They go to his drag show and before the action begins, a waitress played by Alexis Arquette (then Courteney Cox's sister-in-law who identified as a trans woman) comes to take their order. She says she gets that Chandler is straight when he orders a beer in an exaggerated deep voice. Monica, however, does not know whether to refer to the waitresses as her or him, female or male. The same episode has Ross uncomfortably attempting to flirt with a male police officer to try to get out of a ticket (and Rachel suggesting he is providing a bad role model for his son), as well as Phoebe telling Joey that it is important for him to take off the women's panties he tried wearing as he is getting too comfortable (Episode 7.22, "The One with Chandler's Dad"). Monica's uncertainty about language, Ross's flirting with a male cop, and Joey's enjoyment in wearing women's underwear all suggest a level of gender play that could push the boundaries of gendered expectations. However, Chandler's affirmation of his masculinity, Rachel's criticism of Ross as a father of a son, and Phoebe's suggestion that Joey may be too feminine police and reaffirm gender norms.

Their reactions echo Chandler's discomforts with his father and his sexuality. Earlier in "The One with Chandler's Dad," Chandler describes his embarrassment when his father used to come to his swim meets dressed as Hollywood starlets. While Monica tries to emphasize the importance of Chandler's dad cheering for him at all his swim meets, Chandler has a tough time looking beyond how he felt when his father dressed as Carmen Miranda and handed out fresh fruit from his headdress after the meet. Chandler's only retort when Monica tries to emphasize the positive is that his father had sex with Mr. Garibaldi. When Monica asks who that is, Chandler wonders why that matters. When they later go see his father's drag show, Chandler recognizes the piano player as Mr. Garibaldi. It does not seem to matter that his father may have a long-term relationship (though it is unclear if it is platonic or sexual) with Mr. Garibaldi, only that the two men have a relationship. Of course, the fact that Chandler later points out that he played one of the male dancers in his father's "It's Raining Men" number may provide some context for his discomfort. His anxiety may also be motivated by others judgments as well. When Jack and Judy Geller first meet Nora Bing before the wedding, Jack asks if she is his mother or father, says he has never seen "one" before, and suggests he was trying to "act" like he was all right with "it" (Episode 7.23, "The One with Chandler and Monica's Wedding: Part 1").

Through the seasons of *Friends*, when Chandler's father is mentioned, it is unclear if he is gay, trans, a cross-dresser, and/or a drag queen. While attributing multiple identities to a queer man could be interpreted as gender play, it is instead more likely sloppy attribution. It also means that it is unclear what exactly Chandler has a problem with: that his father has sex with men, that his desire for men led to his divorce from his mother, that his father dresses like a woman, and/or that his father performs in a drag show in Vegas. His embarrassment also helps explain his distress with being considered gay or having "a quality" that may suggest he is gay. Chandler *so* does not want to become his parents that when he hears Monica's voice on their answering machine call them the Bings, he nearly runs out on the wedding. As he explains to Ross, being his parents means fighting and using the pool boy as a pawn in their sexual games (Episode 7.24, "The One with Chandler and Monica's Wedding: Part 2").

Using gender confusion as a punchline served as a major plot point in Episode 8.9, "The One with the Rumor." Brad Pitt's character, Will, tells Rachel that his and Ross's "I Hate Rachel Green" club started a rumor about her in high school. The rumor was that she had both male and female reproductive parts. Her parents decided to raise her as a girl, but she still had a "hint of a penis," and Chandler calls her the "hermaphrodite cheerleader from Long Island." Rachel then searches her mind (and yearbook) for evidence of guys she dated only going to second base for fear of what they might find below the waist. Rachel wonders why Monica never told her about the rumor, and Monica says that she was afraid it might have been true and she feared Rachel might show it to her. One signature in her yearbook from Sean McMahon even said, "Sorry about your teeny weenie." Rachel complains that Ross told people she was "half and half." In the end, Monica does tell Rachel she was so popular that some people wanted to be like her regardless of whether she was a girl or boy and that one girl put a Tootsie Roll in her pants to try to emulate her. While this one comment at the end makes Rachel's "teeny weenie" a desirable attribute, the rest of the episode leading up to this one brief moment merely uses sex and gender as a punchline.

Friends is never quite comfortable playing with gender without judging gender play too. When Joey mistakes Ross for Monica in an early naked picture, Ross clarifies that he was just experimenting (Episode 1.8, "The One where Nana Dies Twice"). After Ross gets Ben to play with G.I. Joe instead of Barbie, Monica says she cannot believe he is making such a big deal about Ben playing with Barbie when he used to dress up like a woman when he was a child. He would wear his mother's clothes, including a dress, big hat, and handbag. While Ross does not seem to remember singing a song about being Bea and drinking tea, when Monica cannot remember the rest of the song, the memories come flooding back and he finishes the last line. That it happens in front of Carol and Susan adds to Ross's embarrassment (Episode 3.4, "The One with the Metaphorical Tunnel"). Ross is also the one who criticizes Joey for playing a woman, even as Joey tries to clarify that he is playing a woman in a man's body (Episode 7.17, "The One with the Cheap Wedding Dress").

Playing a woman is one thing, but gender confusion leads to gay panic when the men cross sexual boundaries with other men. Joey explains that when he first moved to the city, he went out with a woman who was really hot and a great kisser but who had a huge Adam's apple. When

Ross points out that women do not have Adam's apples, Joey asks if they are messing with him. When they all say they are, he is thankful and indicates that he would have freaked out otherwise (Episode 2.3, "The One where Mr. Heckles Dies"). In a later season, Monica, Chandler, and Ross trade secrets about one another, including Ross's revelation that Chandler once made out with a guy, which Monica finds more amusing than that Ross shat himself on Space Mountain after eating tacos (Episode 7.4, "The One with Rachel's Assistant").

CONCLUSION

Tijana Mamula created a video posted on YouTube of the seemingly homophobic moments in *Friends*.[12] The video is fifty minutes long and does not even include all the troubling gender-based moments in the series! The comedy genre can be blamed for some of this problematic representation. Comedy, especially on network television, often depends on difference, disruption, and violating expectations for punchlines. While these moments can provide opportunities to push boundaries and present points of view that are not necessarily mainstream, the genre also requires that "normalcy" be returned by the end of the episode. Add to the characteristics of the genre the era in which this show first appeared and the progress-retraction tensions become clearer. Shelley Cobb explains:

> Symptomatic of the depoliticized postfeminist, post-civil rights, post-Stonewall, post-Reagan, and postmodern era of the 1990s and its young adult cohort, Generation X, the ironic jokes appear clever and even progressive as they signal that all that historical conflict is supposedly over now. However, the jokes rely on the normativity of white heterosexuality and stereotypes of the racial other, controverting the joke's assumptions about political progress.[13]

Friends provided many opportunities to laugh at ourselves, but too often it suggested we should laugh at "others." Inclusion of gender-nonbinary characters, a lesbian couple, and sexual women certainly pushes the boundaries of what came before them on network television. In this way, they challenged the values and practices passed down to them from their Baby Boomer parents. But Generation X still had difficulties grappling with gender, sexuality, and sex, and *Friends* embodied these problematic representations as well.

8

FRIENDS MUSIC, FASHIONS, AND LOCATIONS WILL ALL BE THERE FOR YOU

Whether getting a latte in a huge cup at a local coffeehouse while listening to the soundtrack of your favorite television series or buying an outfit to go with your new Rachel haircut, everyday life continues to be impacted by the popular-culture capital created in *Friends*. Popular-culture capital refers to the artifacts or things that come from or are associated with, in this case, media creations that are well-liked by many people. Popular-culture capital from the 1990s generally and *Friends* in particular has seen a resurgence since the series celebrated its twenty-year anniversary five years ago and the full series became available for streaming on Netflix four years ago in the United States. Interestingly, the accumulation of popular-culture capital that continues today emerged along with the show's popularization of particular aspects associated with it. While some may have been intentional, others took on lives of their own that no one involved with the project could have anticipated.

One way for fans to participate in a show they like and relate to the characters they identify with is to accumulate popular-culture capital associated with the series, such as artworks, books, fashion, memorabilia, music, and experiences.[1] "Fans accumulate cultural capital of television programs in ways that affect the physicality of their own lived experience."[2] For fans, this might mean changing the look of their home or clothes to emulate their favorite settings or characters. In the 1990s, for *Friends* fans, this may have meant getting "the Rachel" haircut, shopping at Pottery Barn, spending hours at Starbucks, or buying the latest series soundtrack.[3] Today, this might mean much of the same but may also extend into newer applications of their logos or products, including getting an iPhone case that looks like Monica's apartment door (yellow frame around the peephole and all) or attending the annual *Friends* Fest in the United Kingdom and being able to actually sit and take selfies in a replica of Central Perk. For other international fans of the series, it might also mean learning English by imitating their favorite characters.[4] This chapter takes a walk down memory lane to where it all started. From the music and fashion to the coffee and décor, *Friends* contributed to the cultural history of television by bringing fans into the fold with the products and experiences they could buy and emulate to become part of the furor around the show themselves.

THE MUSIC IS STILL THERE FOR US

It all began with a song and six actors dancing in a fountain; at least that was how it started for fans. How the song came about has as much to do with pressure from fans as it does the economic structures of the music industry. The theme song for *Friends* was recorded just a few short weeks before the series premiered. The song was proposed because if it were popular, it could help to promote the show. Music producer, and husband of co-creator Marta Kauffman, Michael Skloff first drafted a verse and chorus. Then co-producer David Bright asked Warner Brothers to find a lyricist for the demo. Allee Willis agreed to write the lyrics to fulfill the one-seventh of a song obligation she still owed the company. Willis says that she did her research by watching the pilot over and over and taking notes about each of the characters.[5] She was also given the title, "I'll Be There for You." She ended up writing lyrics that focused on the characters' loyalty to one another.[6] But the song did not yet sound like the producers intended; it had a bit of country flare. So Skloff brought in alternative rock band the Rembrandts. Band member Danny Wilde explains, "We saw the pilot and it was kind of funny; it had 'It's the End of The World as We Know It,' the R.E.M. song, sort of temped in."[7] That plus being given some creative control was enough for him and his bandmate, Phil Solem, to agree to be involved. The band met with Skloff on a

Thursday and recorded the song and mixed it the following Saturday; *Friends* premiered less than a week later with the song attached.[8]

The ringing guitar riffs, handclaps, keening harmonies, and friendship-focused lyrics made the theme song a ubiquitous part of 1990s popular culture. Fan response to the song at the time is what led to the full-length version of the song even being written in the first place. The *A.V. Club* reports that a Nashville Top 40 station (Y107/WYHY) DJ, Tom Peace, and program director, Charlie Quinn, spliced together a two-minute version of the theme song by looping the lyrics and adding a guitar riff at the end that they played nearly sixty times a week in early 1995. "The reaction from listeners was immediate and intense: They thought it was a legitimate, commercially released single, and wanted to know where they could buy it."[9] Pressures began to mount from the Rem-

Friends hang out on the fountain. *Warner Brothers / Photofest © Warner Brothers*

brandts' record label and the television studio for them to *stop* playing their version because no one, not the band or Warner Brothers, was making money off it. Additionally, the band was trying to maintain an alt-rock image and did not want that kind of exposure from Top 40 radio. Even so, fans kept requesting it and trying to find out where they could buy it. Quinn said, "At times, it was unpleasant. But the thing is, there was such a ball rolling with other radio stations that it was just an undeniable situation that it was going to become a song." Regrettably the band did not consult Warner Brothers Television on their first attempt to extend the song when they added their own lyrics, verses, and even a "synth-speckled bridge."[10] While their decision may have ruffled some feathers, ultimately, Wilde and Solem worked with Skloff, Crane, and Kauffman to complete a full-length version of the song that was true to the themes of the show, had the Monkees-esque sound they were looking for, and could be released for sale.

There was pressure from the band's record label, Elektra, to put the song on the band's upcoming album despite the fact that it did not fit with the tempo or tone of *L.P.* The label said that despite the Rembrandts' record being done, they were not going to release it without the song on it. The band refused at first but then acquiesced. Fortunately, the Rembrandts did get to put it as a "hidden" track at the end of the album and were able to require fans to buy their whole album by not releasing it as a single. The song spent eight weeks at No. 1 on the Billboard Hot 100 Airplay chart.[11] The Rembrandts earned their first gold (in August 1995) and platinum (by January 1996) albums. From the point of view of the series, the song was a hit and did its job to help promote the show. The band, on the other hand, "were in a bizarre spot, having unwittingly latched on to a pop-culture phenomenon that made them both well known and invisible."[12] They made new fans, sold albums, and became a household name, but at the same time, few knew they were an alt-rock band or listened to their other music. Solem said the song became their "golden albatross,"[13] earning them a great deal of money for a song they were stuck being known for.

Today, many bands clamor for the kind of attention having a theme song for a hit television show that the Rembrandts had. Even so, Solem claims, "Back in those days . . . in 1994 . . . the last thing a serious band would do would be involved in a television show. We went along with it, but the whole idea was, 'We're anonymous, okay? Nobody's going to know.'"[14] Of course, everyone found out. Charlie Quinn suggests that the trajectory of the song and its relationship with the series was actually one of the first experiments in viral marketing. "Its popularity was a byproduct of the '90s monoculture, an era when a cultural phenomenon could still be pervasive," but at the same time, it benefited from the emergence and growing ability people had to access the Internet to find out more about the song and its performers.[15] Add to these factors that the *Friends* actors appeared in a video for the song with the band and that the sound evoked qualities of The Beatles and The Monkees, and you had the recipe for an intergenerational hit to buoy a new television offering.

The popularity of the theme song, in both its short and full-length versions, and the use of popular music in the show led to the release of soundtracks for the series too. Soundtracks for television programs had been available previously. However, popular bands did not often go out of their way to be associated with television, let alone have their songs used in series or released on soundtrack CDs. *Friends* soundtracks began with the *Friends Original TV Soundtrack* (released by WEA in 1995), which included songs used in episodes of the show, such as Hootie & the Blowfish's "I Go Blind" and Grant Lee Buffalo's "In My Room." While most of the songs were from the 1990s and appealed to the twenty-something demographic, such as Paul Westerberg's "Stain Yer Blood," others represented older generations, like Joni Mitchell's "Big Yellow Taxi." The music of *Friends*, including the subsequent soundtracks, appealed to multiple generations who ultimately tuned in to the show.[16]

Beyond the theme song and soundtracks, *Friends* became known as an original music producer as well. While only one of her songs made it to the radio, and only as a kitschy stunt, Phoebe Buffay's musical stylings made an impact on televisual musical culture as well. A quick Google search of Phoebe's songs finds what readers want today, lists of her nearly forty songs, their lyrics, and how they compare to one another.[17] Phoebe wrote songs to make points ("Two of Them Kissed Last Night"), to get what she wanted (like singing songs until Chandler and Monica paid her a deposit to sing at their wedding), to celebrate significant events ("Emma's Birthday Song"), to express her worldview ("Cows in the Meadow"), to share her (literal) worldview ("The Shower Song"), or to break the tension (like when she tried to make the final episodes into a musical). One of her songs even went the 1990s equivalent of viral: "Smelly Cat."

The genius of a Phoebe Buffay song is that seemingly anyone could write one. *Bustle* suggests that all you need is 45 percent analysis of what last happened to you, 20 percent of a public argument no one can respond to, 10 percent unsolicited advice, 7 percent bodily functions, 7 percent made-up words, 5 percent coffee, 2 percent each of La la la la la la, bagpipe sounds, and phlegm.[18] In reality, Lisa Kudrow explained that the writers would write the lyrics and that she would come up with the tune, sometimes with help, such as when Chrissie Hynde guest starred and helped her sing "Smelly Cat" in Episode 2.6, "The One with the Baby on the Bus." Screenwriter Betsy Borns wrote this episode and the song lyrics. Borns incorporated some of her own world into the episode, such as naming Chrissie Hynde's character after her sister, Stephanie (who Phoebe yell-sings about when Stephanie replaces her singing at Central Perk), and singing about a smelly pet. Although Borns had a very stinky dog, named Gouda, that the song is based on, singing about a smelly cat was funnier. Kudrow said that Hynde then helped her work out the tune and play it on guitar (as Kudrow was a famously bad guitar player too) as they sang it together in the episode.[19]

Later in the second season of the series, Phoebe is tapped to make a video for the song. Phoebe appears in the video, but the music producers dubbed over her voice with another singer. While the friends are worried about how Phoebe would react, she feels sorry for the singer because she does not have a video (Episode 2.17, "The One where Eddie Moves In"). The presence of "Smelly Cat" during season 2 and the appearance of the video on television (and subsequently the Internet) meant that it was hard to avoid the catchy refrain. Even so, the producers had learned their lesson about overexposure during the first season of the show (see more on this topic in chapter 1). So in Episode 3.14, "The One with Phoebe's Ex-Partner," they "retired" the song. Instead of rekindling their partnership, Phoebe gives her erstwhile ex-partner, Leslie (E. G. Daily), who currently works as a jingle writer (or "jingle bitch" or "jingle whore" according to one of Phoebe's other songs), "Smelly Cat" to sell to a kitty litter company. The sale of the song brought an end to their partnership and the presence of the song on the show. Even so, fans will continue to sing the refrain when thinking about their smelly pets (or friends).

RACHEL AS FASHION ROLE MODEL

Jennifer Aniston's haircut, after the pilot episode of the series, created a popular-culture splash of its own. A layered shag cut, styled in a modern-day bouffant on Jennifer Aniston, became known as "The Rachel." It did not seem to matter that this was her hairstyle for only the first two seasons of the show; it took on a life of its own. *People Magazine* editor-in-chief, Jess Cagle, says that if the furor over the Rachel had occurred today, it would have its own Twitter feed. We all tried the Rachel at some point. Even Courteney Cox coveted the hairstyle. She appears to be sporting her own version of the Rachel in the music video for the Rembrandt's full-length version of "I'll Be There for You." She later said that she was so jealous of the attention Rachel's hair earned that she kept changing her hairstyle in hopes that one of hers would also catch on, though none did. [20] Beyond just appearing in the series, and the ubiquitous media presence the actors had at the time, Aniston also posed for what became an iconic photo of the 'do. In 1995, knowing how popular her hairstyle was, Robert Trachtenberg asked Aniston to pose in a wig shop window for a photo for *Entertainment Weekly*. She was positioned between multiple wig heads and just her face and hair were featured. As Trachtenberg points out, "It was just a hairdo and it became this national phenomenon. So I threw the dice and suggested we kind of mock it and she loved the idea of making fun of it. . . . In one photo, you sort of mock it, pay tribute to it and salute it."[21] *People Magazine* has since named the photo as one of its Top 100 Celebrity Photos.

Despite how difficult Aniston has since said it was to maintain, there seems to have been a resurgence of the Rachel in recent years. For some reason, possibly because it appeared as a Jeopardy clue, the question, "What is the Rachel?" was a trending Google search as recently as May 4, 2018.[22] Celebrity news reports indicate that stars have been wearing the 'do since the show was still airing: from Tyra Banks, who wore it at the 1997 Victoria's Secret reveal of their $3 million Dream Bra, to Jennifer Lopez who sported the look as recently as 2015. While some argue the Rachel is only the hairstyle Aniston sported during the first two seasons of the show, stars like Christina Aguilera donned the longer-layer version and Meg Ryan wore the more-shag-like version of the style in 1999.[23] With the resurgence of all things 1990s in the new millennium, even Brie Larson as the new Captain Marvel wears the haircut. What better way to

The Rachel. *Warner Brothers / Photofest © Warner Brothers*

indicate the time period the film takes place during than its superhero star sporting the Rachel. As Kaila Hale-Stern suggested in *The Mary Sue*, "The Rachel defined a generation more than babydoll dresses and clear backpacks ever could. In a hundred years, all characters in period pieces set in the '90s will be required to sport the Rachel, regardless of gender or hair length."[24]

The Rachel led Aniston to frequent presence on the cover of celebrity magazines. The fact that her character worked in fashion and Aniston's ever-presence on red carpets led her to become a fashion icon for people in the 1990s. Interestingly, some of her signature pieces included overalls, aprons, and even the color brown. Article upon article discuss how she dresses, how her style has evolved, and how to recreate her looks. Authors have even ranked every single one of Rachel's outfits worn on the show and suggested her fashion through lines for each season. Season 1 could be considered "The One where Rachel Wore Brown," along with denim jackets, bibs, and long vests, whereas by season 4, she may still have been wearing an inordinate amount of brown, but she was also considered chic and simple and was rocking her best hairstyle yet.[25] Top outfits for each season include her tartan mini skirt with half top turtle neck sweater and knee socks in season 1 (Episode 1.19, "The One where the Monkey Gets Away"); (my personal favorite) her Asian-inspired yellow, embroidered strapless dress in season 5 (Episode 5.2, "The One with All the Kissing"); and her black lace-up décolletage shirt from season 10 (Episode 10.3, "The One with Ross's Tan"), which some say Kim Kardashian stole from Rachel years later.[26] Aniston became such a fashion icon that no matter the hairstyle or the outfit, once she wore it, everyone else copied her.

COFFEE SHOP APARTMENTS

When *Friends* premiered in 1994, Starbucks had already been in operation for thirteen years, and their "coffeehouse" concept had been in place since the mid-1980s. Neither *Friends* nor Starbucks can claim they started the idea of a coffeehouse being a comfortable place to sip coffee and enjoy the company of friends (and even strangers) as it has been a part of cultures around the world for hundreds of years. Turkey can be credited with starting the idea and England can be given credit for spreading the idea to the West.[27] What Starbucks and *Friends* can be credited with is creating the perfect storm for the late-twentieth-/early-twenty-first-century explosion of coffeehouse culture. "In 1994, when Starbucks opened its first drive-thru operation, the company ran 425 stores across the country. By 2000, it had 3,501 stores open across the globe; by 2005, it ran 10,241 outposts."[28] Some have suggested that this explosion of Starbucks stores was an elaborate conspiracy between the *Friends* creators and the chain. Twitter user Alex Baker claims that *Friends* was a "meticulously-planned priming exercise to manipulate human behaviour, getting them away from pubs (*Cheers*) and into coffee shops (*Friends*)."[29] If it was, it was definitely successful. Little evidence suggests collusion in this case though.

What the appearance of Central Perk alongside the explosion of coffeehouse culture in the United States did do was to create the conditions for reverse product placement. "Fictional brands are brands that exist only in the world of fiction and not the real physical world. Reverse product placement consists of transforming these fictional brands into products and services in the real physical world."[30] This type of reverse product placement is only possible if they have brand salience and positive brand associations.[31] Central Perk had both. While it would be difficult to gauge just how much time the friends spent at the coffeehouse, Kit Lovelace counted up and posted on Twitter the number of cups of coffee each character poured, purchased, and consumed and the approximate amounts of money spent across the ten seasons of the show.

Phoebe: 227 cups ($408.10)
Chandler: 212 cups ($381.60)
Monica: 198 cups ($356.40)
Joey: 191 cups ($343.70)
Ross: 188 cups ($338.40)
Rachel: 138 cups ($248.40)
Total: 1,154 cups ($2077.20)[32]

Ironically, Rachel, who worked at Central Perk the longest, was actually the one who drank the least amount of coffee. Given that anything other than a black coffee would likely have cost more than the $1.50 base Lovelace used to estimate these costs, these estimates are likely low. But they speak to the amount of time the cast spent at the coffeehouse as they appeared there at least once in most of the 236 episodes of the series.

Given how often the cast were seen in the coffeehouse, it is no surprise that products, especially the large coffee cups with the *Friends* and/or Central Perk logo on them, became top sellers. Fans can still be a part of Central Perk and the *Friends* universe by buying these big cups, T-shirts, aprons, and even phone cases today.

Beyond products to buy, the time the *Friends* spent at Central Perk also inspired fans to want to spend time in their home away from home as well, making the café itself into a reverse product placement opportunity. In various locations, replicas of the Central Perk set have cropped up in both temporary and semi-permanent locales. A pop-up Central Perk occupied bar Replay in Chicago in November 2018, while New York City saw a similar pop-up for one month to celebrate the twentieth anniversary of the show back in 2014. London is privy to an annual *Friends* Fest where fans can inhabit the coffee shop and apartment replicas every year.[33] Chinese entrepreneur Du Xin created replicas of the coffee shop and Joey's apartment on the sixth floor of a Bejing apartment building and plans a second location in Shanghai. The name Central Perk is licensed for thirty-two similar replicas in nearly thirty-two countries.[34] Du's version has the orange couch front and center for fans to sit on, and the apartment includes the oversized TV unit with DVDs of Baywatch on its shelves. Du says that these locations allow fans who treat *Friends* like a religion (as he does) the opportunity to have a moment in the kind of lives they are looking to live, lives where anyone can do anything they want. When Chandler quit his job and found another one he liked better, for example, he inspired Du to make a life of his own choosing.[35]

The fact that the friends were young and attractive, informal yet modern, and lived in trendy apartments and hung out at the coffee shop sitting on the orange couch made them aspirational to many. Being in that café with the plush sofa surrounded by comfy chairs and tables with mismatched chairs recreated the setting of most sitcoms, the living room, which the family usually inhabited. In this case, *Friends* created their own alternate family model (see more in chapter 3), and one of their living rooms was created around the orange couch in the coffee shop. "As the central prop in the sitcom, the orange sofa was so important in representing the *essence* of the *Friends* that it stars in the opening credits. It's the first thing that appears, empty and positioned outside in front of the fountain before being filled up by the characters."[36] It is not just the coffee shop culture that is important but the aesthetic as well. " Bare brick walls, dark floorboards and rugs, blackboard menu, retro signs and, above all, plush, mismatched easy furniture all rapidly became *de rigeur* for every latte-seller."[37] Designing cafés to look like living rooms makes patrons feel comfortable in a place they can consider their home away from home. From the business side of things, the longer the patrons stay, the more money they will spend.

Seeing the *Friends* apartment décor, especially Monica's apartment, makes you wonder whether they brought the coffeehouse into the apartment or vice versa. Arguably, Monica's apartment is the place the friends spend the most time in the series. As such, beyond Central Perk, it is the space fans are most familiar with. It serves as a gathering place for the characters during the holidays, for parties, and for everyday events. Its familiarity and the comfort it provides became part of the series' appeal as well. It was not difficult to recognize the familiarity in this space as its décor echoed that of the coffeehouse, with its four-seat kitchen table, mismatched chairs, comfy sofa accompanied by a cushy chair in the center of the living room, as well as the retro-looking French posters on the walls. Add to the décor the relationships among the group and their explicitly stating that it is "a place of love and laughter" (Episode 10.18, "The Last One: Part 2") and you have another space that fans want to inhabit.

Fans can also (still) purchase the yellow picture frame that surrounded the peephole in Monica's apartment. Putting a piece of her apartment in one's own home allows fans more of a connection to the series by transforming their own space into Monica's place. Unlike a monopoly game based on *The Simpsons* or a bobblehead of characters from *The Big Bang Theory*, "the peephole frame extends the setting for the characters' lives to a fan's own living room. . . . As viewers appropriate physical objects featured in the show, their living rooms become extensions of the *Friends* set, even when the television is off."[38] Warner Brothers' official online forum for *Friends* shows how much fans seek and acquire popular-culture capital from the show. They request information about set decorations, including the names of the posters in Monica's apartment, Rachel's room, and even Joey and Chandler's place. As fans decorate their homes with recognizable objects from the show, they create lasting connections to the series by making the show part of their realities, and their homes also become part of popular culture.[39]

Monica's apartment. *NBC / Photofest © NBC*

CONCLUSION

The music, characters, their storylines and fashions, and the spaces they inhabited all made *Friends* the comfort food fans needed throughout its run. This was especially true after the attacks on the United States on September 11, 2001. Most new seasons of television shows then still began in September. After the attacks, most series delayed their premieres, including *Friends*. However, once it started in late September that year, it had its highest ratings in years and won its only Emmy for Outstanding Comedy Series. By season 8, fans were *in* though. Only one change had to be made in post-9/11 episodes: they took out B-roll scenes of the Twin Towers. Despite its setting in New York City, the show did not explicitly address the attacks. But when they returned, the erasable white board on the door in Joey's apartment read, "I heart NYC." While *Friends* may be a fictional show set in a fictional world, its impact on popular culture and its fans was, and still is, very real. From music and fashion to coffeehouses and home décor, our lives were changed by what we saw and what we wanted to bring into our new realities.

9

FRIENDS AMONG FANS: MEMES AND ALTERNATIVE NARRATIVES

I won't lie: I have always seen myself in *Friends*. I have aspirations to be witty like Chandler and laid-back like Phoebe or Joey. So I was excited when the result of my "Which 'Friends' Character Are You Based on These 'Would You Rather' Questions?" quiz was Joey! This result suggested that I was a "charmer, incredibly likable and while [I] sometimes say dumb things [I'm] still super popular," and that my "life is always good when pizza is around."[1] While I wish my lactose intolerance would allow me to enjoy eating pizza like Joey while charming my friends, the reality is that I am much more like an amalgam of Ross and Monica. I most often identified with Ross because I recognize that I can be "competitive, creative and quick on [my] feet" and "willing to risk it all if [I] can end up on top and have full-time bragging rights."[2] My result from the "Which Famous 'Friends' Episode Defines Your Life?" quiz was consistent with this finding as it indicated that "The One with the Embryos" (Episode 4.12) defined my life, as it includes the quiz game competition that results in Monica and Rachel losing their apartment to Joey and Chandler.

Like me, television audience members identify with characters and their series when "television affirms, authenticates, and reflects fans' social experience."[3] Repeat viewings over the course of twenty-five years allowed fans to develop their relationships with the characters on-screen. Learning about the actors' backstories for their characters and personal lives off-screen provides fans with opportunities to deepen those relationships by "applying their own perspectives to enhance a program's social image and making meaning of their own experience."[4] Viewers can also extend their relationships with series and their characters "by living out these relationships by commiserating with the actors, fantasizing about their lives with friends and using the characters as models for their own lives."[5] Taking quizzes about *Friends*, sharing reactions to the show with scholars, creating memes, and even writing their own alternate narratives for characters are all ways viewers take their fandom to the next level and contribute to the cultural legacy of the series.

Taking these quizzes helps fans to continue their connection with the show even fifteen years after the series ended. The results tell fans which character or episode most relates to their lives. But the fun in taking the quizzes is answering questions related to character traits, activities, or storylines from the show. For example, the "Which 'Friends' Character Are You Based on These 'Would You Rather' Questions?" quiz asked me if I would rather have a third nipple or advertise an STD clinic, have my fake tan look like Ross's or have to massage a friend who makes sex noises, and run like Phoebe or dance like Chandler? In order to even take the quiz, one must have knowledge of the show. For those of us who do, we are taken back to Chandler having his third nipple removed when a woman he was dating with a prosthetic leg thought it was weird (Episode 3.14, "The One with Phoebe's Ex-Partner") and we wonder if this would be better or worse than when Joey's family disinvited him from Thanksgiving dinner because he appeared on a public service poster for venereal disease and they worried he had it (Episode 1.9, "The One where Underdog Gets Away").

Beyond making connections between episodes and characters, another "Would You Rather?" quiz did not even give a result at the end. Rather, once you indicated your answer, it showed how many other fans answered each way.[6] When I indicated that I would rather get a massage from Phoebe than have a meal cooked by Monica, I learned that I was in the minority as 72 percent would rather have the meal from Monica. I was really surprised to find out that more people (52 percent) would rather eat Rachel's trifle (which, if you remember, included lady fingers, jam, beef, peas, and onions!) than spend Thanksgiving in a box (as Chandler did to repent for not being a true friend to Joey). I was not surprised, however, when I learned that 62 percent of us would rather marry Chandler than have a one-night stand with Joey. Taking this kind of quiz brings fans together and makes them wonder whether they are in the majority or minority while immersing them in the stories and characters they still love.

More in-depth, scholarly research has also been conducted about fans' relationships with *Friends*. In their examination of American and Indian fans interpretations of "The One where Dr. Ramoray Dies" (Episode 2.18), scholars[7] found that the discussion of safe sex came across clearly to both Indian and American audiences. However, Indian audiences saw cultural differences in the discussions of sexual activity and partners. Indian audience members said that it was culturally inappropriate for either Monica or Rachel to have premarital sex, for Monica to date a man (Richard) twenty-one years older than her, and for Monica's brother to not only know she was having premarital sex but to have sex in the bedroom right next to hers. Most disturbing, and revealing, was Indian audience members' claims that it was unrealistic to believe that a man (Richard) would call off sex when a condom was not available. While American audiences also saw this as potentially problematic, both audiences saw this message as one to potentially be emulated. Both audiences identified with or wanted to be like particular characters. Phoebe was most talked about as quirky and someone they wanted to be friends with by Indian audiences whereas American audience members identified with successful working mother Rachel and Chandler, who they viewed as always ready with a joke. Interestingly, Indian audience members saw the friends living together, finding love in one another, and supporting each other in their daily lives as most like their own lives, whereas American audience members saw primarily a depiction of twenty-somethings whose lives were too perfect to be considered realistic.

This chapter explores ways that fans identify with and make *Friends* their own. Some may take online quizzes or contemplate how they might apply safe sex messages to their own lives, while others take to the Internet to create memes or write alternative storylines for their favorite (or least favorite) *Friends*. Fan reactions to and interactions with *Friends* continue today, making use of the series, its characters, and connections with popular culture to deepen their connections with the show. They share their quiz results, memes, and theories in order to connect with one another over their shared love for the show.

Early friends. *Warner Brothers / Photofest © Warner Brothers*

FAN CULTURAL PRODUCTIONS: MEMES

Fans also like to engage in their own production of *Friends*-related materials. Some may create fan art or fan fiction, but the most frequently shared fan creations today are memes—images or videos, often taken from popular culture, that are copied, changed in some way, and shared among Internet users. These memes take multiple forms. Some use still photos or gifs (animated or moving images) from the series with added text that indicates the characters are saying what the user wants them to. One image, taken from Episode 5.8, "The One with All the Thanksgivings," shows Monica trying to cheer Chandler up by putting the turkey, hat, and glasses on her head. This scene leads to Chandler telling Monica he loves her for the first time (even though he takes it back right away). Fans, however, have made it into a commentary on drunk behavior during the holidays by suggesting this is what happens when you've had too much spiked cider.[8] In other memes, fans have taken stills of Chandler arriving home to find Joey in his and Monica's refrigerator. Fans added a title that indicates that this type of relationship is "friendship goals" for them and queered Chandler and Joey's friendship by having them greet one another with "Hey, honey," and "Hey, sweetie."[9]

Alternatively, fans use quotes from the show that go with their pictures of the characters but use them in a context that alters the meaning. For example, when Chandler is helping Ross and Rachel move Ross's couch, Ross keeps yelling for them to "Pivot!" and when Chandler cannot take Ross's instructions anymore, he yells, "Shut up! Shut up! Shut up!" (Episode 5.16, "The One with the Cop"). A fan used that image and quote but made the response be one to feeling overwhelmed. In another meme, Ross is drinking and trying to convince Rachel, Joey, and Charlie that he is "fine" (Episode 10.2, "The One where Ross Is Fine"). Instead of this moment being about Ross's inability to deal with Rachel and Joey dating, this fan made it about anytime anyone cannot deal with life but does not want to reveal their true feelings.

Other fan-created memes connect *Friends* images and/or dialogue with other texts, characters, actors, or celebrities to create intertextual and/or self-referential narrative worlds. One brings Dr. Drake Ramoray, Joey's *Days of Our Lives* character in *Friends*, together with Dr. Derek Shepherd from *Grey's Anatomy*. It shows them meeting over their love of fast cars. It does not matter that *Grey's Anatomy* did not premiere until the year after *Friends* ended nor that the two series took place in different locations. Fans of both shows can appreciate the idea that two neurosurgeon characters, and the actors who play them (who both love fast cars), can come together outside of their shows. Just as another meme brings Joey's ad for the Japanese product Ichiban—lipstick for men—together with Kylie Jenner's lipstick to suggest that Joey inspired Kylie's new color. In this case, the world where Joey gets paid to do Japanese lipstick ads for men is also one where Kylie Jenner (who was not even born until 1997, three seasons into the series) pays attention to Japanese fashion trends to inspire what will come next in her makeup line. That it is associated with Joey on *Friends* merely adds to who knows about her products.

Fans create such memes primarily because they find it pleasurable to do so. They can share their creations to enhance connections to other fans who "get" their messages. Fans can also relate these media texts to their personal lives more directly by creating memes that are more specific to their life experiences. They can even reaffirm their feelings of self-worth by creating something new related to a text that means something important to them. The quizzes and fan creations show just how much *Friends* means to its fans, even twenty-five years after the series premiered.

FAN CULTURAL PRODUCTIONS: ALTERNATE NARRATIVES

Some fans take steps to make the series their own by taking their creativity to the next level. Media scholar Stuart Hall suggests that there are multiple possible meanings of media texts determined not just by what appears on the screen, but by the relationship created between texts and fans, including dominant, negotiated, and resistant readings.[10] When fans see what they like and can identify with characters and storylines, their interpretations are often in line with dominant, or intended, readings. On *Friends*, this would be something like fans agreeing that the Rachel and Ross love story was the central relationship of the series. However, when they see differences between themselves and the characters and stories they see, they rework them into something they find more pleasurable that they can relate to more or that seems to make more sense in the current historical, political, and/or cultural climate. A negotiated meaning involves the dominant meaning of the text, but also requires fans to make that meaning their own in some way.[11] For example, fans always wondered how it was that the friends always got to sit on the orange couch in Central Perk until someone noticed there was a "reserved" sign on the table in front of the couch. While somewhat "hidden," this is part of the dominant text as it all appears on the screen. Even so, one fan on Reddit speculated that the *reason* there was a reserved sign was that Gunther put it there "with the intention of keeping his beloved Rachel in close proximity."[12] This part of the interpretation amounts to a negotiated meaning as the reason the sign is there is not part of the show. Resistant meanings, as you might imagine, are those where fans reject the intended dominant meanings of the text and make meanings of their own. Resistant meanings may be counter to what the producers, writers, and actors meant by what they made. For *Friends*, this might involve telling the story from Gunther's point of view instead of that of the primary characters.

Negotiated meanings can involve fans altering small details or larger storylines. For example, some fans critique the small details, such as that the "real" New York would have more ethnic minorities than appear on the series and that struggling twenty-somethings could never afford the apartments the characters inhabit in Manhattan on the show.[13] Other fans focus on how they might extend upon or revise details about the characters themselves. For example, Rachel twice mentioned the role toes can play in sexual pleasure. She cheered for toes being considered an erogenous zone in Episode 4.11, "The One with Phoebe's Uterus." She also once told Ross that she wanted to find a man "who could be your best friend but can also make your toes curl" (Episode 1.19, "The One where the Monkey Gets Away") and painted Ross's toes in Episode 3.25, "The One at the Beach." Reddit user DarthMcree then speculated that Rachel has a foot fetish.[14] Another fan wondered if Monica developed her OCD-like need to keep everything clean and neat, and perhaps even her fertility troubles, because of hormone treatment she received at fat camp.[15] To further extend upon the dominant narrative of the show, comedian Emily Heller tweeted that Ross and Monica had to be related, otherwise the rest of the characters would have sided with Ross's ex-wife, Carol, in the divorce.[16] Within just three days, Heller's post "racked up over 40,000 likes and 8,000 responses."[17] Responses ranged from dissing Ross for not being a "real Friend" to defending Ross's centrality to the group. Heller clarified that she meant the post not "as a Ross burn but a Carol compliment."[18]

Like the Ross and Monica theory, speculation about both Joey's and Phoebe's brain power gained traction in online discussions. Ojcoolj posted on Reddit that Joey was a lot smarter than he may have appeared, and he just manipulated his friends into giving him what he wanted.[19]

Examples from the show that support this theory include speculation about whether Joey only goes on a second date with Erin (Kristen Davis) just to get Rachel to make him pancakes (Episode 7.7, "The One with Ross's Library Book") or Joey assertively, and correctly, amending Ross's grammar (Episode 8.4, "The One with the Videotape"). While there is some evidence to support this theory about Joey, others have more convincingly speculated that it is Phoebe who is the genius. She may not have had a formal education, but she fluently speaks French (Episode 10.13, "The One where Joey Speaks French"), spouts Italian without knowing that she could (Episode 5.19, "The One where Ross Can't Flirt"), plays puppet master to her friends' shenanigans (Episodes 5.14, "The One where Everybody Finds Out" and 9.14, "The One with the Blind Dates"), and controls Monica and Rachel on a regular basis (Episodes 2.13, "The One after the Superbowl: Part 2" and 6.6, "The One on the Last Night"). "This theory contends that Phoebe Buffay is a genius with 'zero ambition' who plays her friends off against one another 'for her own amusement.'"[20] Phoebe's "That was fun—who's hungry?" end to her episode-long argument with Ross about evolution in Episode 2.3, "The One where Heckles Dies," where she makes him question the basis of his own belief system, demonstrates just how smart, savvy, and seemingly heartless she is in exerting her intellectual powers.

Finally, sometimes fans just run with storylines that the series decided to end, such as Rachel and Joey dating. On the show, Joey fell in and out of love with Rachel, but she did not reciprocate his feelings, at least not at first. Then Rachel had a crush on Joey but could not tell him because he was dating Charlie. Once he and Charlie broke up though, Rachel finally told Joey. The two had a barely three-and-a-half episode relationship before Rachel's inability to do more than make out with him made them both realize that perhaps they should just be friends. Twitter user Claire Willett created a more-than-one-hundred-tweet thread where she provided reasons why Rachel and Joey were the ones who were truly meant to be. Many of the posts suggested why Joey was better with Rachel than Ross, giving evidence such as Joey always accepting Rachel for who she is and Ross seeing her more as a possession than a real friend.[21] Others focus on why Rachel and Joey were more appropriate for one another, such as that Joey remained supportive and protective of Rachel as she evolved as a person and that he is the one who noticed what she wanted,[22] as well as that they were more on the same intellectual level as one another. This theory stands in stark contrast to the more commonly accepted theory that had more evidence across all ten seasons that Phoebe and Joey should have ended up with one another.

Most of the resistant fan interpretations of the series take two forms: creating self-referential and intertextual television worlds and constructing alternate narratives for the characters. The simplest intertextual world was created between *Friends*, *Mad about You*, and *Seinfeld*, which were all at one time on NBC's "Must-See TV" together. Lisa Kudrow originated the role of Ursula the bad waitress on *Mad about You* in 1993, the year before *Friends* began. When she was cast on *Friends*, rather than confusing fans by her playing two unrelated characters on the same network on the same night or eliminating her from one of the series, NBC, producers, and writers agreed to have Kudrow play both Ursula and Phoebe and also made them twin sisters who both appear on *Friends*. Further connecting the *Mad about You* and *Friends* universe, Helen Hunt and Leila Kenzle made a cameo as their *Mad about You* characters, Jamie Buchman and Fran Devanow, respectively, stopping into Central Perk for a cup of coffee. This makes sense as both shows take place in New York. To further the connection, Jamie and Fran mistake Phoebe for Ursula and decide not to stay as they may never get their coffee. This moment also served, at the time, to clarify for fans that it is the same Ursula who appears on both shows, but that Phoebe does not know the characters from the other show. Their bad experience at Central Perk also helps to explain why the characters' worlds do not overlap more often.

On *Seinfeld*, Jerry's friend George Costanza (Jason Alexander) and his girlfriend/fiancée, Susan Ross (Heidi Swedberg), watch an episode of *Mad about You* and Jerry's neighbor Cosmo Kramer (Michael Richards) also appears in Episode 1.8, "The Apartment," which creates direct connections between *Mad about You* and *Seinfeld*. To further extend this part of the NBC world, Courteney Cox also guest starred on *Seinfeld* in 1994 as Meryl. Her character and Jerry pretend they are married (Episode 5.17, "The Wife"). Later the same year, Cox premiered as Monica on *Friends*.[23] After *Seinfeld* ended, Jason Alexander then guest starred on *Friends* as a suicidal office worker whose coworkers barely acknowledge his existence and who Phoebe must save (Episode 7.13, "The One where Rosita Dies"). Alexander may not have played his *Seinfeld* character George, but fan speculation that his office worker could very well have been George is legitimate given his emotional instability. It could be further speculated that his appearance on *Friends* also acts as a commentary on what Alexander's life might be like without work post-*Seinfeld* (though an extreme version).

The *Friends* actors have also been associated by fans with media worlds created after the series ended. In Episode 7.9, "The One with All the Candy," Rachel tells Monica that she did not sleep with Tag because it was the first date. Monica then lists the names of men Rachel has slept with on first dates, including Ben Wyatt. Ben Wyatt was also the name of Adam Scott's character on NBC sitcom *Parks and Recreation* (2009–2015). Reddit user Phefflin speculates:

> After doing the math, at the time of season 7 of *Friends* (2000), Rachel is 29 years old. . . . At the same time, Ben would be 26, slightly younger but still within range of a relationship. . . . I think at some point after Ben left Patridge, Minnesota in shame after his failure as mayor, he went to NYC for a brief time, met Rachel, and either had a one night stand, or a relationship. Both shows did air on NBC . . .[24]

While the use of his name and the hypothesis about their ages lend credibility to this theory, neither *Friends* nor *Parks and Recreation* ever created an episode titled, "The One where Rachel Dates Ben Wyatt from *Parks and Rec*."[25]

Other fans have taken the end of *Friends* and speculated about how Rachel's story might have ended differently. Reddit user NotAnAverageTaunTaun wonders if Paris Geller's (Liza Weil) story arc on a later season of *Gilmore Girls* is "actually Rachel Green's redemption story."[26] After all, her character's name is Paris—where Rachel was going to go for her new job—and her last name is Geller—which may be what Rachel changes her name to if and when she and Ross married. Even if Rachel married Ross and did not change her name, the use of the last name Geller creates a connection to what Rachel got (Ross Geller) for giving up her new job (in Paris). In contrast Paris chose to break up with her boyfriend because of her fear that he would interfere with her ability to go away to medical school. Her boyfriend, Doyle (Danny Strong), decides to follow her to medical school to save their relationship and support her career goals. This is what NotAnAverageTaunTaun suggests Rachel and Ross should have done: Rachel should have gone to Paris and Ross should have followed her.[27] The conclusion of their storyline on *Friends* suggests that Rachel has finally gotten to the point where she is ready to settle down and get married, despite her career goals. However, NotAnAverageTaunTaun's theory is more consistent with her story arc over the course of the ten seasons: not ready to settle down until and unless her partner supports her independence and career aspirations.

Another fan theory based on the latter events of the series includes suppositions about the house Monica and Chandler bought and are getting ready to move to in the suburbs. One fan wondered whether they were going to be living near Ted Mosby from *Friends*-inspired *How I Met Your Mother*, as he also bought a house in the New York suburb of Westchester County. Of course, many others speculate that *How I Met Your Mother* was merely a re-telling of *Friends*. Since it only appears in the series a couple of times, Monica and Chandler's house sparked additional guesswork from fans about to whom the house first belonged. The holiday scenes of their house make it look just like the house in Christmas favorite *Home Alone*. Of course, outside of the show, this can easily be explained as a production choice to license the footage of the house, and its attractive suburban neighborhood seen from inside the house, to show an appropriate, for the season and the neighborhood, house for them. But fans have taken it a step further to explain how *Home Alone* premiered fourteen years before the final season of *Friends* aired. This would give enough time for the kids in *Home Alone* to have grown up and moved away. Given that Monica and Chandler just adopted their newborn twins, fans further imagine their kids growing up and defending their home from criminals, just as Kevin (Macauley Culkin) did.[28] No suggestions about who would play the criminals though.

Fans' theories extend to one of the most depicted locations on the show as well: Central Perk. Radio presenter Alex Baker suggests that *Friends* might just be "a mad, elaborate stage-setter for Starbucks" and a "meticulously-planned priming exercise to manipulate human behaviour, getting them away from pubs (like the show 'Cheers') and into Coffee Shops (as with 'Friends')."[29] Further details, such as Rachel's resemblance to the Starbucks logo and her name Green being the Starbucks signature color, are presented as evidence to support this theory. As further evidence is presented, such as that Ross and Monica's last name Geller is near to the German word, *gellen* or yell, being what Starbucks baristas do when your coffee is ready, the less water this theory seems to hold.[30] Even so, *Friends* can be credited with being a part of both the "gentrification of the urban sitcom"[31] and popularizing coffeehouse culture. While Starbucks was founded in 1971, their coffeehouse concept was not created until 1984. Between 1987 and 1994, they went from 17 stores to 425. However, between 1994 and 2004, the years *Friends* initially aired, they increased from 425 stores to 8,569 stores worldwide.[32] At the same time that Starbucks got customers used to paying exorbitant amounts of money for cups of coffee, *Friends* showed their cast drinking that coffee out of giant cups while hanging out at the coffeehouse doing nothing nearly every episode (see more in chapter 4). While there is little to no evidence that *Friends* and Starbucks conspired to move fans from the bar to the coffeehouse, *Friends* holds some responsibility for "marketing cities to young white suburbanites, [which] helped fuel the market-demand side for gentrification to take place in the '90s and 2000's."[33]

Resistant readings that focus on the main characters take them in directions that redefine the series altogether. Chapters 1 through 3 discuss different ways the series privileges the ensemble of all six actors and how their characters depended on one another as an alternative family of friends. In contrast, two similar theories, one focused on Rachel and the other on Phoebe, contend that the narrative was really created by a terribly lonely person looking for that kind of camaraderie. "The One where It All Takes Place in Rachel's Head" was inspired by fans' close reading of the cover of the season 4 DVD boxset where Rachel is the only one awake in the image.

Twitter user Phil Dunne posted his theory:

> Rachel had a dream on the eve of her wedding day, she didn't want to marry Barry so she had a major anxiety dream. She created a fantasy in her mind and the five other Friends characters as a way to escape her spoilt, trapped future life. And also the trauma of her getting married the next day. This cover is her partially waking up from that dream at 5am on the morning of her wedding day. The whole entire series was her anxiety dream.[34]

While the it-all-takes-place-in-Rachel's-head theory did not gain much traction, the similar theory about Phoebe is more believable.

Twitter user @strnks suggested that all ten seasons of the series were actually from Phoebe's "fevered imagination, projecting herself into the lives of the others. All she ever wanted was . . . Friends."[35] This theory speculates that Phoebe is still living on the street and has become a meth addict. From her view outside of Central Perk, she sees people that she

Friends in bed. *Warner Brothers / Photofest © Warner Brothers*

makes into her circle of imaginary friends. Her outsider status in the group, kooky asides, and attempts to make everything about her are the evidence provided to support this hypothesis. According to @strnks,

> The final scene would be Phoebe walking away from Central Perk, with the Ross, Rachel, Joey, Chandler, and Monica characters making a reference to "the crazy lady who always stares at us." They all have different names and personalities. Phoebe walks past a furniture store and catches her reflection in a mirror placed in the window. The name of the store? "Ursula." Finally she returns to the park where she sleeps in front of the fountain. A broken lamp stands next to her bench. It starts to rain. From behind, we see her put up six dirty, but brightly coloured umbrellas. Fade to black.[36]

Some of the main reasons that fans continue to follow the show are the relationships among the six friends, the creation of their alternative family, and how they can relate to them. So making their relationships the result of a lonely, drug-addled, homeless woman's unachievable dream to have friends is what co-creator Marta Kauffman said is the "saddest thing" she's ever heard.[37] Even so, trying to figure out how each member of the cast fits, or does not, continues to be a way that fans engage with the show beyond just watching it. As a non-relative, who is only a part of the group because she was once Monica's roommate, a pairing she left without even telling Monica because the two clashed so terribly, it is easier to see how this type of theory could be true in an alternate reality.

Even more critical viewers of the series speculated about why it was that after Rachel and Ross's daughter, Emma, was born, Ross's son, Ben, never appeared again. Ben is born during the first season of the show and appears every year through season 8. Smokingcage posted on Reddit that the reason he does not appear in the last two seasons is that Ross lost custody of Ben.[38] This poster has a point: Ben does not even ever meet his half-sister, Emma. One blogger suggests the reason for losing custody is his being a bad father and his disturbing antics—such as his trying to kiss his cousin, at-times uncontrolled rage (that gets him fired), dating students (that gets him threatened to be fired), and treatment of women and homophobia.[39] His treatment of Carol and Susan is discussed further in chapter 7. Suffice it to say here that viewers' connections to and extensions of the series into alternate narratives are not always positive. Sometimes they try to provide correctives for issues they see as wrong in the series.

CONCLUSION

Believing these fan theories is not required. What is important is recognizing how fans develop, enhance, and extend their relationships with *Friends* by engaging in these forms of cultural production. Viewers of all generations participate in creating and engaging in these relationships. Despite fan demand for a *Friends* reunion, that is unlikely to happen, even in this age of reboots from 1980s and 1990s television (such as *Will & Grace*, *Roseanne*, and *Murphy Brown*). That does not stop fans from speculating about what the show would be like if it were on the air today. Younger fans' criticisms of the show for its representations of sexuality and race (see chapter 7), for example, could be addressed (although in another twenty-five years it would likely need to be updated again). Perhaps changes might incorporate suggestions Netflix made when fans criticized the series for just these reasons, such as episodes focused on Joey having to go to the hospital because he ate Tide Pods; Chandler's inability to stop making Vines; Ed Sheeran cameoing to sing with Phoebe at the coffeehouse; and Ross trying to get everyone to buy bitcoin.[40] Alternatively, changes could reflect Millennial culture and practices, such as Central Perk becoming a juice bar; everyone blocking Rachel on Facebook for posting too many baby photos; Monica and Chandler Photoshopping their engagement picture; Phoebe's "Smelly Cat" video going viral on YouTube; Joey using Tinder to enhance his dating prospects; and Ross getting a flat-pack sofa from IKEA that would allow him not to have to "PIVOT!"[41] These strategies of fan engagement with the series allow them to become a part of the cultural history of the show. While *Friends* was a show that aired on NBC from 1994 to 2004, its characters are still a part of its fans' lives today. Fans engage in production of popular culture related to the series as a way to keep it alive and incorporate it into their changing lives still today.

10

FRIENDS FOREVER

One major reason that *Friends* remains a part of the popular imagination is that it has always been there for us. The show has continued to be shown in syndication since it first qualified for that status in 1998. Additional access to the show via DVDs and streaming services allows anyone with the Internet and a screen to access the series twenty-five years after it first aired. With its premiere on Netflix in the United States in 2015 (and the United Kingdom in 2018), fandom for the show expanded exponentially to include those who watched it the first time around (Baby Boomers and Generation X) and Millennials, many of whom were experiencing it for the first time. The impacts of the availability of the series to new generations is only just starting to be understood, as are the availability of countless "Which Friend Are You?"–like quizzes online. But it is unquestionable that there is an impact. Recently, Netflix changed the tab on the series to indicate that it would only be available through January 1, 2019 (likely so that it could be offered exclusively through Warner Brothers' new streaming service).[1] The news motivated fans to protest online. Within twenty-four hours, Netflix announced that it would not be saying good-bye to our *Friends* for at least another year. Rumors are that they had to pay no less than $100 million for the privilege of continuing to offer the series.[2]

Beyond mere access, the cultural impact of the series also continues today through its appeal to multiple generations. Most fan connections come through multiple viewings of the show, continual consumption of media coverage of the actors and their characters, intertextual references to the show across multiple media (see chapters 2 and 9), and fan productions related to the series (see chapters 8 and 9). Immersive fan experiences have also started to crop up all around the world to bring fans one step closer to being a part of the show. Whether it is a two-week pop-up bar in Chicago where fans can drink show-themed cocktails in replicas of Monica's and Joey's apartments and Central Perk[3] or the annual *Friends* Fest in the United Kingdom, fans can take their connections to the show to the next level. Fans can also now, since 2015, tour a replica of Central Perk on the Warner Brothers Studio lot. They may also visit the coffee shop in China, Australia, and the UK.[4]

As exciting as such experiences may be, fans' access is limited and impacts are short-lived. What has had a lasting and continual influence from the series is the lexicon created in *Friends* that has become part of everyday language and the post-*Friends* media creations from the actors themselves. This chapter focuses on one particularly significant concept coined in the series—the friend zone—as well as phrases the characters said and how they said them that have become part of the cultural landscape since the series began. Beyond the language impacts, the stars of the series offer a unique cultural legacy connected to the show with their more recent projects. Their post-*Friends* work offers a unique intertextual and self-referential view of the (primarily) television landscape that will continue to shape popular culture for decades to come.

THE FRIEND ZONE

In Episode 1.1, "The One where Monica Gets a Roommate," which first aired on November 3, 1994, Rachel Green runs out on her wedding to Dr. Barry Farber (Mitchell Whitfield) because she realizes that she is not in love with him and is merely marrying him to fulfill her family's expectations. By the end of the first episode, we also learn that Ross Geller has had a crush on Rachel since high school. When he asks if she might want to go out with him sometime, she says maybe. This moment sets up what arguably becomes the central love story in the series as one where the man has romantic feelings for the woman who may or may not feel the same way about him.

By Episode 1.7, "The One with the Blackout," Ross has not asked Rachel out yet. He wants to, but so far he has been wallowing in his secret (to her) desire for her. He does, however, give her advice about her love life and the potential for passion in her future. While Ross sees these moments as moving him toward a relationship with Rachel, Joey points out the flaw in his plans: that he has already entered the "friend zone." In this moment, Joey originated the concept of the "friend zone,"[5] which is now defined in the *Oxford English Dictionary* as a platonic relationship where one person wants to be more than just friends, whereas the other does not.[6]

Since it was first uttered, the concept has become popularized and taken on a life of its own. Some applications of the term are firmly rooted in its use on *Friends* in the relationship between Rachel and Ross, but in other instances it has been extended, making it more insidious in practice than the writers on *Friends* likely ever intended. As early as 2002, an Internet forum appeared asking female users if the friend zone was fact or fiction,[7] and by 2003 definitions of the term appeared in the *Urban Dictionary*.[8] It was not until 2008 that use and analysis of the term began to explode, especially online. Advice threads appeared, a web comic critiquing the term was published, memes were created,[9] books were published about escaping the zone,[10] and psychologists began studying perceptions both women and men have of romantic and platonic relationships and how to get out of the zone.[11] Chris Rock focused a stand-up routine on the concept, and MTV even aired the series *Friendzone* for five seasons from 2011 to 2015. A more recent Internet pastime includes listing the "most heartbreaking" friend-zoned characters in popular culture, from the ultimate 1980s friend Duckie Dale's unrequited love for Andie Walsh in *Pretty in Pink* to Professor Severus Snape's declaration of "always" loving unattainable Lily Potter in the *Harry Potter* series and from Jacob Black's unfulfilled desires for Bella Swan in the *Twilight* series to William Miller's unanswered declarations of love for Penny Lane in *Almost Famous*.[12]

Each of these characters' desires for the women they saw as unattainable or who were unavailable to them mimic Ross Geller's behavior toward Rachel when he believed they should be together and she did not see him as anything other than a friend. For example, later in "The One with the Blackout," Rachel meets sexy Italian neighbor Paolo (Cosimo Fusco). When Ross sees Rachel flirting with Paolo, he perceives his chances with her are threatened and he tries to keep them apart. Despite Ross's best efforts to prevent it, Rachel does end up dating Paolo—that is, until he hits on Phoebe. When Ross finds out that Paolo grabbed Phoebe's butt and exposed himself to her, Ross contends that Phoebe must tell Rachel as it is a feminist issue (Episode 1.12, "The One with the Dozen Lasagnas"). This behavior comes to define how Ross reacts when he gets jealous of other men who date or want to date Rachel.

After Ross breaks up with Julie (Lauren Tom) in the second season, but before he and Rachel get together, Ross tries to impede Rachel's chances with Russ by diminishing his professional credentials (Episode 2.10, "The One with Russ") and Casey by hiding his number and then interrupting her flirting with him (Episode 2.14, "The One with the Prom Video"). He uses the same strategy later when Ross and Rachel are living together platonically to co-parent their child. A man calls for her and Ross does not give Rachel the message. When she finds out, she ends up moving out (Episode 9.9, "The One with Rachel's Phone Number"). Ross even goes so far as to not tell Rachel that they are still married (after a drunken night in Vegas) when she expects him to get their marriage annulled. While Ross says it is because he does not want to be the guy who has been divorced three times before he is thirty, Phoebe calls him out for still being in love with Rachel (Episode 6.2, "The One where Ross Hugs Rachel").

Ross's justification for being a good friend to Rachel and for not asking her out too soon was that he was laying the groundwork for a future romantic relationship. This means that he expected a pay-off (romance and sex) from Rachel in return for the work he exerted for her. Unfortunately, this rationalization for his behavior puts Rachel in the position of either acting as he expects her to (by eventually paying him off for his efforts with sex and a relationship) or attempting to continue to be his friend and his being perpetually disappointed that he never got what he thought he deserved for his efforts. What this interpretation reveals is that either way, the relationship must be reciprocal. However, "the term itself has some problematic implications, mostly because it's often used as a talking point for heterosexual men voicing their frustrations with the opposite sex."[13] It is not necessarily because women are friend-zoned less than men, but "because women are conditioned to be less vocal about their sexual desires."[14]

This gendered perspective of the friend zone is reflected in much of the advice given about and popular-culture representations of the concept. Much of the material published about the friend zone focuses on how to escape it. Based on his psychological research, the "Attraction Doctor," Jeremy Nicholson, suggests that the following actions can help you escape the zone: (1) be less interested, (2) make yourself scarce, (3) create some competition, (4) get them to invest, (5) be rewarding,[15] (6) be attractive, (7) find an equal match (in terms of physical attractiveness, education, social status, etc.), (8) be bold and ask, and (9) make them work instead of doing all the work yourself.[16] These nuggets of advice all focus on games one partner can play to try to create the conditions under which the other will "fall" for them, leaving one partner as the actor and the other as acted upon. Additionally, all of this advice also assumes that the goal of relationships (especially between men and women) is *not* friendship. Questioning this basic assumption behind the friend zone would allow for better advice for improving relationships not based on achieving the goal of sex and romance.

The emergence of memes based on the concept demonstrates its problematic gendered representations. As early as 2008, memes began to appear in the Advice Animal image macro series on Reddit. On August 15, 2011, the "Friend Zone Fiona" series began being posted. A year later, more than 2,500 submissions appeared on the page.[17] One sequence of memes suggests that Fiona appreciates a man who makes her smile but not in a romantic way. One says that Fiona "Totally wants you . . . to meet the right girl someday," while another suggests that Fiona "Thinks you're the perfect guy . . . for anyone else."[18] Friend Zoned Phil followed shortly after. These memes were supposed to provide a male version of the friend zone memes. However, their messages still placed the onus on the woman for having "friend zoned" Phil. For example, in one Phil says that she "Asked me if I wanted to go out with her . . . to find an outfit for her date on Friday," and another has Phil "Help her move out of her dick boyfriend's" while "she asks why she can't find a nice guy."[19]

In reference to a particular person or relationship, it might be easier to see the humor in these memes. When used to characterize an entire gender and expectations in relationships between men and women, this concept has been distorted into an unnecessarily harmful one. Some memes have even gone so far as to advocate violence against women who do not respond in the ways the men expect them to, such as when Friend Zoned Phil posted, "Said I love you . . . Ended up burying her in the woods,"[20] or when an image of a woman with a sloth whispering in her ear is accompanied by the words: "She put me in the friend zone. . . . I put her in the rape zone."[21]

Fortunately, resistance to such characterizations are also present in the online world. On July 23, 2012, Redditor ChicagoRunner submitted a post to the /r/Feminism subreddit titled "The Friend Zone," which featured Matrix Morpheus image macros deriding the concept: "What if I told you . . . Friendzoning is bullshit because girls are not machines that you put kindness coins into until sex falls out." Even so, the extended shelf-life of this particular popular-culture trope seems based on its continued cultural relevance as people around the world continue to contend with (especially heteronormative) gendered expectations for relationships. E. J. Dickson contends that the friend zone needs to die as it is lazy and unimaginative, is inherently sexist, implies a lack of agency for women, perpetuates the myth that men and women cannot be friends without sex being a factor, and posits that sex is the ultimate end of any relationship.[22]

While Joey coined the term and Ross embodies it, we cannot put all the blame for the negative uses of the concept on *Friends*. There were times in Rachel and Ross's relationship that Rachel had romantic feelings for Ross but he did not feel the same way. For example, Rachel flew all the way to London to tell Ross she loved him just as he was about to marry Emily (Episode 4.24, "The One with Ross's Wedding: Part 2"). While she did not actually disrupt his impending nuptials, she did end up telling him *after* he was married that she loved him (Episode 5.2, "The One with All the Kissing"). In both of these instances, however, she did not demand a response from him and, in the second example, actually laughed out loud at how ridiculous she was for telling a newly married man that she had feelings for him. In later episodes, when Rachel was pregnant with his child, she admitted that while it was unreasonable, she did not want Ross to date while she was pregnant. Instead she requested that he be at her beck and call and he agreed (Episode 8.21, "The One with the Cooking Class"). It could be argued that her demands and his capitulation embody the spirit of the friend zone. But, in this case, neither of the parties wished to be in a romantic relationship. In this way, it may have been unreasonable, but given the circumstances, Rachel asked for what Ross thought was reasonable given that she was growing their child for them. While their relationship may have begun in the friend zone, and went in and out of it throughout the series, in the end it was their friendship and shared love for their daughter and for one another that brought them together, not the need to trick one or the other into sex and romance.

WHAT THE *FRIENDS* SAID

An Internet search of the most memorable quotes from the show elicits pages of lists. A survey of the top ten most visited sites[23] suggests some agreement about the most memorable quotes we still use today. Although many quotes could be included, the following entries appeared on at least half of the most-visited sites. Here are those words and phrases, why they were so impactful in the show, and how they continue to be used today. While this list is certainly not exhaustive,[24] it should give you a taste of how *Friends* dialogue has impacted popular culture and the ways we still talk today.

"We were on a break!"

Rachel's success at work meant she had less time to spend with boyfriend Ross. Ross, however, feels threatened, not by her work but by her work-mate Mark. Their conflict comes to a head in Episode 3.15, "The One where Ross and Rachel Take a Break," when Rachel suggests they take a break and Ross walks out. Ross, believing that Rachel is with Mark, ends up sleeping with Chloe the copy girl. The next day, after Rachel finds out about Ross and Chloe, Rachel is actually the one who says to Ross that they were on a break (Episode 3.16, "The One with the Morning After"). Interestingly, Rachel and Ross both agree initially that they were on a break. However, Ross uses their break as justification for sleeping with Chloe whereas Rachel claims it is a mere technicality that does not justify Ross cheating on her. Ross uses "We were on a break!" in multiple episodes across the next seven seasons of the show to try to explain why it was that he did not actually cheat (Episode 3.17, "The One without the Ski Trip," Episode 4.1, "The One with the Jellyfish," Episode 6.5, "The One with Joey's Porsche"), including as a joke in the very last episode when he and Rachel finally get back together (Episode 10.18, "The Last One: Part 2").

For viewers, the simple refrain "We were on a break!" can be used whenever discussing someone's unsuccessful relationship, cheating, and especially when two parties in a relationship have different perceptions of that relationship. In a broader context, anyone at any time can take a break. For example, the phrase can be your answer when a friend asks why you ordered pizza or ate ice cream during your cleanse.[25] Still others take Rachel's side. In the movie *How to Be Single* (2016), the character Alice says that she is not single as she and her beau are "just on a break." Her friend Robin replies, "Uh, there's no such thing as a 'break,' season-three-Ross."[26] There was no need to actually say *Friends* as the line has become part of our cultural lexicon.

"How you doin'?"

Even though it became a defining line for Joey, he said it less than twenty times through the run of the series and did not actually utter his famous pick-up line for the first time until Episode 4.13, "The One with Rachel's Crush." He tells Rachel, "What I do is, I look a woman up and down and I say, 'Hey . . . how *you* doin'?'" While neither Rachel nor Phoebe is impressed at first, when Joey looks a very pregnant Phoebe up and down and says the line, she giggles like a schoolgirl. How he says it is just as important as what Joey says. When he is hitting on one of Emily's brides-maids in England, she asks him to speak in his New York accent to her and Joey puts on his best New York Italian accent to utter the line. It's a line that encapsulates everything we know to be true about Joey: he is "a man so confident in his looks and general appeal that he'd rarely pass up an opportunity to approach a beautiful woman."[27] In a later episode, he tries to teach the line to another actor, Karl, who is trying to learn how to be his twin. But Karl gives himself away in (how he looks as well as) how he says the line: "How you *doing*?" rather than "How *you* doin'?"

There is no hidden meaning here. Joey's famous pick-up line functions still today as a pick-up line. When used, the intention may be to ask someone out or let them know you think they are hot. But using the line from *Friends* adds layered meaning to it. If someone just tried to use this line and the recipient of the line did not get the reference, they may just think that some creep is trying to pick them up with a cheesy line. But if the recipient of the line gets the reference, then it comes with the *Friends* connection. The humor and companionship with which Joey says the line comes with it. While the line is typically used in the dating context, it can also be used toward any desirable object, person, or interaction.

"She's your lobster." / "He's her lobster."

Phoebe first tells Ross that he and Rachel belong together by using the metaphor of lobster love in Episode 2.14, "The One with the Prom Video." She claims that it is a known fact that lobsters mate for life and that you can see them at the bottom of the tank holding onto one another's claws. When logical, academic Ross tries to use flighty Phoebe's metaphor to explain to Rachel why they should be together, something is lost in translation. However, when Rachel later sees that Ross was ready to take her to her prom when he thought her prom date had stood her up, she crosses the room and kisses him for the second time. Phoebe responds, "See? He's her lobster."

When you see a couple that seemingly belongs together, one of the best *Friends* compliments you can give them is to say that they are one another's lobsters. Using the phrase properly requires taking the character whose theory it is into account. When Phoebe says it, it means that our lobster is the one who accepts us for all of our quirks and weird habits, someone who loves us that we can love right back. It does not matter if you are overbearing and a neat freak like Monica, a cynical comic like

Rachel and Ross together. *Warner Brothers / Photofest © Warner Brothers*

Chandler, selfish and fashion-obsessed like Rachel, overly analytical like Ross, or comically dim like Joey.[28] We all deserve the love of the person who accepts us for who we are and wants to be with us for life.

"It's a moo point."

Joey says this line to Rachel in Episode 7.8, "The One where Chandler Doesn't Like Dogs," when Rachel asks how long she has to wait before she asks her assistant Tag out. While Monica and Phoebe tell her that she needs to wait longer, Joey says that she only needs to wait a half an hour. However, Joey wisely suggests that if Tag does not like her, then "it's a moo point." While the audience knows that he means "moot," Rachel, who wants to use Joey's timeline for asking Tag out, says that Joey's point makes sense and heads out to find out if Tag likes her too.

While the line could be used anytime to replace the word "moot," it could also be used to end an argument quickly that you realize you cannot win.[29] For example, when you show your significant other your new fashion-forward ensemble and he does not seem to understand it, you can tell him that his opinion is moo.[30] Alternatively, this is a great opportunity to introduce *Friends* to your children and then just say moo to them whenever they say anything that you think is irrelevant. Of course, the danger is then that your kids will say it right back to you.

"Pivot!"

Ross buys a new couch in Episode 5.16, "The One with the Cop." When he sees how exorbitant the delivery charge will be, he decides on the spot not to pay and for him and Rachel to carry the couch to his apartment. When they arrive back at Ross's apartment and have to carry the couch up the stairs, Ross continually shouts the key word, "Pivot!" as he attempts to give Rachel, and then Chandler as well, directions for how to maneuver the couch up the curved staircase. His directions fail miserably and the couch gets stuck, falls off the banister, and ultimately ends up cut in half.

"Pivot!" is a must when you are moving furniture with friends. Their response will indicate whether they are *Friends* fans or not. If they are fans, the laughter that ensues can help you all get through the tough job of moving. If they are not, their response may lead to a twenty-two-minute break to watch the episode before your friend refuses to help you move furniture again! It can also be a helpful driving direction when trying to get out of a tough spot. Although Ross's instructions when trying to move his sports car out of a too-small parking spot may also be helpful here: "Lift and slide" (Episode 7.14, "The One where They All Turn Thirty"). The instruction also works when someone has talked themselves into a corner and cannot seem to get out. A strategically placed "pivot" can help them redirect their point to try another tack.

"JOEY DOESN'T SHARE FOOD."

Beyond his relationships with the friends, Joey is also known for his love of food and sex. There are plenty of opportunities to see just how much Joey loves food, such as when we learn that the "Joey special" is two pizzas (Episode 6.20, "The One with Mac and C.H.E.E.S.E."); that his favorite food is sandwiches, which can be used to placate him when he is upset (Episode 8.10, "The One with Monica's Boots"); or even when he meets his food Everest: a whole Thanksgiving turkey (Episode 8.9, "The One with the Rumor"). When faced with the choice between food and sex, Joey finds it so difficult to choose (Episode 10.10, "The One where Chandler Gets Caught"). However, fans who watched the previous episode see that when actually given the choice between food and a woman, he chose food.

In Episode 10.9, "The One with the Birth Mother," Joey first refuses to go on a second date with a woman, Sarah (Annie Parisse), that Phoebe set him up with because on their first date she ate French fries off his plate. Joey declares that he does not share food. When Phoebe suggests ordering a plate of fries for the table to share, Joey gives her another try. However much Sarah enjoys the "table fries," she still tries to taste Joey's food. Joey then admits to her that he does not share food.

This is the perfect refrain for anyone who does not share food. I subscribe to the Joey Tribianni philosophy of shared food—order what you want and I will order what I want. Unlike Joey, I will share if we make plans to do so while we are ordering. But eat my fries after not ordering your own and you will hear: "JENNIFER DOESN'T SHARE FOOD!" This refrain is also useful for parents whose kids try to eat their food. The results may not be the same as kids sometimes just do not listen or respect boundaries, but it is worth a try if you feel as strongly as Joey about food.

"SEVEN!"

Chandler falls for a woman, Kathy (Paget Brewster), that Joey is dating. After Joey magnanimously steps aside so that she and Chandler can be together, they should be thrilled, right? Wrong! In Episode 4.11, "The One with Phoebe's Uterus," Chandler admits that he is intimidated to have sex with Kathy because she had been with Joey before. Then they have sex and it is less than spectacular. Chandler admits to Monica and Rachel that he feels he cannot do what he needs to live up to what she is used to with Joey. Monica tells Chandler what most guys do not know: that there are seven erogenous zones he should attend to. She then draws a picture of a woman, marking the erogenous zones, and takes him through a hilarious "how to" please a woman that ends with repeated visits to "SEVEN!" Chandler takes Monica's advice. After having sex with Chandler, Kathy enthusiastically thanks Monica for that advice.

Just saying "SEVEN!" is a terrific strategy to tell any *Friends* fan about your sex life without being too explicit. But you would have to share an understanding about what each number refers to. When asked on Yahoo! Answers what the seven erogenous zones were, answers included "Wallet – Credit Cards – Cash – Nice House – Fancy Clothes – Foreign Vacations," "eye's ears nose throat back of neck inside thighs ankles," and "1) Penis 2) Penis 3) Penis 4) Penis 5) Penis 6) Penis 7) Penis What? Guys can have erogenous zones too!"[31] Such answers merely confuse the issue, making the reference unusable (and probably belie men's limited understandings of women's bodies). The most common list of the seven erogenous zones Monica labels is: (1) ears (2) lips (3) neck (4) breasts (5) butt (6) inner thighs, and (7) vagina.[32] Although we can give them some leeway (it is the Internet after all), it is notable that the clitoris is not listed at all. While we might assume that the vagina encapsulates all of "that area," it still suggests a limited understanding of the female body. I guess we have to admit that women have different tastes in sex and perhaps "SEVEN!" merely refers to whatever body part and interaction gets you there!

HOW THE *FRIENDS* SAID IT

Friends' impact on popular culture and communication comes not just from *what* the characters said but for *how* they said it. In this way, language used in media both reflects language of the time but also paves the way for innovation in the *ways* that people say what they say.[33] As noted in the previous section, "How *you* doin'?" just would not have the same impact without Joey's emphasis on the *you* and the nod of the head that accompanied the line. There were certainly words, phrases, and delivery that impacted popular culture at the time the show aired, but that are not used frequently today. Others, such as Chandler's unique emphasis and Ross's overarticulation, became defining features of their characters throughout the series that trickled into our communication even today. Other *Friends* also had particular lines that they delivered in specific ways that have fans continuing to mimic them as well. The following exemplars demonstrate some of the impacts methods of delivery have had on our communication today.

"Could I *be* wearing any more clothes?"

Chandler has a particular way of emphasizing certain words in his sentences that is unique to his character. In the pilot episode of the show, Chandler says, "She should *not* be wearing those pants" about a character in the Spanish-language telenovela they are watching. So begins ten years of overarticulation of particular words in sentences that marked Chandler's character and humor. His delivery became so much a part of his character and popular culture that even the series started to poke fun at it as early as the end of the first season. In Episode 1.22, "The One with the Ick Factor," Phoebe pokes fun when she asks if a report could "*be* any later." While Chandler objects, he does so by saying, "That is so *not* true," and cannot stop saying the line the same way. When he finds out that his former workmates, now subordinates, do not like him and overhears them making fun of him, he finally owns this feature of his delivery when he tells them they need to get their work done "*by* nine o'clock." Although they laugh as they walk away, Chandler tells Phoebe that he did it on purpose to give them something to criticize him for. By the time the third season highlight, Episode 3.2, "The One where No One's Ready," airs, it is no surprise when Joey walks into Monica's apartment wearing all of Chandler's clothes and says, "Could I *be* wearing any more clothes?" While this latter line could be useful "when the weather dips below 20, but you can't cancel your plans,"[34] Joey's emphasis on "be" highlights the *way* Chandler talks that has become part of communication around the world.

"OH. MY. GOD!"

The one line not delivered by one of the central cast to make this list is from Chandler's on-again-off-again girlfriend Janice (Litman-Goralnik neé Hosenstein). Interestingly, Janice's first line in her first appearance on the series in Episode 1.5, "The One with the East German Laundry Detergent," is "Oh my god" as she complains about how bad her day was, just before Chandler is about to break up with her. But the line is delivered with so little emphasis that it is unremarkable. Her signature staccato laugh, "ha ha ha ha" in her nasally Janice voice, comes a few minutes later. Maggie Wheeler explains that Janice's voice and laugh were her choices as an actress and that the laugh came out during rehearsal when Perry drank his espresso like a shot and immediately asked her if she wanted another drink before she took her first sip.[35] Janice appears next when Chandler invites her to the New Year's Eve party that none of the friends is supposed to bring dates to. When he breaks up with her *again*, in the middle of the party, she again reacts with some staccato "Oh. No."s and a nonchalant "Oh my god." While her staccato delivery of "Oh. No." suggests what is to come, the "Oh my god," once again, almost goes unnoticed.

Despite having said these words in both of her first two appearances on the series, it is not until her third appearance in Episode 1.14, "The One with the Candy Hearts," that her signature delivery occurs. Joey fixes Chandler up on a double date. The woman Joey is seeing brings a friend for Chandler. They learn that the friend's name is Janice just before Wheeler's character enters to learn that she has been set up with Chandler. Upon her entrance, she stops dead in her tracks and says, "OH. MY. GOD." in her unique way for the first time. Wheeler says that when she went in to audition for the first time, at the top of the script, it said, "fast talking New Yorker." Wheeler said, "I saw the language, and I just thought yeah, I know that girl. So I made the choice and it turned out to be the right one."[36] While few remember the first two times she subtly said the line, once she said it the way we have come to remember, it became her signature and fans continue to yell it to her on the street and over social media.

"I'm *fine*."

Ross is known for overarticulating everything he says. But it is his delivery of the line, "I'm fine," in all its incarnations that demonstrates his overarticulation, changes in pitch, and the accompanying physical comedy that make this line and its delivery continue to be remembered today. Episode 10.2, "The One where Ross Is Fine" begins where the previous episode left off: with Ross walking into Joey's apartment to see Rachel and Joey kissing. When he gets over his initial shock, he insists, "I'm *fine*." As he repeats it over and over again, his voice continues to get louder and squeakier, until he attempts to modulate the key in which he is speaking by saying it in a deeper voice. In an attempt to prove how fine he is with their being together, he ends up inviting Rachel and Joey over for a double dinner date with him and Charlie (who Joey was dating up until the previous episode). When Charlie, Joey, and Rachel arrive for dinner at his apartment, the evidence that he is *not*, in fact, fine takes the form of making (and drinking) multiple pitchers of margaritas, insisting that there is no weirdness, suggesting they all take a trip together, overzealously answering each kitchen timer when it dings, carrying the sizzling fajita pan out to the living room without oven mitts, making toasts to love, and continuing to insist that he is *fine*.

Ross's phrase can be used by anyone at any time they are uncomfortable, such as when someone tells you a secret you never wanted to know or when you are the only single person at a wedding.[37] Although if someone were feeling more annoyed about the situation, they might use Ross's response to Rachel when she tells him, "We are *so* over!" Ross replies, "FINE BY ME!" (Episode 4.1, "The One with the Jellyfish"). This earlier variation on his use of "fine" can be helpful when the situation warrants more overt anger. But the line must have Ross's emphasis (and possibly even the squeaky pitch) to have significant impact.

"I KNOW!"

The running gag in Episode 5.14, "The One when Everybody Finds Out," is the continuing extension of the line, "They don't know that we know they know." While this line certainly made its mark in this episode, the use of the shorter, more concise "I know" by Monica Geller across all ten seasons made it a phrase that could be used in almost any context depending on the delivery. The most common usage of the phrase emerged whenever Monica was angry and trying to make a point. The first utterance occurred when Phoebe mistakenly cuts Monica's hair to look like actor Dudley Moore's instead of Demi Moore's. When Phoebe notes how cute Demi's hair is, Monica screams, "I KNOW!" (Episode 2.1, "The One with Ross's New Girlfriend"). When Monica is upset, she does not always shout the line though. When Joey wonders why she's been in the airplane bathroom for "like a half an hour," he does not know that she was waiting for Chandler. Her response to Joey, while looking at Chandler, is saying the line through clenched teeth (Episode 5.1, "The One after Ross Says Rachel"). Leave it to Courteney Cox to have a whole range of using what could be argued to be Monica's signature line. Monica says those two little words when she is upset (Episode 6.2, "The One where Ross Hugs Rachel"); in response to compliments (Episodes 3.20, "The One with the Dollhouse"; 4.20, "The One with the Wedding Dresses"; 6.18, "The One where Ross Dates a Student"; and 7.24, "The One with Monica and Chandler's Wedding: Part 2"); and even when she is excited (Episodes 3.16, "The One with the Morning After"; 5.9, "The One with Ross's Sandwich"; 6.16, "The One That Could Have Been: Part 2"; and 9.11, "The One where Rachel Goes Back to Work").

If you are wondering if Monica yells a lot, she does. But she also has a sweeter version of her acclamation. When Chandler points out that she is naked in a picture she gives him (Episode 5.9, "The One with Ross's Sandwich"), when Rachel compliments her new boots (Episode 8.10, "The One with Monica's Boots"), or when Joey tells Monica and Chandler how cute they are when they are doing a crossword puzzle together (Episode 5.16, "The One with the Cop"), Monica responds with her frequent refrain. But when she says it in these cases, it is with a smile, a raise of the shoulder, and/or sweetness in her eyes. The point is: regardless of the situation, Monica's response is most often "I know!" and Courteney Cox knows just how to deliver the line so that it is right for the situation.

"Oh, no."

Phoebe is known for going to extremes at times, such as when she first sees Monica and Chandler having sex though the window of Ugly Naked Guy's apartment and screams (Episode 5.14, "The One where Everybody Finds Out"), or when she suggests she and Joey escape to Mexico when their plan to get Rachel and Ross back together by setting them up on bad dates is revealed (9.14, "The One with the Bad Dates"). However, it is her use of the much more subtle "Oh, no" and the way she delivers it that made its impact on how we see Phoebe. In line with her "out there" character, there are times when she uses it that seem incongruous with the situation. For example, in a flashback to a previous life, she serves as an infantry nurse during World War I and ends up having her arm blown off and blood gushing from her wound. Instead of yelling and screaming, she merely pauses in her work and laments, "Oh, no" (Episode 5.8, "The One with All the Thanksgivings"); or the first morning she wakes up with Gary the cop (Michael Rapaport) after they move in together and he reacts to a singing bird by shooting it, Phoebe's response is a quiet one (Episode 5.21, "The One with the Ball") just as when she sees the end of the movie *Old Yeller* for the first time. As her mother always turned off the TV before the conclusion, she never knew (spoiler alert!) that Travis had to shoot the dog because he had rabies. The humor is not just from those two little words, but from Phoebe's lackadaisical delivery of those two little words in such extreme situations.

Even so, Phoebe uses the familiar refrain, and her delivery of it, to communicate different messages depending on the context. At times, it comes when something bad happens that she usually caused. When she gets caught doing something wrong, her subtle delivery of those two words tends to land the joke most effectively, such as when Monica realizes that she is secretly moving out (Episode 3.6, "The One with the Flashback"); when she lets slip to Chandler that Monica saw her ex Richard (Episode 5.23, "The One in Vegas, Part 1"); when she realizes her cab is out of gas (Episode 3.17, "The One without the Ski Trip"); and when she calls out Tag as father of Rachel's baby but realizes he is not the father (Episode 8.2, "The One with the Red Sweater"). With two words Phoebe effectively communicates the sentiment "Sorry, not sorry" as she is sorry she got caught but not sorry she did it in the first place.

POST-*FRIENDS* META-SPIN-OFFS AND MEDIA CRITIQUES

Beyond the language and delivery *Friends* contributed to our contemporary lexicon, the actors have continued to contribute to television culture through their careers beyond the series. NBC, Warner Bros., and the show's creators worked around the cast members' other projects whenever possible when the show was still in production. Their flexibility allowed the cast to work on other projects while filming *Friends* and was a significant factor in keeping all of the original cast together for the duration of their decade-long show. All of the actors, with the exception of LeBlanc, found success in films while the series was still on the air. Lisa Kudrow entertained indie audiences with *Romy and Michele's High School Reunion* (1997) and *The Opposite of Sex* (1998) and held her own with Billy Crystal and Robert DeNiro in *Analyze This* (1999) and its sequel *Analyze That* (2002). Similarly, Jennifer Aniston impressed critics in smaller, independent films like *She's the One* (1996), *Picture Perfect* (1997), *The Object of My Affection* (1998), and *The Good Girl* (2002) and played a supporting role in Jim Carrey's blockbuster *Bruce Almighty* (2003). Courteney Cox found success (and a husband—David Arquette) with the *Scream* franchise, filming four movies between 1996 and 2011. Matthew Perry also saw a string of hit movies with *Fools Rush In* (1997), *The Whole Nine Yards* (2000), and *The Whole Ten Yards* (2004) and still found time to guest star in a few episodes of *The West Wing* (2003). While David Schwimmer dabbled a bit in film while new episodes of *Friends* were still on the air, playing Anne Heche's fiancé in *Six Days Seven Nights* (1998), he made a bigger splash in the award-winning miniseries *Band of Brothers* (2001). Unfortunately, Schwimmer's performance as the morose Tom Thompson in *The Pallbearer* (1996) earned him a nomination for the Golden Raspberry Award (or Razzie) for Worst New Star rather than the critical acclaim he had hoped for. Likewise, LeBlanc's movie career was not very successful either. Neither *Ed* (1996) nor the *Lost in Space* (1998) remake wowed critics or audiences. Even so, he was still the one actor to score a spin-off from *Friends*.

In her post-*Friends* work, Jennifer Aniston's success first seemed to exploit Rachel's romantic foibles to create a star persona that appealed to fans.[38] Movies such as *Rumor Has It* (2005), *The Break-Up* (2006), and *He's Just Not That into You* (2009) lament Aniston's girl-next-door characters' difficulties in finding love and commitment with her male partners, much as Rachel spent ten years doing on *Friends*. These storylines also tap into the media coverage of Aniston's off-screen love life (see more on this topic in chapter 2) with varying degrees of success. However, the roles she has taken that contrast with her *Friends* persona have also helped her distance her film self from her television character, even as they rely on the incongruence between Rachel and these roles to do so. Roles like Dr. Julia Harris in *Horrible Bosses* (2011) and *Horrible Bosses 2* (2014), Rose O'Reilly in *We're the Millers* (2013), and Claire Bennett in *Cake* (2014) allowed audiences to laugh (and cry) at how much her characters were unlike Rachel. Since Dr. Julia Harris was a dentist, it is difficult not to compare her character with Rachel's ex-fiancé, Dr. Barry Farber, D.D.S. (Mitchell Whitfield). In Episode 1.20, "The One with the Evil Orthodontist," Rachel visits Barry to return the engagement ring and finds that he has gotten hair plugs and went on their honeymoon to Aruba with her best friend/maid of honor, Mindy. Instead of running for the hills, Rachel finds him irresistible and ends up having sex with him in the dental chair. Fast-forward sixteen years to Dr. Julia Harris sexually harassing her assistant Dale (Charlie Day) and his fiancée (Lindsay Stone). Julia's filthy language, nudity in the office, and attempts at blackmailing Dale with photos of her taking advantage of him while under anesthesia in the dentist's chair take Rachel's sex with Barry in the chair to a new level that Rachel would never have engaged in, even as *Friends* fans may compare the two situations. Add to this portrayal her role as a stripper-turned-would-be-drug-trafficker in *We're the Millers*, and seeing Aniston's character perform a striptease, and you have the perfect recipe for casting against type in order to heighten the humor in these films. *Cake* represents a different type of role for Aniston. As Claire Bennett, she has to deal with living in chronic pain, addiction, and the suicide of a friend. Bennett has to decide whether to fight to live a meaningful life or to escape her pain by ending her life. The film capitalizes on its cast's ability to invoke humor in the face of tragedy (William H. Macy and Felicity Huffman, in particular), while still allowing the audience to understand and feel Bennett's pain in her every move. While Aniston had some opportunities to show dramatic range with Rachel (see Episode 3.16, "The One with the Morning After"), roles such as Claire in *Cake* give her the opportunity to distance herself from Rachel.

What is particularly interesting about the *Friends* actors' post-*Friends* work is how its impact on contemporary popular culture depends largely on how it built upon and/or critiqued the celebrity they developed in the show. The actors experienced the vortex of celebrity culture surrounding the series, their characters, and their personal lives (see chapter 2) and the popular-culture capital available to fans together (see chapter 8). "Their subsequent work shows them semi-autobiographically reflecting on the experience. Together (though apart), they've produced . . . some of the most interesting philosophizing on (and reckoning with) the intersection of reality, gossip, television, and celebrity on the small screen."[39] While this is true of their film as well as their television work, their television series often seemed like a new kind of spin-off. While LeBlanc's actual spin-off, *Joey*, lasted only two seasons and took place in the same universe as *Friends*, the other series acted like spin-offs but were "orthogonal to the source text."[40] That is, they could be considered "meta-spin-offs," or series that are not actual spin-offs of the original (like *Joey* was to *Friends*), but projects with the same actors as the original that have characters, actions, settings, and so on that are close enough to the original that they invite viewers to make connections between the original and the new. In suggesting such connections, meta-spin-offs end up blending audiences' knowledge of actors in their real lives with their celebrity status, their characters, and shows they are on.[41] While Aniston's post-*Friends* work certainly evoked intertextual and self-referential connections to the series, the other actors' work demonstrates this concept of the meta-spin-off.

LeBlanc's film career did not amount to much while the show was filming. But the fact that Joey begged for a part in *Outbreak 2: The Virus Takes Manhattan* alongside Ross's former pet, the monkey Marcel, in Episode 2.13, "The One after the Superbowl: Part 2," was prescient as "LeBlanc broke into movies *alongside* a monkey (in *Ed*), a career choice that further connects him to his *Friends* character, and suggests he is more suited to television work."[42] His nomination for a Razzie for Worst Screen Couple in 1997 alongside the monkey merely punctuated this point. However, the actual *Friends* television spin-off, *Joey*, failed after two critically maligned seasons even though it took over the *Friends* time slot on Thursday nights. In the pilot episode of *Joey*, Joey chooses to star in a violent cop cable show instead of a network show called *Nurses*. His show fails, but *Nurses* succeeds. "Here *Joey* suggests that Joey could be a much more successful, popular actor if he had done the mass market program, at once valorizing LeBlanc's decision to participate in the spin-off while predicting his move to the more prestigious *Episodes*."[43]

Episodes (2011–2017), created by *Friends*' co-creator David Crane and his life partner, Jeffrey Klarik, focuses on a romantically involved British screenwriting couple who are brought to Hollywood to recreate their hit show that takes place at an English boarding school. In true Hollywood fashion, the network forces them to hire Matt LeBlanc to play the "erudite, dexterous headmaster of an elite boys' academy."[44] The lack of believability of "Joey" playing this headmaster leads to tension between the network, writers, and star. The incongruent pairing of two seemingly uptight British writers, Sean and Beverly (Tamsin Greig and Stephen Mangan), in Hollywood with a swearing, philandering, self-involved version of Matt LeBlanc (playing Matt LeBlanc!) was the basis for the humor of the series. The real genius of *Episodes* though was how it functioned as a meta-spin-off. The "Matt LeBlanc" character shared characteristics from the actor's real life, such as having money from having starred on *Friends*, having been married and divorced, having

Episodes' **Matt LeBlanc, Tamsin Greig, and Stephen Mangan.** *Showtime / Photofest* © *Showtime*

children, and a penchant for sports cars. Using these "facts" as a basis for the character capitalized on comparisons between Joey and the "real" Matt LeBlanc.

These similarities also suggested to the audience that the other characteristics of "Matt LeBlanc" on *Episodes* might also be true, including his womanizing (like Joey) and being a spoiled, self-centered asshole (unlike Joey). "*Episodes* self-consciously collapses Matt and Joey, and suggests that Matt uses Joey strategically in his career and in his personal life."[45] "Matt LeBlanc" on *Episodes* is divorced; sleeps with his stalker, his costars, and the wives of his writers and studio executives;[46] and is fired from a game show (which he only hosts for the money) after having a sexual encounter with one of the contestants on the set. In Episode 1.4 of *Episodes*, Matt tells Sean that he will just "throw the judge a couple of 'How you doin's'" to gain favor in his custody hearing. By starring in a show on cable, LeBlanc is able to appeal to a niche audience with a heightened, more obnoxious version of himself. His love for fast cars, a small part of *Friends* and a larger part of *Episodes*, also led to LeBlanc's guest hosting (and later hosting the British version of) car enthusiasts show *Top Gear*. While he never won an individual award for playing Joey, he won the Golden Globe in 2011 for playing "Matt LeBlanc." Now LeBlanc stars in the family comedy *Man with a Plan* (2016–present). While the show does not really break any new comedic ground, it could be considered the antidote to or anti-*Episodes*, as it returns LeBlanc to a lovable and somewhat dim character, while also adding the new characteristic of his being a committed husband and father, which provides its audience with a dose of "Joey-with-a-family" every week. While there are outliers, LeBlanc has had a harder time leaving his iconic character behind than Aniston did, but he has found great success playing hybrid versions of himself and Joey on television.[47]

Kudrow continued the trajectory she started while on *Friends* by taking smaller roles in larger films, including *P.S. I Love You* (2007) and *Easy A* (2010). She always garnered critical praise in these smaller roles and did not risk having the success or failure of a film placed on her shoulders. Since she seemed to have just as hard a time as LeBlanc in leaving Phoebe behind, she not only capitalized on her *Friends* character by playing characters related in some way, but actually created hybrid versions of herself and Phoebe.[48] She took significant risks with her post-*Friends* forays into cable television and early Internet streaming content by producing, creating, and playing Valerie Cherish on *The Comeback* (2005, 2014) and Fiona Wallace on *Web Therapy* (2008–2014). Kudrow starred in HBO's *The Comeback* less than a year after the end of the *Friends*. On it she starred as Valerie Cherish, a fading sitcom star, and the comedy was shot as a faux-reality series. Her character's name refers to Episode 10.14, "The One with Princess Consuela," where Phoebe changes her name to Princess Consuela Banana Hammock but reassures Monica that she is going to have her friends call her Valerie, "creating an intertextual link between the two shows."[49] Further, actress Cherish became famous from starring in a *Friends*-like hit sitcom, *I'm It*. *The Comeback* represents what Cherish has been "reduced to" since that sitcom ended: reality television. Cherish plays "herself" in this reality show as well as a wacky character like Phoebe, in a clear *Friends* spin-off called *Room and Board*, where she is set up as a foil to the hotter, younger leads in the show and is criticized for her crazy behavior at her age (in her forties).[50]

While the first premiere and episodes of HBO's *The Comeback* did not fare well with audiences, critics loved it and Kudrow earned Emmy nominations. Critics saw the genius of Lisa Kudrow, just a year after *Friends* ended, playing a washed-up sitcom star trying to find an audience in a "reality" series. Unfortunately, audiences may still have seen her as Phoebe and found the washed-up part difficult to understand. It only lasted one season. This is the danger of the meta-spin-off: the parts cannot be too close to the actor or character's public life. If they are too close and the storyline is not consistent with the actor or character it is built upon, it may not resonate with audiences. However, with the explosion of reality TV in more recent years and ten years passing after the conclusion of *Friends*, *The Comeback* came back in 2014 with more new episodes. *The Comeback* can now be seen as it was intended: as a comment on the challenges sitcom actors face when their hit shows end. In contrast to LeBlanc's turn in *Episodes*, where he still benefits from his role as Joey when it comes to series he is offered and relationships off-screen, *The Comeback* focuses in particular on challenges Valerie faces as a female star. She *has to* turn to reality TV and accept the role of the older, advice-giving foil against the younger stars of her new sitcom *because* she has no money and cannot get starring roles anymore.

Between incarnations of *The Comeback*, Kudrow teamed up with Dan Bucatinsky (who played an annoyed waiter in Episode 9.5, "The One with Phoebe's Birthday Dinner") to create *Web Therapy*. The premise of this initially Internet-only series had Fiona Wallace offering clients three-minute therapy sessions online in order to avoid having to hear them ramble on about their dreams and feelings. After four seasons online (2008–2011), Showtime expanded the premise and made it into a pay-cable sitcom, where it ran for another four seasons (2011–2014). On Showtime, Fiona turned to web therapy after quitting her job in finance for dubious reasons (somewhat like the alternate-reality version where Phoebe, who works for Merrill Lynch, is fired after losing $13 million in Episodes 6.15 and 6.16, "The One That Could Have Been: Parts 1 and 2"). Instead of turning to singing and songwriting as a career, as Phoebe does, Fiona decides to become an online therapist, who still offers clients efficient three-minute sessions. The format of the series allowed Kudrow to capitalize on her Hollywood contacts for guest "clients." Her *Friends* costars Courteney Cox, Matt LeBlanc, Matthew Perry, and David Schwimmer all made appearances on the series as well as Bob Balaban (who played Phoebe's birth father), Dan Bucatinsky, and fellow Must-See-TVer, Julia Louis-Dreyfus. Kudrow created, starred in, and produced these series. She also developed and serves as producer on the ongoing *Who Do You Think You Are?* (2010–present).

Courteney Cox turned her attention to developing, producing, and starring in her own series as well. Her first post-*Friends* series, *Dirt* (2007–2008), garnered mixed reviews. Some found the dark themes, sexually explicit material, and morally ambiguous content exciting while others did not enjoy Cox in her role as an ethically bankrupt tabloid editor. This series, which premiered the same year as *Keeping Up with the Kardashians*, allowed Cox to talk back to the paparazzi and celebrity culture that plagued the *Friends* actors, "effectively reclaiming the narrative from the forces that hounded her and her pal Aniston. By the end of the first season her character ends up bleeding and stabbed by a star who's been blackmailed and pushed too far."[51] Having Aniston guest as a rival magazine editor, who happens to be a lesbian who kisses Cox's character good-bye on the lips (Episode 1.13, "Ita Missa Est"), further situates *Dirt* as a comment on *Friends*, where Rachel and Monica only said they kissed, but whose kiss did not appear on-screen (Episode 4.19, "The One with All the Haste"). The stabbing at the end of the first season also sent a clear message: that the other morally questionable folks in the paparazzi machine deserved what they get.

But many *Friends* fans rejoiced when she produced and starred in *Cougar Town* (2009–2015), as it played like a spin-off: *Friends*-in-a-cul-de-sac-in-Florida. Cox directed many episodes of the show and played Jules Cobb, a woman in her forties who shared custody of her teenage son, Travis (Dan Byrd), with her ex-husband, Bobby (Brian Van Holt). She lived next door to her best friend, Ellie (Christa Miller); her husband, Andy (Ian Gomez); and their infant son, Stan (Sawyer Ever). Along with Jules's other neighbor Greyson (Josh Hopkins) and work assistant, Laurie (Busy Phillips), Cox had a new group of friends who hung out at each other's houses in their cul-de-sac drinking wine out of giant glasses and playing penny can. The first three seasons aired on ABC. Instead of canceling the show after low ratings, they instead sold it to TBS where it aired for another three seasons. Some called it a grown-up *Friends* while others appreciated that these friends were not too grown up to have fun just hanging out. Having Jennifer Aniston guest star as a crystal-wearing, Buddha-worshipping, flower-child-like therapist to Cox's character at once evoked images of what a Rachel/Phoebe offspring might be like as an adult and allowed fans to enjoy seeing Monica/Jules and Rachel/Glenn on-screen together again. She and ex-husband David Arquette also produced the short-lived *Celebrity Name Game* (2014–2017) by turning their home game nights into a Craig Ferguson–hosted game show.

LeBlanc's, Kudrow's, and I would add Cox's continued relevance on television in general and sitcoms specifically demonstrates how the memorability and recognizability of their characters did not kill their careers. Rather, they were able to "capitalize on their own television histories to produce critically acclaimed programs that keep their past and present images in circulation."[52] At the same time, it is important to recognize the limitations that starring on *Friends* for a decade had on the careers of its cast. As noted, Cox's biggest acting success post-*Friends* was a show touted as a grown-up *Friends*.

David Schwimmer and Matthew Perry have also experienced some difficulties with roles in front of the camera. Schwimmer was deeply hurt by the reception of his first big movie, *The Pallbearer*, which costarred then rising star Gwyneth Paltrow. Some blamed it on the film itself, while others believed that Schwimmer's stardom as Ross interfered with audiences' ability to see him as anyone else. As writer/producer/director Kevin S. Bright contends, "It was David Schwimmer in *The Pallbearer*, not Ross in *The Pallbearer*. That's really unfair and hard for an actor."[53]

However, Schwimmer began directing while he was still on the series. He is credited as director on ten episodes, including hilarious episodes such as "The One on the Last Night" (Episode 6.6), "The One with the Truth about London" (Episode 7.16), and "The One with Phoebe's Birthday Dinner" (Episode 9.5). He also continued to be a part of the Lookingglass Theatre Company, which he cofounded in 1988 and for which he still acts, produces, and directs today.

Most recently, Schwimmer received praise for starring as Robert Kardashian in the Emmy Award–winning miniseries *American Crime Story: The People vs. O.J. Simpson* (2016) and has guest starred on the reboot of *Will & Grace* (2018–present). As Lily Loofbourow suggests in "The End of the *Friends* Era of Gossip, Fame, and Meta-Spinoffs," Schwimmer's role as Kardashian brings him full circle as he plays "Kardashian as [O. J.] Simpson's hapless but earnest cheerleader whose initial authentic gestures of support—like reading Simpson's bizarre farewell note to the news cameras during the Bronco chase—collapse into a frozen *performance* of friendship (or Friendship) he's unable to escape."[54] Beyond performing friendship to a man he later believes killed Nicole Brown Simpson and Ronald Goldman, Schwimmer portrays the patriarch of the Kardashian family before they ever dreamed of becoming the first family of reality TV (Robert Kardashian died four years before *Keeping Up with the Kardashians* premiered). His character's advice to his children about how being "pure of heart" is more important than fame is consistent with Schwimmer's feelings about fame and celebrity culture.[55]

Schwimmer's feelings about life in front of the cameras has led to his increasingly working behind the cameras in production and directing. Even so, his guest role as Noah, a grumpy and grungy Internet reviewer, in a few episodes of the *Will & Grace* reboot is a plausible forty-something version of Ross Geller.[56] Both Noah and Ross have a repressed rage that motivates their actions. Where Ross had to repress his rage, Noah's job allows him to use his rage to entertain his followers. Even so, Ross's rage came out at inconvenient times, such as when Rachel continues not to be ready to go to his work engagement (Episode 3.2, "The One where No One's Ready"), when his boss eats his sandwich at work (Episode 5.9, "The One with Ross's Sandwich"), and when he tries to get his job at the museum back but sees Chandler making out with his sister (Episode 5.14, "The One where Nobody's Ready"). Interestingly, Noah's ability to speak back to a public that irritates him gives Schwimmer the same opportunity as Cox had with *Dirt*: to speak back to celebrity culture. Without such an outlet, it is no wonder that Ross's anger burst out at times.

Despite Matthew Perry's film successes while *Friends* was still on the air, he has also faced similar challenges since the show ended. Since *Friends* he has starred in four since-canceled series, including *Studio 60 on the Sunset Strip* (2006–2007), *Mr. Sunshine* (2011), *Go On* (2012–2013), and *The Odd Couple* (2015–2017). As a *Friends* fan, I have watched each of these shows and have a hard time understanding why none stayed on the air. Perry starred with Bradley Whitford (hot off of *The West Wing*), Amanda Peet (with whom Perry starred in *The Whole Nine Yards*), and pre-*American Horror Story* and *American Crime Story: The People vs. O.J. Simpson* Sarah Paulson in the Aaron Sorkin–created *Studio 60*. The cast, creator, and premise—a dramedy set behind the scenes of a *Saturday Night Live*–like sketch comedy show—seemed destined for success. However, audiences did not seem ready for dramedies just yet, nor for a non-Chandler, more serious Perry.

In his subsequent sitcoms, he played Chandler-like characters, including the manager of a second-rate events arena in *Mr. Sunshine* (2011) and as a sportscaster who joins a support group to try to deal with the death of his wife in *Go On* (2012–2013). Both characters had Chandler/Matthew's dry wit, often motivated by self-loathing, and inability to initiate or commit to relationships. Fortunately, he had better luck as Oscar Madison with Thomas Lennon's Felix Unger (who Perry also starred with in *17 Again*) in the reboot of *The Odd Couple* (2015–2017) as it lasted two seasons. But the chemistry and comic timing seemed lacking. Perry does not stop working or trying to find the right character and project though. Most recently he produced and starred as Ted Kennedy in the television mini-series *The Kennedys: Decline and Fall* (2017). We can only hope that he finds the right project at the right time as we all know how talented he is. He does seem to be having a harder time than most of the cast finding just the right project in his post-*Friends* career.

CONCLUSION

The language used and created in the series has had a significant impact on our culture by influencing what *Friends* fans (and non-fans alike) say, and even how we say it, today—from new ways to conceive of mixed romantic/platonic relationships like the "friend zone" and methods to hit on someone like Joey's famous "How *you* doin'?" to instructions for unsuccessfully carrying a couch up a flight of stairs ("Pivot!") and reactions for getting caught knowing something you are not supposed to know ("Oh, no."). Beyond the words we use and how we say them, the *Friends* actors also continue to influence popular culture with their post-*Friends* projects. Rather than continuing our relationship with the series through merely re-watching it or its sequel, *Joey*, we can instead engage with media creations like meta-spin-offs that extend the *Friends* world into one where Courteney/Monica now lives in a cul-de-sac with an older group of friends and where Matt LeBlanc, who once played kind, caring, womanizing Joey, now plays a swearing, philandering, self-absorbed actor, "Matt LeBlanc." While the language impacts may fade over time, the ones noted in this chapter still hold sway twenty-five years after the series ended. The media creations the series actors continue to create will only stop once they retire or stop making series and films that capitalize upon, extend, and critique the world they created in *Friends*.

APPENDIX

The One with the Twenty-Five Best Episodes

Friends aired a total of 236 episodes. What follows is my list of the twenty-five best episodes. Why twenty-five? Because it is constitutes just over 10 percent of the total number of episodes. What make them the "best"? I started with my own list and then consulted others' lists of their favorites.[1] The episodes that made the list that follows were ones that (1) appeared on at least two of these lists and (2) were funny, smart, and entertaining from start to finish. There are other more significant and/or funny moments not included on this list as they were not deemed quality from start to finish. The episodes appear in chronological order according to their air dates. Feel free to rank them yourself, though I did note my absolute favorite moment too!

Episode 1.7: "The One with the Blackout" (November 3, 1994)

When the power goes out, Chandler ends up trapped in an ATM vestibule with Jill Goodacre (playing herself) trying to figure out how to talk to her. His voice-over reveals his discomfort and self-criticism until he accepts the offer of gum from Jill by saying it would be "perfection." As his voice-over critiques his choice of the word, he chokes on the gum only to have Jill save him. While trapped in the apartment building, the other five friends sit by candlelight discussing the strangest places they have had sex. Meanwhile, Ross tries to hit on Rachel, when Joey points out that it's never going to happen because he waited too long and is now in the "friend zone" (more on the friend zone in chapter 10). While Joey encourages Ross to take advantage of the moonlight and candles to woo Rachel, when he goes out onto the balcony to do so, he gets attacked by a cat. The appearance of the lost cat leads the cast to search the building for its owner. Rachel and Phoebe find the cat's owner: a hot Italian man named Paolo (Cosimo Fusco). Ross's attempts to woo Rachel are then thwarted when Paolo and Rachel kiss.

Why This Episode Is in the Top 25

When (nearly) the whole cast is stuck in the apartment, magic happens: the reveal of personal information, intensification of Ross's desire for Rachel even as she kisses Paolo for the first time, a song from Phoebe, and even some physical comedy (when Ross gets attacked by a cat). Chandler's awkward attempts to interact with a supermodel add the cherry on top of the cake.

Episode 1.18: "The One with All the Poker" (March 2, 1995)

In this episode, the men and women are together, but the game of poker divides them by gender lines and, supposedly, by skills in poker too. The secondary storylines are intertwined within this primary storyline: Rachel applies for jobs; Ross and his pet monkey, Marcel, are in conflict; and the gang fears Monica's ultra-competitive side will come through when they play poker.

The women's stereotypically girly style of play loses them their first two games. During the third and final game, Rachel hears that she did not get the job and takes her frustration out in the game. She keeps betting until she is out of money and then turns to Monica and Phoebe for more money to stay in the game. Ross, being the only one left in the game, does not shirk from upping the bet. When he runs out of money, Joey and Chandler kick in some funds as well, making the final hand the guys against the gals. Rachel shows a full house and Ross folds. As she celebrates with the other women, the guys lament the loss but Ross also notes how happy Rachel is, which makes the other guys suspicious but Ross won't show them his hand.

Why This Episode Is in the Top 25

The gender stereotypes may provide much of the humor, but the details we learn about the characters add depth to them as well. Add in some great repartee between Ross and Rachel, especially during the final poker game, and you have a good time. Also, the women win in the end (whether legitimate or not), bringing the traditional sex role stereotypes into question.

Episode 2.7: "The One where Ross Finds Out" (November 9, 1995)

Monica's overzealous attempts to motivate Chandler to lose weight lead him to list all the problems she is currently facing to convince her to just go back to bed. Phoebe's boyfriend becomes Joey's hero when he gets Phoebe to beg him to sleep with her with the promise that he did not have to call her afterward and her believing it was a good idea. Meanwhile, Rachel tries to get over Ross by going out on a date. Instead of enjoying her date, she drinks heavily; obsesses about Ross, Julie, and the cat they plan to get together; and ultimately leaves Ross a phone message telling him she is over him. The next day, Ross hears the message and ends up not getting a cat with Julie. Before the episode concludes, Ross and Rachel argue at Central Perk after closing about the timing of Rachel's revelation and Ross's inability to tell Rachel about his feelings for over a decade. Ross walks out; Rachel locks the door. Ross cannot actually leave. Rachel re-opens the door and they kiss for the first time in the rain.

Why This Episode Is in the Top 25

This episode is one of most significant as Ross and Rachel kiss for the first time. The comedy gold of Rachel going on a date, getting drunk, throwing a stranger's phone in an ice bucket, leaving her drunken "closure" message for Ross, and jumping on his back to prevent him from hearing it make it one of the most enjoyable to watch. Add in Phoebe talking a guy into sex and Monica's attempts to help Chandler lose weight and you have laughs from start to finish.

Episode 2.14: "The One with the Prom Video" (February 1, 1996)

Joey pays Chandler back some money and gives him a bonus gold brace-let engraved with "Best Bud" to thank him. Unfortunately, Joey is hurt when he overhears Chandler complaining about the bracelet. When Chandler loses the bracelet and buys a new one so Joey won't find out and then Rachel finds the original bracelet, Chandler gives the new bracelet to Joey so that they can be, as Joey says, "bracelet buddies." Monica and Ross's parents, Jack and Judy Geller (Elliot Gould and Christina Pickles), visit to bring her some of her stuff, including the videotape from her prom night. When Monica reveals that she lost her job, they make her feel guilty. So Ross ends up loaning her money. Despite Ross's best attempts to get Rachel to forgive him for making a list about her faults (in a previous episode), she still rejects him—that is, until they watch the prom video. While watching the video, the friends get to see high school "fat Monica" and Rachel with her old nose, as well as college student Ross with his Mr. Kotter curly hair. In the video, it appears that Rachel's date stood her up. Judy and Jack convince Ross to take Rachel instead. Before he comes downstairs, Rachel's date shows and they all leave while Ross stands on the stairs in his father's tuxedo holding a bouquet of flowers. In present day, Rachel, without saying a word, crosses the room and passionately kisses Ross. Phoebe highlights the moment by reminding everyone that "she's his lobster." During the closing credits, Monica watches the rest of the video, which includes her father teaching her to dance and a sex tape of Judy and Jack!

Why This Episode Is in the Top 25

This episode is primarily about Ross and Rachel finally getting together. Seeing their passionate kiss at the end could not have garnered more studio (and at home) audience cheers. Along the way to their kiss, we get to see Joey and Chandler be friends, fight, and make up; uncomfortable interactions between Monica and her parents; and high school and college-aged Monica, Rachel, and Ross for the first time, which make this a stellar episode.

Episode 3.2: "The One where No One's Ready" (September 26, 1996)[2]

This particular episode takes place in Monica and Rachel's apartment in real time (twenty-two minutes) as the ensemble gets ready to leave for Ross's museum benefit. Joey and Chandler fight over who possesses a chair. When Joey gets out of the chair, he takes the cushions. Then Joey puts on all of Chandler's clothes when he learns that Chandler hid all his underwear as ransom for the cushions, forcing him to go "commando." Although Phoebe shows up dressed and ready to go, their fight results in hummus being thrown on her dress. Monica freaks out because she hears an answering machine message from her ex-boyfriend Richard. While the friends try to prevent her from calling him back, Monica tries to leave him a new message, hears another woman on his machine, and ultimately ends up changing Richard's outgoing message to her confession about dialing into his machine because she was on her period. Rachel cannot figure out what to wear. Ross, stressed that no one is ready, ends up yelling at and humiliating her. She decides not to go to the benefit. When Ross says he will do anything to get her to go, including drinking a cup of leftover fat, Rachel lets him off the hook.

Why This Episode Is in the Top 25

The brilliance of *Friends* was its ensemble nature and made this one of my top three favorite episodes. This particular episode foregrounds the whole ensemble while still highlighting Joey and Chandler's roommate relationship, the negative and positive parts of Ross and Rachel's relationship, Phoebe's role as comic relief, and Monica's obsession with being liked.

Episode 4.8: "The One with Chandler in a Box" (November 20, 1997)

Chandler agrees to spend six hours in a giant box to think about what he did (kiss Joey's girlfriend) and prove his friendship to Joey. When Kathy comes to tell Chandler that she does not want to come between him and Joey, he cannot talk back. But Joey lets Chandler out so that he can chase after Kathy. The friends decide to do Secret Santa gifts for Christmas to save money. As the cast members all try to trade who they are giving gifts to, they learn that Rachel returns all gifts she is given. When Ross gives Rachel a hard time about exchanging gifts, she proves she is sentimental by showing Ross all the things she saved from when they went out. While preparing Thanksgiving dinner, Monica gets ice in her eye and has to go to the eye doctor. She avoids seeing her ex-boyfriend/eye doctor, Richard, but ends up seeing the on-call doctor, Richard's son, Tim (Richard Vartan). Tim and Monica flirt during the appointment and she invites him over. The friends point out how twisted it is for Monica to be with Richard's son. When Monica and Tim kiss, she realizes it reminds her of Richard and they both realize it is icky.

Why This Episode Is in the Top 25

This episode allows us to see Ross and Rachel argue (again!) and remember how special their time was together. Monica talking like a pirate before Tim puts her eye patch on is enough to make one guffaw. Watching her make out with Richard's son is enough to make one go ewwwwww. Chandler's time in the box provides a sight gag as well as proving that Kathy and Chandler's relationship will not threaten Chandler's relationship with Joey. The emotional roller coaster makes this episode.

Episode 4.12: "The One with the Embryos" (January 15, 1998)

Joey and Chandler and Monica and Rachel end up betting about whether the men or women know each other better. If the guys lose, they have to get rid of their birds. If the gals lose, they have to give the guys their apartment. Questions in the quiz-show-style game reveal details we never knew before such as that Monica's biggest pet peeve is animals dressed as humans; Michael Flatley, "Lord of the Dance," scares Chandler; the *TV Guide* the women steal is addressed to Ms. Chanandler Bong; and Chandler's father's all-male burlesque show is called Viva Las Gaygas. The women lose when they cannot name Chandler's job. Meanwhile, Phoebe's brother, Frank (Giovanni Ribisi), and his wife, Alice (Debra Jo Rupp), visit the gynecologist's office where Phoebe has their embryos implanted. Back at the apartment, Phoebe tries to help their chances by laying down with her feet up. Frank and Alice show up with a lollipop and pregnancy test in hopes that they can find out if she's pregnant. The guys and other gals stop fighting over the apartment when Phoebe comes out of the bathroom telling them all that the test was positive.

Why This Episode Is in the Top 25

Two storylines, two winners! When Lisa Kudrow was pregnant in reality, *Friends'* producers and writers decided to write her pregnancy into the show. Not ready to give any of the friends a live-in child, they chose to have her carry the child of her brother and his wife instead and capitalized on the humor of a sister having her brother's child. Rachel and Monica losing their apartment and the guys moving into their apartment provides enough visual humor for any episode, but add the questions and answers during the actual quiz and you have comic gold!

Episode 4.24: "The One with Ross's Wedding—Part 2" (May 1998)

At the end of the previous episode, Rachel heads to London to tell Ross she loves him before he marries Emily. A very pregnant Phoebe, who had to stay in New York, continually tries to call London to try to get one of the friends to stop Rachel from ruining the wedding. Rachel sits next to an Englishman on the plane who tells her what a horrible person she is trying to ruin her friend's wedding and that he agrees with Phoebe that this is a terrible plan. After a drunk guest at the rehearsal dinner mistakes Monica for Ross's mother, Chandler tries to comfort her while she drinks to excess. Immediately after, the scene cuts to the next morning as Ross barges into Chandler's hotel room shouting, "I'm getting married today!" Ross leaves and Monica emerges from under the covers asking if Ross knew she was there. Although Phoebe tasks Joey with intercepting Rachel so that she does not ruin the wedding, Joey misses her when he is making out with a bridesmaid. When Rachel enters the ceremony space, however, she immediately sees Ross and Emily kissing. Instead of ruining the wedding, she hugs and congratulates Ross. At the wedding, Monica and Chandler talk about their night together as they walk down the aisle and decide that they are getting together again. During the ceremony, Ross mistakenly says "I, Ross, take thee, Rachel." Although he corrects himself, the pastor asks, "Shall I go on?" and the episode ends. Spoiler Alert: Ross and Emily still get married in the next episode.

Why This Episode Is in the Top 25

Seeing Jack Geller and Mr. Waltham nearly come to fisticuffs over the bill for the wedding is enough to rank this episode in the top twenty-five. Monica emerging from under the covers of Chandler's bed, Rachel racing to stop Ross's wedding, and, of course, Ross saying Rachel's name during the ceremony create a recipe for excellence. *Friends* was already a worldwide hit, but including so many famous English actors and having the wedding set in London solidified the series' role in American *and* English culture.

Episode 5.8: "The One with All the Thanksgivings" (November 19, 1998)

The friends compete for who has had the worst Thanksgiving. The flashback stories begin with Chandler's mother (Morgan Fairchild) explaining to nine-year-old Chandler (Joshua Duvall Preston) that his father would rather sleep with the houseboy than her. Then Phoebe tells a story from a past life when she was a nurse during World War I. Rachel sparks a competition among the friends to guess which of Monica's Thanksgivings were her worst. Phoebe suggests it was when Joey got a turkey stuck on his head trying to scare Chandler. The second nominee takes us to the 1980s at the Gellers', where Monica is fat, Rachel has her old nose, and Ross and Chandler (home from college) look like members of Flock of Seagulls. Monica attempts to flirt with Thanksgiving-hating Chandler by making him macaroni and cheese but is mad enough to stop eating when she overhears him call her fat. Rachel points out that it was actually Thanksgiving 1988 that was Monica's worst. In this flashback, we learn that Rachel has her new nose, Ross and Chandler arrive in Miami Vice suits, and a thin Monica makes Chandler drool all over her. Monica wants to get back at him for calling her fat so Rachel advises her to make Chandler *think* she wants to have sex by acting like everything around her turns her on. When she picks up a knife and rubs it against her body, she drops the knife and it cuts off Chandler's toe. Back in the present, Monica assures Chandler it was an accident and tries to cheer him up by putting a turkey on her head and doing a dance for him. He tells her that he loves her and then takes it back.

Why This Episode Is in the Top 25

Providing some backstory for Monica and Chandler's relationship in this episode gave the audience reasons why their getting together might not have been so surprising after all. The sights of the flashback friends on past Thanksgivings gave a potentially serious topic—fat bias—a humorous frame. It might have been a bit far-reaching to give Chandler's advice to Monica as the reasons for her becoming a chef and losing weight though.

Episode 5.9: "The One with Ross's Sandwich" (December 10, 1998)

The friends keep finding evidence of Monica and Chandler's secret relationship. To keep their secret, they blame Joey. But when Rachel catches Joey with a naked picture of Monica, she calls him out. Joey turns the tables and lies, telling the group that Monica has been obsessed with him ever since they slept together in London. When asked why she would keep Joey's underwear, Monica admits that she is disgusting. Phoebe invites Rachel to join her for a literature class at the New School. But Rachel frustrates Phoebe when she does not do her homework and steals Phoebe's answers. Rachel tells Phoebe that she only wanted to have fun, not learn, and suggests she bring Monica instead. Monica ends up humiliating Phoebe by being an overzealous student.

Ross, already depressed because of his divorce from Emily and being evicted, is triggered further when someone at work eats his Thanksgiving leftover sandwich. He freaks out at his boss when he reveals he ate it. Ross later arrives at the coffeehouse, sedated by a psychiatrist, and tells the friends he has been put on leave but does not care about his sandwich anymore.

Why This Episode Is in the Top 25

David Schwimmer's performance of increasing rage and mood swings while he gets over Emily reaches a fever pitch from this episode through Episode 5.14, "The One where Everyone Finds Out." Just that one storyline would not be enough to qualify this episode for the top twenty-five. Add Monica and Chandler's continued sloppiness in hiding their relationship; Joey's taking the blame, until Monica has to admit she is the disgusting one; and Phoebe's trials and tribulations trying to learn with Rachel and Monica, and you have an overall quality episode.

Episode 5.11 "The One with All the Resolutions" (January 7, 1999)

This episode follows the friends as they try to keep their New Year's resolutions: Ross does something new every day; Phoebe wants to pilot a commercial jet; Ross bets Chandler he cannot stop making fun of them; Phoebe teaches Joey to play guitar; Rachel tries not to gossip; and Monica starts to take more pictures. On the first day, Ross asks out a woman named Elizabeth Hornswaggle. On the second, Ross wears leather pants on his date. After getting overheated in the pants, he goes to Elizabeth's bathroom, pulls his pants down, and cannot pull them back up. Ross then puts powder and lotion on his legs and still cannot get the pants back on. He comes out of the bathroom with paste on his head and legs with his pants in hand. Joey ends up firing (and later apologizing to) Phoebe as his guitar teacher as she uses questionable methods. Rachel hears Monica on the phone flirting with Chandler, but Joey will not let her tell him the news (even though he already knows it). Chandler has trouble with his resolution from the start as he cannot make fun of the name Hornswaggle, the hand positions Phoebe teaches Joey, or Ross's leather pants. Ultimately, he calls them all out and loses the bet.

Why This Episode Is in the Top 25

While Rachel finding out about Monica and Chandler is humorous, the highlight of this episode is Ross doing everything he can to try to pull his leather pants back up. Add to it the ridiculousness of Phoebe and Joey's interactions as he tries to learn guitar and Chandler's inability to tell jokes, and the laughter in this episode does not stop.

Episode 5.14: "The One where Everybody Finds Out" (February 11, 1999)

When Phoebe and Rachel accompany Ross to Ugly Naked Guy's apartment, which Ross hopes to rent, Phoebe sees Monica and Chandler undressing each other through the window. Rachel and Phoebe prevent Ross from looking out the window as he does not know about them yet.

Later Ross tries to set himself apart from all the competitors for Ugly Naked Guy's apartment by using what the friends know about his likes and dislikes. Ross arrives at Ugly Naked Guy's apartment and applauds his nakedness. Then the gang sees that Ugly Naked Guy has a naked friend: "naked Ross." Meanwhile, Phoebe and Rachel hatch a plan to mess with Monica and Chandler rather than tell them they know about their relationship. Rachel has them do her laundry, and Phoebe flirts with Chandler. This incites a game of chicken where Chandler and Phoebe make increasingly bold sexual moves toward each other to see who will admit what they know first. Ultimately, Phoebe wins when Chandler stops kissing her and shouts that he loves Monica. Monica enters and tells him she loves him too. After Ross secures Ugly Naked Guy's apartment, Ross brings his boss to see it and assures him his rage is over. But then Ross sees Monica and Chandler getting together through the window and freaks out again.

Why This Episode Is in the Top 25

The intertwined nature of the action in this episode emphasizes the ensemble nature of the writing in the series. Having Joey be the sane one in the "They don't know that we know that they know we know!" competition between the mess-ers and mess-ees is a sight to see. It gets better and increasingly awkward the closer Phoebe and Chandler get to the culminating moment.

Episode 6.9: "The One where Ross Got High" (November 25, 1999)

Monica tells Chandler not to tell her parents that they are living together because they do not like him. He decides to try to win them over but ends up confused when Judy wonders if he is stoned again. Ross then tells Monica and Chandler that he got high in his bedroom in college and told his parents that it was Chandler. Due to pages stuck together in the cookbook, the dessert Rachel makes is half an English trifle and half a shepherd's pie. Anxious to leave for a day of drinking with his roommate Janine's dancer friends, Joey and Ross decide not to tell Rachel and get everyone to eat and act like they like the trifle. Since Ross refuses to tell their parents about his smoking pot, Monica tells them. Her revelation leads to rapid-fire competing confessions that culminate with Monica revealing that Ross lost his job and married Rachel in Vegas and Ross disclosing that Monica and Chandler are living together. Along the way, Phoebe admits loving Jacques Cousteau and Rachel realizes she was not supposed to put beef in the trifle. In the end, Judy and Jack turn to Chandler to bring some sanity back to the room and their family.

Why This Episode Is in the Top 25

The vision of the gang acting like they like Rachel's trifle would be enough to put this episode in the top twenty-five (and my top three favorites). To see all of the main and secondary storylines—each entertaining in themselves—come together in the end through the hilarious, rapid-fire Ross and Monica confessions, Joey's plea to leave, Rachel's revelation about the trifle, Phoebe's declaration, and especially Judy Geller's response to each and every one of them makes this episode a triumph in the genre.

Episode 6.15: "The One That Could Have Been—Part 1" (February 17, 2000)

What would have happened if: Rachel married Barry, Ross never divorced Carol, Chandler quit his job, Joey had not been fired from *Days of Our Lives*, Monica were still fat, and Phoebe accepted a job from Merrill Lynch? After Ross introduces Rachel to Joey Tribbiani from *Days of Our Lives*, she decides to have an affair with him. Ross says he is still doing karate to release his sexual tension as he laments his dry spell with Carol. Carol is not receptive to some of the sex games Ross suggested but loves the idea of a threesome. Out-of-work Chandler works as Joey's assistant to make some money. Joey treats him like his "bitch." Chandler ends up quitting working for Joey when he sells a comic to Archie comics. "Fat Monica" is dating Dr. Roger, who is really boring. She reveals to Rachel that she is a thirty-year-old virgin. Rachel strongly encourages Monica to just do it! Phoebe smokes like a chimney, heartlessly fires people, and then loses $13 million and has a heart attack. Ross does not tell her that she got fired as she is still in the hospital and at risk.

Why This Episode Is in the Top 25

Many of the storylines in this episode merely serve as set-ups for part 2 (see below). However, the ways the actors embodied the not-so-far-from-their-real-selves roles of what might have been made them believable and entertaining and allowed this episode its own place on this list. Listening to the conversation between Rachel and Monica over Monica's virginity shows their comfort with one another as actors and demonstrates the similarities and differences between their real selves and these imaginary ones with amusing results.

Episode 6.16: "The One That Could Have Been—Part 2" (February 17, 2000)

The episode opens with "Could Have Been" credits. As each actor's name appears, the scenes shown reflect this could-have-been world: Rachel shops while blowing on her freshly manicured nails before appearing in bed with Barry as he clips his toenails; "Fat Monica" wears a chef's hat while dancing with donuts; Phoebe dons a suit, smokes while talking on a cell phone, and then throws the phone; Joey is shown as Dr. Drake Ramoray and then wearing a leather jacket and sunglasses flirting with a woman and checking her out as she walks away; Chandler writes outside, gets pooed on by a bird, and then falls asleep writing on a laptop; finally, Ross does karate and tries to make out with a resistant Carol.

When Ross and Carol's choice, Susan, arrives for their threesome, she and Carol go directly to the bedroom as Susan hands Ross her coat. Later Ross tells Joey that his part of the threesome was over pretty quickly because Susan kept kicking him away. Phoebe escapes the hospital and goes in to work where she learns that she was fired. She has another heart attack. During the closing credits, she sings at Central Perk, but in this reality the songs are about heart attacks, coming to her senses, and wanting the people she worked for to die. Rachel's attempts to have an affair with Joey are thwarted when she drinks too much and ends up vomiting and passing out at his apartment. But when Rachel arrives home early, she finds Barry in bed with someone else. She tries to track down Joey to go through with the affair but instead helps Ross realize that his wife is actually a lesbian. Dr. Roger gets called into the hospital before Monica can seduce him. She ends up sharing the aphrodisiac-filled dinner with

Chandler instead and loses her virginity to him. The next day Chandler comes back to Monica's apartment and tells her he beeped Roger again so that he could come over and tell her that she should be with him and not Roger.

Why This Episode Is in the Top 25

This episode finds just the right balance between the reality we have seen these characters in for six seasons and who they might have been had certain details of their lives changed. It allows us to appreciate how much they have each grown. The cast also gets to play with their characters, from Rachel's spoiled Long Island princess trying to get her way to Phoebe's competitive edge, in a way that adds humor to their less-desirable traits.

Episode 6.17: "The One with Unagi" (February 24, 2000)

Joey needs money for new head shots. He cannot earn enough working at the coffee shop, so he tries to volunteer for a new medical experiment for identical twins that pays $2,000. He finds a "twin" at an audition. When they actually go to the study, the doctor immediately says they are not identical twins and Joey blames Carl. Ross tells Rachel and Phoebe that their self-defense class is useless unless they have "unagi," or a state of total awareness that would prepare them for an attack. Phoebe and Rachel correct Ross by telling him that unagi is freshwater eel. The rest of the episode shows Ross trying to scare Rachel and Phoebe and then Phoebe and Rachel trying to get back at him. Chandler and Monica both forgot they agreed to make Valentine's gifts for one another. Before Chandler tells Monica that he forgot, she offers to make him whatever he wants in the kitchen and do whatever he wants to in the bedroom. So he does not tell her he forgot. One night when Monica cooks for him, she puts on the mixtape he gave her and finds their song, "The Way You Look Tonight," is on it. Then his ex-girlfriend's, Janice's, voice comes on wishing him a happy birthday and saying that she made the tape for him. Monica is pissed.

Why This Episode Is in the Top 25

The physical comedy in this episode, from seeing Joey with his twin to Ross's attempts to attack Rachel and Phoebe (and vice versa), make it necessary to be on this list. Add to the physical humor the ridiculousness of "unagi" being anything but freshwater eel and Phoebe's sock bunny becoming a sex toy for Chandler and Monica and you have the makings of a terrific episode.

Episode 6.24: "The One with the Proposal—Part 1" (May 18, 2000)

Chandler tells all the friends that he is going to take Monica out to dinner to propose to her. However, Monica's ex-boyfriend, Richard (Tom Selleck), shows up with a date and the four of them end up having dinner together, which prevents Chandler from proposing. Rachel brings Phoebe and Joey to a charity event to impress her boss. At the event, Joey accidentally wins the silent auction for a sailboat. Since Joey cannot afford the boat, Rachel tries to convince the second-highest bidder to buy the boat instead. Rachel's speech backfires and convinces Joey to buy the boat. Ross feels like a babysitter when he arrives to ask his former-student-cum-girlfriend to go to a play and finds her engaged in an alcohol-filled balloon fight. After weighing the many cons and few pros of staying with Elizabeth, Ross breaks up with her. When Monica and Chandler return home from dinner, their friends try to congratulate them, but since he did not propose, Chandler has to divert each of them as they come in so that Monica will not find out about the proposal. Phoebe suggests Chandler try to throw her off track by making her believe marriage is the last thing on his mind and that he is afraid of commitment. However, Richard visits Monica at her restaurant and tells her that he still loves her.

Why This Episode Is in the Top 25

While the audience looks forward to Monica and Chandler's engagement, Richard's disruption also allows us to compare and contrast Monica's options. Seeing Rachel attempt to corral Phoebe and Joey at the auction while trying to impress her boss and Ross finally break up with Elizabeth provides additional entertainment.

Episode 6.25: "The One with the Proposal—Part 2" (May 18, 2000)

This episode begins with Richard telling Monica that he wants to marry her and have kids. She tells him he is too late and lies saying that Chandler wants to marry her. Rachel and Phoebe express their happiness about Monica and Chandler's imminent engagement. But they feel the need to secure backups, or someone they can marry if they are not betrothed by the time they are forty. Rachel, Joey, and Ross learn that Phoebe already has backup deals with both Joey and Ross. Rachel ends up writing Joey and Ross on napkins for her and Phoebe to draw. When Rachel picks Joey and Phoebe picks Ross, they switch. Monica goes to Richard's and tells him she wishes he had wanted to marry her three years ago or that Chandler wanted to marry her now. Although he arrives after Monica leaves, Chandler arrives at Richard's and tells Richard about his plan to surprise Monica with a proposal. Richard tells Chandler to go get her and not let her go. Upon his return, Chandler finds Monica surrounded by candles in their apartment waiting to propose to him. Monica gets down on one knee to propose to Chandler but cries and cannot finish. So Chandler gets down on his knees with her and proposes to her. She says yes.

Why This Episode Is in the Top 25

Monica getting engaged to commitment-phobic Chandler is the headline here. The fact that we get to compare and contrast Monica's chemistry and relationship with the man she once wanted to marry and Chandler suggests to the audience that she does indeed belong with Chandler. Add the humor of seeing Chandler challenge Richard and the very real ambivalent feelings of Monica's female friends, and you have the recipe for a monumental episode.

Episode 7.23: "The One with Monica and Chandler's Wedding—Part 1" (May 17, 2001)

When Chandler hears Monica's voice in their outgoing message refer to them as "the Bings," he suddenly gets the jitters. Later, at the rehearsal dinner, the end of Ross's best man speech, "To the Bings!" freaks Chandler out further. Later, the gang realizes Chandler is missing. Phoebe joins Ross to look for the still-missing Chandler the next morning while

Rachel tries to stall Monica to keep her from getting ready. Rachel begins to panic about how they are going to handle Monica. When Phoebe pulls her into the bathroom to try to calm her, Phoebe pulls tissue out of the trash to give to the crying Rachel and finds a positive pregnancy test. Phoebe says Monica is pregnant. Filming begins on Joey's World War I movie the day before the wedding. When he rehearses with his costar, Richard Crosby (Gary Oldman), Crosby keeps spitting in Joey's face. Crosby tells him that of course he is spitting on him as enunciation is the key to good acting. They then film a scene spitting in each other's faces. At the end, Joey finds out that he has to work the next day, the day of the wedding he must officiate.

Why This Episode Is in the Top 25

While this episode just prepares us for the wedding, it does so with humor, anxiety, and comfort. The writers' and actors' choices allow the audience to experience the anxiety of will-Chandler-or-won't-Chandler-show-up without also freaking Monica out about it by having the friends keep his escape quiet as they distract her. The bonus in this episode is getting to see Jack and Judy Geller be just as randy when discussing Gunther and Rita Moreno as they are with one another and seeing Nora and Charles Bing spar over their femininity.

Episode 7.24: "The One with Monica and Chandler's Wedding—Part 2" (May 17, 2001)

Rachel tries to stall Monica getting ready for the wedding while Ross and Phoebe look for Chandler. They finally find Chandler at his office and convince him to shower and get dressed. When Chandler goes for a smoke, he overhears Phoebe and Rachel say that Monica is pregnant. He freaks out and takes off again. When they find him, he reveals that he knows about Monica's pregnancy and is no longer afraid. Joey tries to get out of filming his movie so that he will be able to officiate the wedding. When Crosby shows up drunk, Joey calls Rachel to tell her that he cannot get out yet. As it is one hour until the wedding, she finds a Greek Ortho-dox priest to do the ceremony. The director tells Joey that as long as Crosby is conscious, they will still be shooting. Joey tells Crosby they are done, puts Crosby over his shoulder, and carries him out. Joey bursts in to take over from the Orthodox priest and completes the ceremony. Afterward, Chandler tells Monica that he knows about the baby. When she questions, "What baby?" the camera focuses on a nervous-looking Rachel.

Why This Episode Is in the Top 25

Rachel's anxieties about her own love life and her selfishness become assets when trying to delay Monica. Interactions between Joey and Richard Crosby are hilarious. Chandler coming to his senses, the actual wedding, and then the surprise (Spoiler Alert: Rachel is the one who is pregnant!) all make the episode the perfect culmination of the planning Monica has done for the wedding all season and a cliff-hanger for the next.

Episode 8.4: "The One with the Videotape" (October 18, 2001)

Monica and Chandler return from their honeymoon excited to have met another couple they can hang out with, only to learn that the other couple gave them a fake phone number. Phoebe suggests they may have given them fake names too, and we learn that hers is Regina Phalange and Joey's is Ken Adams. In telling their friends the story of how Rachel got pregnant, no one believes Ross when he says Rachel came onto him until he says that he has it on videotape. Ross explains that he was recording himself practicing Joey's "magic story" (that always gets him laid) when Rachel walked in. Embarrassed, Ross did not tell her the camera was still recording. Ross's objections to watching the tape before destroying it end up convincing Rachel to watch it to prove who came on to who(m). On the tape, they see Ross and Rachel reminiscing over wine when Rachel starts to tell the "magic story," which reveals that she came onto Ross. Joey asks how she knows the story. She says that she heard it from her friend who "heard it from some guy." Joey says that he is the "some guy"; he is Ken Adams.

Why This Episode Is in the Top 25

This episode of the series is my absolutely favorite! Why? The way the writers wove multiple stories (Monica and Chandler getting wrong-numbered by another honeymoon couple, Joey and Phoebe's fake names, Ross's inability to get laid, and who came onto whom to lead to Rachel's pregnancy) that came together in the end, with call-backs, laugh-out-loud moments, and surprising reveals. The bonus is the end of the episode: getting to watch Rachel's and Ross's reactions to their own sex tape!

Episode 8.9: "The One with the Rumor" (November 22, 2001)

Monica invites everyone over for Thanksgiving and tells them that her friend from high school, Will, is coming too. When they are all seated at the table for dinner, Will (Brad Pitt) reveals that Rachel made his life miserable in high school and that he cofounded the "I Hate Rachel Green Club" with Ross. Will is dismayed when he learns that Ross broke their pact never to date Rachel. Ross explains to Rachel that for him it was really an "I Love Rachel" club for the stupidly-in-love teenager that he was. Then Will reveals that their club made up a rumor about Rachel having male and female parts and Monica points out that Rachel also started a rumor that Ross kissed their fifty-year-old librarian. Ross then decides he is back in the club—that is, until Monica assures Rachel that the rumor about her made other people want to be like her and the rumor about Ross put him on the social map. When Ross says that they should let bygones be bygones since they are having a baby together, Will gets excited that Ross "knocked her up" but is not going to marry her.

Why This Episode Is in the Top 25

The running joke of the episode is, of course, how hot Will/Brad Pitt is. This joke and the tension between Rachel and Will are compounded with the audience's knowledge that Jennifer Aniston and Brad Pitt were married at the time. Pitt's little-seen comedic skills, including his delivery and timing as he mocks Rachel for her "typical" spoiled behavior, add unexpected laughs. Unfortunately, a running joke about a person being intersexed has not aged well.

Episode 9.5: "The One with Phoebe's Birthday Dinner" (October 31, 2002)

Phoebe's boyfriend, Mike (Paul Rudd), has to work on her birthday and all the friends arrive late for her birthday dinner. The waiter will not let Phoebe and Joey order their food until their whole party arrives and makes them move to a table for two. Rachel and Ross were delayed because they both ended up getting locked out of their apartment with Emma inside. Chandler and Monica were late because they had a fight about him smoking while working in Tulsa and Monica "tricking" Chandler into having sex while they were still fighting. Once everyone arrives and orders, Rachel continues to be distracted by Judy and Emma and Monica and Chandler are still fighting. Phoebe tells off the friends for being late. But then Mike calls and she decides to spend her birthday with him. Rachel and Ross decide to go home to Emma, and Monica suggests she and Chandler go home for more sex. Joey then has "the best birthday ever" when all the food for all six of them, and a birthday cake, comes just for him.

Why This Episode Is in the Top 25

Although episodes with the whole ensemble together tend to be the best, this one highlights moments of Lisa Kudrow's comedic skills and Joey's love of food. Their dynamic as they interact with the waiter and try to save the table while starving serves as the center of this episode. But the interpersonal dynamics between Monica and Chandler as they deal with the difficulties of conceiving a child (and Chandler's bad habits) and fears of a new mother about leaving her child (and the credibility of babysitters) add depth, heart, and more humor.

Episode 10.2: "The One where Ross Is Fine" (October 2, 2003)

Ross walks in on Joey and Rachel kissing and invites them over for dinner with him and Charlie. During the dinner, Ross drinks too much and continues to insist that he is "fine." The next morning Joey assures Ross that he and Rachel will not continue their relationship without Ross's blessing. But Ross realizes that he and Rachel have not been a couple for six years and that it is time to move on. Frank Jr. visits Phoebe at the coffee shop with the out-of-control triplets. When the triplets finally sleep, Franks admits that he has not slept in four years and wonders if Phoebe could take one. When Phoebe asks which one, Frank goes through each kid's qualities and realizes that he could not give up any of them. Phoebe offers to help by babysitting more often.

Phoebe refers a frustrated Monica and Chandler to friends of hers who can help them navigate adoption. Chandler runs into their son on the way to the bathroom and tells him that they are learning about his adoption but finds that Owen did not know. Chandler and Monica try to escape before Owen rats Chandler out, but they are too late. Later, they tell Phoebe how badly things went and Chandler mistakenly reveals to the triplets that Phoebe gave birth to them.

Why This Episode Is in the Top 25

Chandler's bumbling revelations about adopted children and surrogate mothers amuse, but drunk, uncomfortable Ross is the highlight of this episode. From his uncomfortable silent reaction when he first sees Rachel and Joey kissing to his frenetic fajitas, margaritas, and flan feast, David Schwimmer is at his comedic best. One thing that could have made this episode better: seeing Ross's drunk striptease to the *Chicago* soundtrack!

Episode 10.8: "The One with the Late Thanksgiving" (November 20, 2003)

When Monica and Chandler say they do not want to host Thanksgiving this year, Phoebe stokes Monica's competitiveness by getting her to try to outdo her last Thanksgiving dinner. Despite the fact that it may make them late for dinner, Phoebe convinces Rachel to bring Emma to a baby beauty pageant and Joey and Ross go to a Rangers game. Rachel, Phoebe, Ross, and Joey run into each other in the hallway when they all arrive forty-five minutes late. They try to come up with an explanation for their lateness (other than the truth). Ross tries to lie about the subway breaking down, but Joey's foam Rangers finger gives them away. Rachel unlocks the door with her old key, but the chain keeps the door from opening all the way. The four of them put their heads through the door and Joey tries to "eye contact" them into submission. Then Joey cannot get his head out of the door. Monica goes to answer the phone while the rest of them end up breaking the door down and knocking Thanksgiving dinner on the floor. Monica does not care though because the adoption agency called with the news that she and Chandler are getting a baby.

Why This Episode Is in the Top 25

While Monica and Chandler make their final Thanksgiving in the apartment together, the audience gets to reflect on ten years of those holidays in the apartment. Meanwhile, we get the pleasure of seeing what were once unlikely friendships (the spoiled rich girl with the flighty homeless hippie and the actor/ladies' man with the geeky academic) flourish in yet another situation they have to try to get out of.

Honorable Mentions

Episode 4.23: "The One with Ross's Wedding—Part 1" (May 7, 1998)

Friends do London.

Episode 6.6: "The One on the Last Night" (November 4, 1999)

Ross and Chandler hit Joey in his bubble-wrapped head while Phoebe stokes a fight between Monica and Rachel that ends with their incomprehensibly making up.

Episode 6.22: "The One where Paul's the Man" (May 4, 2000)

Bruce Willis being a "neat guy" and "the man."

Episode 7.1: "The One with Monica's Thunder" (October 12, 2000)

Ross and Rachel almost . . . Monica and Chandler cannot . . . Phoebe tries to book herself as the wedding band and Joey spurs her along.

Episode 8.20: "The One with the Baby Shower" (April 25, 2002)

The baby shower itself is amusing, but seeing Joey practice hosting a new game show, *Bamboozled*, on Chandler and Ross makes this episode.

Episode 9.1: "The One where No One Proposes" (September 26, 2002)

Monica and Chandler try to have sex all over a hospital while Joey and Ross try to work out which one of them is engaged to Rachel.

NOTES

INTRODUCTION

1. David Wild, *Friends . . . 'til the End* (Burbank: Warner Brothers Entertainment Inc., 2004).

2. Anne Marie Todd, "Saying Goodbye to *Friends*: Fan Culture as Lived Experience," *Journal of Popular Culture* 44, no. 4 (2011): 871.

I. *FRIENDS* CHANGES THE SITCOM LANDSCAPE

1. Anne Marie Todd, "Saying Goodbye to Friends: Fan Culture as Lived Experience," *The Journal of Popular Culture* 44, no. 4 (2011): 854–71.

2. Neil Postman, *Amusing Ourselves to Death: Public Discourse in the Age of Show Business* (New York: Penguin, 1985): 87.

3. John Fiske and John Hartley, *Reading Television* (London: Methuen, 1978): 24.

4. Todd, "Saying Goodbye."

5. "Why Monica and Chandler Are Secretly the Heroes of 'Friends,'" *Hello Giggles*, October 5, 2015, https://hellogiggles.com/reviews-coverage/monica-and-chandler-relationship-model/.

6. Today this amounts to approximately twenty-two minutes of show with eight minutes of advertisements spread through commercial breaks. *Friends* experimented with sitcom formatting by filming and airing what they called "supersize" episodes. These episodes aired over the course of forty-five minutes instead of thirty, making the actual episode time approximately thirty-three min-

utes instead of twenty-two. These episodes appeared the first time the episodes aired (and in some repeats during the season they aired) but are now only available on the first DVD box sets of the seasons. These longer episodes did not show up on the BluRay releases nor are they the episodes that air in reruns on cable or on Netflix.

7. Lauren Jade Thompson, "'It's Like a Guy Never Lived Here!': Reading the Gendered Domestic Spaces of *Friends*," *Television & New Media* (2018): 4.

8. Lawrence Mintz, "Ideology in the Television Situation Comedy," *Studies in Popular Culture* 8, no. 2 (1985): 42–51.

9. Mintz, "Ideology," 44–45.

10. Richard F. Taflinger, "Sitcom: What It Is, How It Works: A History of Comedy Television: Beginning to 1970," https://public.wsu.edu/~taflinge/comhist.html.

11. Amanda Lotz, "Segregated Sitcoms: Institutional Causes of Disparity among Black and White Comedy Images and Audiences," in *The Sitcom Reader: Viewed and Skewed*, edited by Mary M. Dalton and Laura R. Linder, 139–50 (New York: State University of New York Press).

12. Shelley Cobb, "'I'd Like Y'all to Get a Black Friend': The Politics of Race in *Friends*," *Television & New Media* (2018): 3.

13. Cobb, "I'd Like Y'all." Cobb refers to the "slumpy" audience identified by Ron Becker, *Gay TV and Straight America* (New Brunswick, NJ: Rutgers University Press, 2006): 81.

14. Cobb, "I'd Like Y'all," 2.

15. Warren Littlefield (with T. R. Pearson), *Top of the Rock: Inside the Rise and Fall of Must See TV* (New York: Anchor Books, 2012): 182–83.

16. David Wild, *Friends . . . 'til the End* (Burbank: Warner Brothers Entertainment Inc., 2004): 85.

17. Wild, *Friends . . . 'til the End*, 122.

18. Wild, *Friends . . . 'til the End*, 40.

19. Wild, *Friends . . . 'til the End*, 53, 55.

20. Littlefield, *Top of the Rock*, 176.

21. Littlefield, *Top of the Rock*.

22. Littlefield, *Top of the Rock*, 166.

23. Littlefield, *Top of the Rock*, 169.

24. Littlefield, *Top of the Rock*.

25. Littlefield, *Top of the Rock*.

26. Jasmine Lee, "What Did 'Friends' Say about '90s Dating Culture?" *Screen Prism*, December 1, 2015, http://screenprism.com/insights/article/what-did-friends-say-about-90s-dating-culture-what-has-changed-since-then.

27. Littlefield, *Top of the Rock*, 177.

28. Littlefield, *Top of the Rock*, 180–81.

29. "Let the BackLash Begin!" *Newsweek*, February 11, 1996, https://www.newsweek.com/let-backlash-begin-179758.

30. "Let the BackLash Begin!"

31. Littlefield, *Top of the Rock*, 188.

32. Wild, *Friends . . . 'til the End*.

33. Radio presenter Alex Bake suggested *Friends* was an elaborate marketing strategy employed by Starbucks to promote coffeehouse culture (and their business), summarized by Ruth Kinane, "Friends: 7 of the Craziest Fan Theories," *Entertainment Weekly*, September 1, 2017, http://ew.com/tv/2017/09/01/friends-craziest-fan-theories/.

34. Todd, "Saying Goodbye," 262.

35. Jonathan Bernstein, "Friends at 20: How Ross and Rachel started a TV Revolution," *Telegraph*, September 22, 2014, http://www.telegraph.co.uk/culture/tvandradio/11110627/Friends-at-20-how-Ross-and-Rachel-started-a-TV-revolution.html.

36. Thompson, "It's Like a Guy," 4.

37. Andrew Harrison, "The Hunting of the Snark: *Friends*, 20 Years On," *New Statesman*, September 12, 2014, http://www.newstatesman.com/culture/2014/09/hunting-snark-friends-20-years.

38. John DellaContrada, "'Friends' Reflected Change in American Society, Among First TV Shows to Portray 'Youth on Their Own,'" *UB News Center*, April 16, 2004, http://www.buffalo.edu/news/releases/2004/04/6680.html.

39. Littlefield, *Top of the Rock*, and Harrison, "The Hunting of the Snark."

40. Littlefield, *Top of the Rock*.

41. Littlefield, *Top of the Rock*, 154.

42. Littlefield, *Top of the Rock*, 170.

43. Littlefield, *Top of the Rock*.

44. Mike D'Avria, "The Sexual Proclivities of Friends," *Vulture*, July 27, 2011, http://www.vulture.com/2011/07/the-sexual-proclivities-of-friends.html.

45. Ketan S. Chitnis, Avinash Thombre, Everett M. Rogers, Arvind Singhal, and Ami Sengupta, "(Dis)similar Readings: Indian and American Audiences' Interpretation of *Friends*," *The International Communication Gazette* 68, no. 2 (2006): 131–45.

46. Wild, *Friends . . . 'til the End*, 216.

47. Bernstein, "*Friends* at 20."

48. Alice Leppert, "*Friends* Forever: Sitcom Celebrity and Its Afterlives." *Television & New Media* (2018): 2.

49. Harrison, "The Hunting of Snark."

50. Wild, *Friends . . . 'til the End*, 190.

51. Wild, *Friends . . . 'til the End*, 192.

52. Adam Sternbergh, "Is Friends Still the Most Popular Show on TV? Why So Many 20-Somethings Want to Stream a 20-Year-Old Sitcom about a Bunch of 20-Somethings Sitting around in a Coffee Shop," *New York Magazine*, March 21, 2016, http://www.vulture.com/2016/03/20-somethings-streaming-friends-c-v-r.html.

53. Amanda Lotz, *The Television Will be Revolutionized*, 2nd ed. (New York: New York University Press), as cited in Shelley Cobb, Neil Ewen, and Hannah Hamad, "*Friends* Reconsidered: Cultural Politics, Intergenerationality, and Afterlives," *Television & New Media* (2018): 3.

54. Harrison, "The Hunting of Snark."

55. Leppert, "*Friends* Forever," 3.

56. Cobb, "I'd Like Y'all," 4.

2. *FRIENDS* ON-SCREEN AND OFF

1. David Wild, *Friends . . . 'til the End* (Burbank: Warner Brothers Entertainment Inc., 2004): 119.

2. Lily Loofbourow, "The End of the *Friends* Era of Gossip, Fame, and Meta-Spinoffs," *Week*, August 21, 2017, http://theweek.com/articles/719464/end-friends-era-gossip-fame-metaspinoffs.

3. Jeffrey Toobin, "Gawker's Demise and the Trump-Era Threat to the First Amendment," *New Yorker*, December 19 and 26, 2016, https://www.newyorker.com/magazine/2016/12/19/gawkers-demise-and-the-trump-era-threat-to-the-first-amendment.

4. Toobin, "Gawker's Demise."

5. Toobin, "Gawker's Demise."

6. Loofbourow, "The End of the *Friends* Era."

7. Jillian Sandell, "I'll Be There for You: *Friends* and the Fantasy of Alternative Families," *American Studies* 39, no. 2 (Summer 1998): 143.

8. Alice Leppert, "*Friends* Forever: Sitcom Celebrity and Its Afterlives," *Television & New Media* (2018): 1–17. doi: 10.1177/15274764188778424: 3.

9. Wild, *Friends . . . 'til the End*.

10. Wild, *Friends . . . 'til the End*.

11. Wild, *Friends . . . 'til the End*.

12. Leppert, "*Friends* Forever," 13.

13. Leppert, "*Friends* Forever," 4.

14. Stephanie Webber, "Tate Donovan Was 'Dying Inside' Working with Ex Jennifer Aniston on 'Friends,'" *Us Magazine*, September 5, 2018, https://www.usmagazine.com/celebrity-news/news/tate-donovan-dying-inside-working-with-ex-jennifer-aniston-on-friends/.

15. Leppert, *"Friends* Forever."

16. Wild, *Friends . . . 'til the End*, 35, 37.

17. Andy Borowitz, "The Big Pitch: Six Ways to Keep Our Favorite Friends Around," *TV Guide*, October 22, 2002: 24–25.

18. Leppert, *"Friends* Forever," 3.

19. Leppert, *"Friends* Forever," 13.

20. Wild, *Friends . . . 'til the End*, 229.

21. Wild, *Friends . . . 'til the End*, 230.

22. *The Phil Donahue Show* aired from 1967 to 1996.

23. Leppert, *"Friends* Forever," 4.

24. Loofbourow, "The End of the *Friends* Era."

25. Lauren Yapalater, "A Timeline of Jennifer Aniston's Relationships," *Buzzfeed*, August 13, 2012, https://www.buzzfeed.com/lyapalater/a-timeline-of-jennifer-anistons-relationships.

26. Sarah Weldon, "A Definitive Timeline of Jennifer Aniston and Justin Theroux's Relationship," *Cosmopolitan*, February 16, 2018, https://www.cosmopolitan.com/entertainment/celebs/a18208604/jennifer-aniston-justin-theroux-relationship-timeline/.

27. Leppert, *"Friends* Forever," 1–17.

28. Leppert, *"Friends* Forever," 13.

29. Wild, *Friends . . . 'til the End*, 51.

30. Wild, *Friends . . . 'til the End*, 57.

31. Wild, *Friends . . . 'til the End*, 185.

32. Zach Johnson, "Courteney Cox and Brian Van Holt Break Up, David Arquette Reveals," *E! News*, October 31, 2013, https://www.eonline.com/news/476095/courteney-cox-and-brian-van-holt-break-up-david-arquette-reveals.

33. "The Real Life Partners of the Friends Cast," *Go Social*, http://www.gosocial.co/the-real-life-partners-of-the-friends-cast/.

34. Wild, *Friends . . . 'til the End*, 186.

35. Jessica Kane, "13 Reasons David Schwimmer Is Ross Geller," *Huffington Post*, December 6, 2017, https://www.huffingtonpost.com/2013/07/22/david-schwimmer-ross-geller_n_3636512.html.

36. Deborah Behrens, "Hal Linden and Christina Pickles Summer *On Golden Pond*," *LA Stage Times*, October 3, 2017.

37. Scott Fishman, "Christina Pickles on Winning Her First Emmy at 83, 'St. Elsewhere' & 'Friends' Memories," *TV Insider*, September 14, 2018, https://www.tvinsider.com/716066/christina-pickles-interview-break-a-hip-web-series/.

38. James Mottram, "Elliott Gould: 'I Didn't Have a Drug Problem. I Had a Problem with Reality,'" *Independent*, July 22, 2012, https://www.independent.co.uk/news/people/profiles/elliott-gould-i-didnt-have-a-drug-problem-i-had-a-problem-with-reality-7956788.html.

39. Mottram, "Elliott Gould."
40. Wild, *Friends . . . 'til the End*, 146.
41. Wild, *Friends . . . 'til the End*, 208.
42. Wild, *Friends . . . 'til the End*, 208.
43. Wild, *Friends . . . 'til the End*, 146.
44. Wild, *Friends . . . 'til the End*, 148.
45. Wild, *Friends . . . 'til the End*, 186.
46. Jethro Nededog, "Matthew Perry Says He Can't Remember 3 Years of Shooting 'Friends' Because of Alcohol and Drug Abuse," *Business Insider*, January 25, 2016, https://www.businessinsider.com/matthew-perry-friends-drug-abuse-2016-1.
47. Samantha Allen, "How Matthew Perry Forgot Three Years of 'Friends,'" *Daily Beast*, January 27, 2016, https://www.thedailybeast.com/how-matthew-perry-forgot-three-years-of-friends.
48. Allen, "How Matthew Perry Forgot."
49. Wild, *Friends . . . 'til the End*, 70.
50. "Matthew Perry: 'My Drug and Alcohol Addiction Was So Public,'" *News.com.au*, August 21, 2015, https://www.news.com.au/entertainment/celebrity-life/matthew-perry-my-drug-and-alcohol-addiction-was-so-public/news-story/f74e61177a59bbdaa119a079c2de8968; Mangala Dilip, "The Tragedy of Matthew Perry: Pornstars, Drugs and the Decline of an Icon," *Media, Entertainment, Arts Worldwide*, June 11, 2018, https://meaww.com/the-sad-tragic-life-of-mathew-perry-you-did-not-know-about.
51. Allen, "How Matthew Perry Forgot."
52. Wild, *Friends . . . 'til the End*.
53. Dilip, "The Tragedy of Matthew Perry."
54. Wild, *Friends . . . 'til the End*, 75.
55. Wild, *Friends . . . 'til the End*, 156.
56. Leppert, "*Friends* Forever."
57. Wild, *Friends . . . 'til the End*, 92.
58. Carina Chocano, "A Circle of 'Friends,'" *Los Angeles Times*, April 25, 2004: E1, E28–E29.
59. Leppert, "*Friends* Forever," 5.
60. Leppert, "*Friends* Forever," 5.
61. Wild, *Friends . . . 'til the End*, 43.
62. Leppert, "*Friends* Forever," 5–6.

3. *FRIENDS* AS FAMILY

1. Ella Taylor, *Prime-Time Families: Television Culture in Postwar America* (Berkeley: University of California Press,1989).

2. See Stephanie Coontz, *The Way We Never Were: American Families and the Nostalgia Trap* (New York: Basic Books, 1992).

3. Jillian Sandell, "I'll Be There for You: *Friends* and the Fantasy of Alternative Families," *American Studies* 39, no. 2 (Summer 1998): 144.

4. Sandell, "I'll Be There for You."

5. Claire Cain Miller, "The Divorce Surge Is Over, but the Myth Lives On," *New York Times*, December 2, 2014, https://www.nytimes.com/2014/12/02/upshot/the-divorce-surge-is-over-but-the-myth-lives-on.html.

6. Shelley Cobb, "'I'd Like Y'all to Get a Black Friend': The Politics of Race in Friends," *Television & New Media* (2018): 6.

7. Appeared in ad publicity material on nbc.com in 1998 according to Sandell, "I'll Be There for You," 147.

8. Sandell, "I'll Be There for You," 147.

9. For a discussion of which of the friends spent the most time with the others on-screen, see Ben Blatt, "Which Friends on Friends Were the Closest Friends?" *Slate*, May 4, 2014, http://www.slate.com/articles/arts/culturebox/2014/05/friends_chandler_joey_ross_rachel_monica_phoebe_which_friends_were_closest.html.

10. I call them "Monica's apartment" and "Joey's apartment" as Monica is the only friend who lives in #20 for the whole series and Joey is the only friend who lives in #19 for the whole series, with the exception of a few episodes in season 2. Rachel, Phoebe, and Chandler live with Monica and Chandler, Ross, Phoebe, and Rachel live with Joey for periods throughout the series.

11. The people sitting on the couch were not actors but the writers for the third season of the show: http://friends.wikia.com/wiki/The_One_With_The_Princess_Leia_Fantasy.

12. Tanya Ghahremani, "The Central Perk Couch on 'Friends' Was Always Unoccupied for a Reason You Never Noticed," *Bustle*, January 16, 2015, https://www.bustle.com/articles/59138-the-central-perk-couch-on-friends-was-always-unoccupied-for-a-reason-you-never-noticed.

13. Sandell, "I'll Be There for You," 151.

14. David Wild, *Friends . . . 'til the End* (Burbank: Warner Brothers Entertainment Inc., 2004).

15. Jonathan Bernstein, "Friends at 20: How Ross and Rachel started a TV Revolution," *Telegraph*, September 22, 2014, http://www.telegraph.co.uk/culture/tvandradio/11110627/Friends-at-20-how-Ross-and-Rachel-started-a-TV-revolution.html.

16. Andrea So, "Why Monica and Chandler Are Secretly the Heroes of 'Friends,'" *Hello Giggles*, October 5, 2015, https://hellogiggles.com/reviews-coverage/monica-and-chandler-relationship-model/.

17. Laura Hurley, "Friends Almost Let Joey and Phoebe Have the Best Sex Joke Ever," *Cinema Blend*, 2015, https://www.cinemablend.com/television/Friends-Almost-Let-Joey-Phoebe-Have-Best-Sex-Joke-Ever-84947.html.

18. Sandell, "I'll Be There for You," 143.

19. Wild, *Friends . . . 'til the End*, 207.

4. *FRIENDS* HAPPY NOT DOING TOO MUCH

1. "The Year 1994 from the People History," *People History*, July 10, 2018, http://www.thepeoplehistory.com/1994.html.

2. Neil Ewen, "If I Don't Input Those Numbers . . . It Doesn't Make Much of a Difference: Insulated Precarity and Gendered Labor in *Friend*," *Television & New Media* (2018): 1–17.

3. Ewen, "If I Don't Input," 2.

4. Ewen, "If I Don't Input," 2.

5. Peter Hanson, *The Cinema of Generation X: A Critical Study* (Jefferson, NC: McFarland, 2002).

6. Helene A. Shugart, "Isn't It Ironic? The Intersection of Third-Wave Feminism and Generation X," *Women's Studies in Communication* 24, no. 2 (2001): 131–68.

7. Andrew Harrison, "The Hunting of the Snark: Friends, 20 Years On," *New Statesman*, September 12, 2014, http://www.newstatesman.com/culture/2014/09/hunting-snark-friends-20-years.

8. Anne Marie Todd, "Saying Goodbye to *Friends*: Fan Culture as Lived Experience," *Journal of Popular Culture* 44, no. 4 (2011): 856.

9. Jonathan Bernstein, "Friends at 20: How Ross and Rachel started a TV Revolution," *Telegraph*, September 22, 2014, http://www.telegraph.co.uk/culture/tvandradio/11110627/Friends-at-20-how-Ross-and-Rachel-started-a-TV-revolution.html.

10. The creators of the show were cowriters on the song. The complete song played on the radio at the time.

11. Ewen, "If I Don't Input," 4.

12. David Wild, *Friends . . . 'til the End* (Burbank: Warner Brothers Entertainment Inc., 2004): 82.

13. Wild, *Friends . . . 'til the End*.

14. David Graeber, *Bullshit Jobs: A Theory* (New York: Simon & Schuster, 2018).

15. Rebecca Schuman, "You've Reached the Winter of Our Discontent," *Longreads*, March 2018, https://longreads.com/2018/03/27/youve-reached-the-winter-of-our-discontent/.

16. Ewen, "If I Don't Input," 14.

17. Hannah Hamad, "The One with the Feminist Critique: Revisiting Millennial Postfeminism with *Friends*," *Television & New Media* (2018): 1–16. For additional readings about popular culture and postfeminism that informed my analysis, see Kim Akass and Janet McCabe, editors, *Reading "Sex and the City"* (London: I.B. Tauris, 2003); Jane Arthurs, "*Sex and the City* and Consumer Culture: Remediating Postfeminist Drama," *Feminist Media Studies 3*, no. 1 (2011): 83–98; Angela McRobbie, "Post-Feminism and Popular Culture," *Feminist Media Studies* 4, no. 3 (2004): 255–64; Yvonne Tasker and Diane Negra, "Introduction: Feminist Politics and Postfeminist Culture," in *Interrogating Postfeminism: Gender and the Politics of Popular Culture* (Durham, NC: Duke University Press, 2007).

18. Cole Sprouse has worked regularly as an actor since his departure from *Friends*. It is possible that his work schedule outside of *Friends* made him coming back to the show difficult. However, see chapter 9 for fan theories as to why Ben never appeared again.

19. Hamad, "The One with the Feminist."

20. Ewen, "If I Don't Input," 2.

21. Harrison, "The Hunting of the Snark."

5. *FRIENDS* HAPPY NOT THINKING TOO MUCH

1. Aaron S. Lecklider, "The Real Victims of Anti-Intellectualism," *Chronicle of Higher Education*, September 2017, https://www.chronicle.com/article/The-Real-Victims-of/241101.

2. David Hopkins, "How a TV Sitcom Triggered the Downfall of Western Civilization," *Medium*, March 21, 2016, https://medium.com/@thatdavidhopkins/how-a-tv-sitcom-triggered-the-downfall-of-western-civilization-336e8ccf7dd0.

3. Hopkins, "How a TV Sitcom."

4. Lecklider, "The Real Victims."

5. "*Friends* (1994–2004): Awards," *Internet Movie Database*, https://www.imdb.com/title/tt0108778/awards.

6. *Friends* ended as #8 in the Nielsen ratings for its first season.

7. Bill Carter, "'Friends' Finale's Audience Is the Fourth Biggest Ever," *New York Times*, May 8, 2004, https://www.nytimes.com/2004/05/08/arts/friends-finale-s-audience-is-the-fourth-biggest-ever.html.

8. Hoang Nguyen, "The One where We Ran a Poll on Friends," *Today*, March 5, 2018, https://today.yougov.com/topics/entertainment/articles-reports/2018/03/05/one-where-we-ran-poll-friends; and UK poll: Rhian Daly, "This Is the Nation's Favourite 'Friends' Character," *NME*, January 31, 2018, https://www.nme.com/news/tv/new-yougov-poll-got-nation-vote-favourite-friends-character-2232879.

9. Hopkins, "How a TV Sitcom."

10. Hopkins, "How a TV Sitcom."

11. For more on the racial implications of this moment, see chapter 7.

12. Shelley Cobb, "'I'd Like Y'all to Get a Black Friend': The Politics of Race in *Friends*," *Television & New Media* (2018): 9.

13. Hopkins, "How a TV Sitcom."

6. THIN, WHITE, UPPER-MIDDLE-CLASS *FRIENDS*

1. In Katherine Sender and Margaret Sullivan, "Epidemics of Will, Failures of Self-esteem: Responding to Fat Bodies in *The Biggest Loser* and *What Not to Wear*," *Continuum: Journal of Media and Cultural Studies* 22 (2008): 573–84, they "use 'fat' in accordance with the practice of fat acceptance advocates such as National Association for the Advancement of Fat Acceptance" (573). I, too, use "fat" in this chapter in keeping with the same perspective. However, there are times when fat is used in this chapter when it is still associated with negative judgments in the context of the series.

2. An investigation by Todd Van Lulling reported in "My Year-Long Quest to Uncover the Identity of 'Ugly Naked Guy,'" *Huffington Post*, June 1, 2016, https://www.huffingtonpost.com/entry/ugly-naked-guy-friends_us_573caa4ae4b0ef86171cef1f, found that Jon Haugen likely played the role.

3. Holly Harper, "Fat Monica from 'Friends' Isn't Even Fat," *Odyssey*, April 5, 2016, https://www.theodysseyonline.com/fat-monica-from-friends-isnt-even-fat.

4. Mathilda Gregory, "Fat Monica Was The TV Role Model I Never Expected," *BuzzFeed*, August 16, 2015, https://www.buzzfeed.com/mathildia/why-i-loved-fat-monica.

5. Gregory, "Fat Monica."

6. Gregory, "Fat Monica."

7. Gregory, "Fat Monica."

8. Shelley Cobb, "'I'd Like Y'all to Get a Black Friend': The Politics of Race in *Friends*," *Television & New Media* (2018): 9.

9. Nora Lee Mandel, "Who's Jewish on 'Friends,'" *Lilith*, Summer 1996, https://www.lilith.org/articles/whos-jewish-on-friends/.

10. Mandel, "Who's Jewish."

11. Lindsey Weber, "Friends Countdown: Is Rachel Green Jewish?" *Vulture*, December 17, 2014, https://www.vulture.com/2014/12/friends-countdown-is-rachel-green-jewish.html.

12. Cobb, "I'd Like Y'all," 2.

13. Jillian Sandell, "I'll Be There for You: *Friends* and the Fantasy of Alternative Families," *American Studies* 39, no. 2 (Summer 1998): 143.

14. John Doyle, "Is Nostalgia for *Friends* All About White Privilege?" *The Globe and Mail*, May 12, 2018, https://www.theglobeandmail.com/arts/television/is-nostalgia-for-friends-all-about-white-privilege/article21149416/.

15. Cobb, "I'd Like Y'all," 4.

16. Docfuture1, "A Semi-Alphabetical Listing of Black Actors with Speaking Roles on Friends," *YouTube*, December 16, 2010, https://www.youtube.com/watch?v=oUc0vbSlanM.

17. Cobb, "I'd Like Y'all," 7–8.

18. Rob Fishman, "*Friends*: Discrimination and Mediated Communication," *Discoveries: John S. Knight Institute for Writing in the Disciplines* 7 (Spring 2006): 107–14.

19. Cobb, "I'd Like Y'all," 5.

20. Cobb, "I'd Like Y'all," 9.

21. Sandell, "I'll Be There for You," 152.

22. David Wild, *Friends . . . 'til the End* (Burbank: Warner Brothers Entertainment Inc., 2004): 243.

23. Cobb, "I'd Like Y'all," 10.

24. Cobb, "I'd Like Y'all," 10.

25. Cobb, "I'd Like Y'all," 11.

26. Cobb, "I'd Like Y'all," 11.

27. Cobb, "I'd Like Y'all," 12.

28. Cobb, "I'd Like Y'all."

29. Doyle, "Is Nostalgia for *Friends*."

7. STEREOTYPES, SEXUALITY, AND
FRIEND-LY TENSIONS

1. Hannah Hamad, "The One with the Feminist Critique: Revisiting Millennial Postfeminism with *Friends*," *Television & New Media* (2018): 1–16.

2. Jasmine Lee, "What Did 'Friends' Say about '90s Dating Culture?" *Screen Prism*, December 1, 2015, http://screenprism.com/insights/article/what-did-friends-say-about-90s-dating-culture-what-has-changed-since-then.

3. Lauren Jade Thompson, "'It's Like a Guy Never Lived Here!': Reading the Gendered Domestic Spaces of *Friends*," *Television & New Media* (2018): 8.

4. Thompson, "It's Like a Guy," 5.

5. Carol and Susan mention their friends Deb and Rona in Episode 1.12, "The One with the Dozen Lasagnas," as well.

6. David Wild, *Friends . . . 'til the End* (Burbank: Warner Brothers Entertainment Inc., 2004): 216.

7. David Wild, *Friends . . . 'til the End.*

8. David Wild, *Friends . . . 'til the End*, 43.

9. *Friends* won Outstanding Comedy Series in 1995 and 1997 and was nominated in 1996.

10. Jillian Sandell, "I'll Be There for You: *Friends* and the Fantasy of Alternative Families," *American Studies* 39, no. 2 (Summer 1998): 151–52.

11. David Wild, *Friends . . . 'til the End.*

12. Tijana Mamula, "Homophobic Friends," YouTube, October 9, 2011, https://www.youtube.com/watch?v=SsQ5za-J6I8.

13. Shelley Cobb, "'I'd Like Y'all to Get a Black Friend': The Politics of Race in Friends," *Television & New Media* (2018): 5.

8. *FRIENDS* MUSIC, FASHIONS, AND LOCATIONS WILL ALL BE THERE FOR YOU

1. John Fiske, "The Cultural Economy of Fandom," in *The Adoring Audience: Fan Culture and Popular Media*, edited by Lisa A. Lewis (New York: Routledge, 1992): 43.

2. Anne Marie Todd, "Saying Goodbye to *Friends*: Fan Culture as Lived Experience," *Journal of Popular Culture* 44, no. 4 (2011): 860.

3. Todd, "Saying Goodbye to *Friends*," 860.

4. Shelley Cobb, Neil Ewen, and Hannah Hamad, "*Friends* Reconsidered: Cultural Politics, Intergenerationality, and Afterlives," *Television & New Media* (2018): 3.

5. Willis says she still has the twenty-six single-spaced pages she typed as she watched the pilot over and over.

6. Annie Zalenski, "The Rembrandts' 'I'll Be There for You' Was a Golden Albatross," *AV Club*, June 11, 2015, https://music.avclub.com/the-rembrandts-i-ll-be-there-for-you-was-a-golden-al-1798280808.

7. Zalenski, "The Rembrandts'."

8. Zalenski, "The Rembrandts'."

9. Zalenski, "The Rembrandts'."

10. Zalenski, "The Rembrandts'."

11. Jon Burlingame, *TV's Biggest Hits: The Story of Television Themes from "Dragnet" to "Friends"* (New York: Schrimer Books, 1996).

12. Zalenski, "The Rembrandts'."

13. Zalendski, "The Rembrandts'."

14. Zalenski, "The Rembrandts'."

15. Burlingame, *TV's Biggest Hits*, 198.

16. *Friends Again*, released in 1999 by WEA, and *Friends: The Ultimate Soundtrack*—the last soundtrack released by Reprise/WEA in 2005 after show ended.

17. Hillary Busis, "'Friends': We Ranked All of Phoebe's Songs," *Entertainment Weekly*, May 7, 2014, https://ew.com/article/2014/05/07/friends-phoebe-songs-ranked/.

18. Alexis Rhiannon, "How Phoebe from 'Friends' Comes Up with Her Ridiculous, Hilarious Songs," *Bustle*, May 22, 2015, https://www.bustle.com/articles/83675-how-phoebe-from-friends-comes-up-with-her-ridiculous-hilarious-songs.

19. Shaun Kitchener, "Friends Writer Reveals Surprising Secret behind Phoebe Buffay Song Smelly Cat," *Express*, March 30, 2016, https://www.express.co.uk/showbiz/tv-radio/656725/Friends-writer-Smelly-Cat.

20. Claire Hodgson, "Courteney Cox Reveals She Was REALLY Jealous of the Rachel Haircut," *Cosmopolitan*, September 24, 2014, https://www.cosmopolitan.com/uk/entertainment/news/a29907/courteney-cox-jealous-rachel-haircut-friends/.

21. Natalie Stone, "Jennifer Aniston's 'Rachel' Haircut: The Story behind the Iconic Photo of Her Wildly Popular Friends Hairdo," *People*, October 25, 2017, https://people.com/tv/jennifer-aniston-story-behind-friends-rachel-haircut-photo/.

22. Molly Thomsom, "People Are Weirdly Googling 'What Is the Rachel?' Today, and We Feel 10,000 Years Old," *Hello Giggles*, May 4, 2018, https://hellogiggles.com/news/what-is-the-rachel/.

23. Marianne Mychashiw, "In Honor of the Friends Reunion, See 13 Celebrities Who Have Also Rocked 'The Rachel' Haircut," *In Style*, https://www.instyle.com/beauty/honor-friends-reunion-13-celebrities-who-have-also-rocked-rachel-haircut.

24. Kaila Hale-Stern, "Brie Larson's Captain Marvel Has the Same Haircut We All Had in the '90s," *Mary Sue*, January 25, 2018, https://www.themarysue.com/captain-marvel-the-rachel/.

25. Kat George, "703 Outfits Rachel Wore on 'Friends,' Ranked from Worst to Best (yes, that's every single outfit)," *Bustle*, May 19, 2015, https://www.bustle.com/articles/84388-703-outfits-rachel-wore-on-friends-ranked-from-worst-to-best-yes-thats-every-single-outfit.

26. George, "703 Outfits Rachel Wore."

27. Sean Paajanen, "The Evolution of the Coffee House," *Spruce Eats*, November 9, 2018, https://www.thespruceeats.com/evolution-of-the-coffee-house-765825.

28. Brentin Mock, "What Made Coffeehouse Culture Go Boom?" *City Lab*, January 23, 2017, https://www.citylab.com/life/2017/01/the-cafe-tipping-point/513656/.

29. Alim Kheraj, "This 'Friends' Theory Suggests That the Show Is Actually an Elaborate Set Up for Starbucks, and Huh?" *Hello Giggles*, July 5, 2017, https://hellogiggles.com/lifestyle/food-drink/friends-theory-suggests-show-actually-elaborate-set-starbucks-huh/. See more on this theory in chapter 9.

30. Laurent Muzellec, Christopher Kanitz, and Theodore Lynn, "Fancy a Coffee with Friends in 'Central Perk'?: Reverse Product Placement, Fictional Brands and Purchase Intention," *International Journal of Advertising* 32, no. 3 (2013): 399.

31. Muzellec, Kanitz, and Lynn, "Fancy a Coffee," 400.

32. @kitlovelace, https://twitter.com/kitlovelace/status/879705598367064064?lang=en, as discussed in Eric King, "How Much Coffee Did They Drink?" *Entertainment Weekly*, June 28, 2017, https://ew.com/tv/2017/06/28/friends-coffee-breakdown/; Lovelace figured out the cost of the coffee based on a bill Monica gets in Episode 2.5, "The One with the Five Steaks and an Eggplant." For a cup of coffee and a scone, her bill was $4.12. Lovelace estimated $1.50 per cup as the base cost and added a 20 percent tip.

33. Rosa Prince, "Friends Coffee Shop Opens to Mark 20th Anniversary of Hit Sitcom," *Telegraph*, September 17, 2014, https://www.telegraph.co.uk/news/worldnews/northamerica/usa/11102423/Friends-coffee-shop-opens-to-mark-20th-anniversary-of-hit-sitcom.html.

34. "The Central Perk Orange Sofa in Friends—A History of Culture in 100 Sofas (No. 7)," *Sofa.com*, February 11, 2015, https://www.sofa.com/inspiration-corner/the-central-perk-orange-sofa-in-friends/.

35. Louisa Lim, "'Friends' Will Be There for You at Beijing's Central Perk," *NPR*, January 23, 2013, https://www.npr.org/2013/01/23/170074762/friends-will-be-there-for-you-at-beijings-central-perk.

36. "The Central Perk Orange Sofa."

37. "The Central Perk Orange Sofa."

38. Todd, "Saying Goodbye to *Friends*," 261.

39. Todd, "Saying Goodbye to *Friends*," 261–62.

9. *FRIENDS* AMONG FANS: MEMES AND ALTERNATIVE NARRATIVES

1. Kimberley Dadds, "Which 'Friends' Character Are You Based on These 'Would You Rather' Questions?" *Buzzfeed*, August 10, 2015, https://www.buzzfeed.com/kimberleydadds/which-friends-character-are-you-would-you-rather?utm_term=.bg6jNpnJK#.ao1PmaBlx.

2. Dadds, "Which 'Friends' Character Are You Based on These 'Would You Rather' Questions?"

3. Ann Marie Todd, "Saying Goodbye to *Friends*: Fan Culture as Lived Experience," *The Journal of Popular Culture* 44, no. 4 (2011): 855.

4. Todd, "Saying Goodbye to *Friends*," 855.

5. Todd, "Saying Goodbye to *Friends*," 867.

6. Ali Velez, "'Friends' Fans Beware: This 'Would You Rather' Test is Pretty Brutal," *Buzzfeed*, October 30, 2017, https://www.buzzfeed.com/alivelez/friends-would-you-rather?utm_term=.gx57qnJY6#.nhvgO4yvw.

7. Ketan S. Chitnis, Avinash Thombre, Everett M. Rogers, Arvind Singhal, and Ami Sengupta, "(Dis)similar Readings: Indian and American Audiences' Interpretation of *Friends*," *International Communication Gazette* 68, no. 2 (2006): 131–45.

8. See meme at https://www.elitedaily.com/p/10-friends-thanksgiving-memes-that-define-your-squad-perfectly-13145919.

9. All other memes discussed in this section can be seen at https://www.cosmopolitan.com/uk/entertainment/g17046737/friends-funniest-memes/.

10. Stuart Hall, Jessica Evans, and Sean Nixon, editors, *Representation*, 2nd edition (Thousand Oaks, CA: Sage, 2013).

11. Hall, Evans, and Nixon, *Representation*.

12. Ruth Kinane, "Friends: 7 of The Craziest Fan Theories," *Entertainment Weekly*, September 1, 2017, http://ew.com/tv/2017/09/01/friends-craziest-fan-theories/.

13. Todd, "Saying Goodbye to *Friends*," 854.

14. Larry Bartleet, "11 of the Wildest Friends Fan Theories," *NME*, January 3, 2018, http://www.nme.com/blogs/tv-blogs/11-wildest-friends-fan-theories-2202741.

15. Bartleet, "11 of the Wildest Friends."

16. @MrEmilyHeller posted May 12, 2015.

17. Aurelie Corinthios, "Friends Fans Divided Over Theory Explaining Why Monica and Ross Had to be Siblings," *People*, May 15, 2018, https://people.com/tv/friends-fans-divided-over-ross-monica-theory/.

18. Corinthios, "Friends Fans Divided."

19. Megan Daley, "Friends Fan Theory: Super Dark Interpretation Could Ruin Your Memories," *Entertainment Weekly*, August 27, 2015, http://www.ew.com/article/2015/08/27/friends-fan-theory/.

20. Bartleet, "11 of the Wildest Friends."

21. Kinane, "Friends."

22. Karen Belz, "This 'Friends' Fan Sent Out 100 Tweets about Why Joey and Rachel Should Have Ended Up Together," *Hello Giggles*, August 10, 2017, https://hellogiggles.com/reviews-coverage/tv-shows/this-friends-fan-sent-out-100-tweets-about-why-joey-and-rachel-should-have-ended-up-together/.

23. Bartleet, "11 of the Wildest Friends."

24. Kinane, "Friends."

25. Kinane, "Friends."

26. Christopher Rosa, "The *Gilmore Girls* and *Friends* Worlds Combine in This Fan Theory about Paris Geller," *Glamour*, November 5, 2016, https://www.glamour.com/story/gilmore-girls-friends-fan-theory-paris-geller.

27. Rosa, "The *Gilmore Girls*."

28. Jacob Hall, "The Weird Connections between 'Home Alone' and 'Friends,'" *Slash Film*, December 30, 2016, http://www.slashfilm.com/home-alone-friends-connection/.

29. Andrew Trendell, "New 'Friends' Conspiracy Fan Theory Links the Show to the Rise of Starbucks," *NME*, July 5, 2017, https://www.nme.com/news/tv/new-friends-conspiracy-fan-theory-links-show-rise-starbucks-2098758.

30. Trendell, "New 'Friends' Conspiracy."

31. Brentin Mock, "What Made Coffeehouse Culture Go Boom?" *CityLab*, January 23, 2017, https://www.citylab.com/life/2017/01/the-cafe-tipping-point/513656/.

32. "Starbucks Company Timeline," *Starbucks*, https://www.starbucks.com/about-us/company-information/starbucks-company-timeline.

33. Kenyon Farrow as quoted in Mock, "What Made Coffeehouse Culture Go Boom?"

34. @thetedfox as quoted in Kinane, "Friends."

35. Daley, "Friends Fan Theory."

36. Daley, "Friends Fan Theory."

37. Kinane, "Friends."

38. Daley, "Friends Fan Theory."

39. Bartleet, "11 of the Wildest Friends."

40. @Netflix posted 12:29 PM on January 24, 2018, as quoted in Paul Moore, "Netflix Are Trolling Any New Friends Fans that Find the Show Offensive," *Joe*, https://www.joe.ie/movies-tv/netflix-are-trolling-any-new-friends-fans-that-find-the-show-offensive-614145.

41. Robin Edds, "If 'Friends' Had Been Set in 2015," *BuzzFeed*, February 18, 2015, https://www.buzzfeed.com/robinedds/if-friends-had-been-set-in-2015? utm_term=.tvbYogLE8#.jrq7NLdJP.

10. *FRIENDS* FOREVER

1. James Hibberd, "Friends Is Not Leaving Netflix Jan. 1 after Fandom Panic," *Entertainment Weekly*, December 3, 2018, https://ew.com/tv/2018/12/03/friends-leaving-netflix/.

2. Erin Crabtree, "Netflix Reportedly Paid $100 Million to Keep 'Friends' Throughout 2019," *US Weekly*, December 5, 2018, https://www.usmagazine.com/entertainment/news/netflix-paid-how-much-to-keep-friends-throughout-2019/; Netflix originally paid $118 million for the rights to stream all ten seasons of the series for four years according to Hibberd, "Friends Is Not Leaving."

3. In Chicago in November 2018.

4. Shelley Cobb, Neil Ewen, and Hannah Hamad, "*Friends* Reconsidered: Cultural Politics, Intergenerationality, and Afterlives," *Television & New Media* (2018): 1–9.

5. Margaret Lyons, "*Friends* Invented the Term *Friend Zone*," *Vulture*, December 30, 2014, https://www.vulture.com/2014/12/friend-zone.html.

6. "Words with Friends: The Language of a Sitcom," *Oxford Dictionaries*, September 17, 2013, https://blog.oxforddictionaries.com/2013/09/17/the-language-of-friends/.

7. FunLvnCriminal, "Friend Zone, Truth or Fiction? Ladies?" *Straight Dope*, July 17, 2002, https://boards.straightdope.com/sdmb/showthread.php?t=126060.

8. "Friendzone," *Urban Dictionary*, https://www.urbandictionary.com/define.php?term=Friendzone.

9. For an excellent summary of the timeline of the popularization of the term, see "Friend Zone," *Know Your Meme*, 2012, https://knowyourmeme.com/memes/friend-zone.

10. Including romance novels based on escaping the zone, including Camilla Isley's *Friend Zone: A New Adult Romance* (Pink Bloom Press, 2017) and Kristen Callihan's *Game On Series: The Friends Zone* (Amazon Digital Services, 2015) and multiple advice books about how to get out of the zone, including Raven Wright's *How to Get Out of the Friend Zone* (Amazon Digital Services, 2015) and The Wing Girls' *How to Get Out of the Friend Zone: Turn Your Friendship into a Relationship* (Chronicle Books, 2013).

11. Jeremy Nicholson, "Escape the Friend Zone: From Friend to Girlfriend or Boyfriend," *Psychology Today*, December 15, 2011, https://www.

psychologytoday.com/us/blog/the-attraction-doctor/201112/escape-the-friend-zone-friend-girlfriend-or-boyfriend; and Jeremy Nicholson, "Avoiding the Friend Zone: Becoming a Girlfriend or Boyfriend," *Psychology Today*, March 1, 2013, https://www.psychologytoday.com/us/blog/the-attraction-doctor/201302/avoiding-the-friend-zone-becoming-girlfriend-or-boyfriend.

12. "35 of the Most Heartbreaking (and Hilarious) Friendzones on Film," *Your Tango*, October 25, 2016, https://www.yourtango.com/2014223890/love-dating-absolute-worst-friendzones-film-and-tv.

13. E. J. Dickson, "6 Reasons the 'Friends Zone' Needs to Die," *Salon*, October 12, 2013, https://www.salon.com/2013/10/12/6_reasons_the_friend_zone_needs_to_die/.

14. Dickson, "6 Reasons."

15. Nicholson, "Escape the Friend Zone."

16. Nicholson, "Avoiding the Friend Zone."

17. "Friend Zone," *Know Your Meme*, 2012, https://knowyourmeme.com/memes/friend-zone.

18. See Friendzone Fiona Memes here: https://knowyourmeme.com/memes/friend-zone-fiona.

19. See Friend zoned Phil memes here: http://www.quickmeme.com/Friend-Zoned-Phil/page/1/.

20. http://www.quickmeme.com/Friend-Zoned-Phil/page/1/.

21. http://i.qkme.me/3tbxx5.jpg.

22. Dickson, "6 Reasons."

23. As of December 12, 2018, these were the most visited sites with lists of memorable *Friends* quotes: "10 Unforgettable Lines from Friends," *Channel 24*, November 10, 2016, https://www.channel24.co.za/ShowMax/10-unforgettable-lines-from-friends-20161109; "38 Most Memorable 'Friends' Quotes That Will Always Be There for You—Friends Quotes," *Viralscape*, http://viralscape.com/friends-quotes/; "55 Memorable and Funny Friends TV Show Quotes," *Good Morning Quote*, July 21, 2015, https://www.goodmorningquote.com/funny-friends-tv-show-quotes-sayings/; Candace Ganger, "10 'Friends' Quotes That We Now Use in Everyday Conversation," *Hello Giggles*, March 9, 2016, https://hellogiggles.com/reviews-coverage/friends-quotes-we-love/; Finlay Greig, "50 of the Funniest Friends Quotes and Jokes," *INews.co.uk*, January 5, 2018, https://inews.co.uk/culture/television/friends-quotes-jokes/; "How YOU Doin'? 20 Friends Quotes that Still Won't Answer the Age Old Question," *Brostrick*, June 9, 2015, https://www.brostrick.com/viral/funny-quotes-from-friends-tv-show/; Becky Kirsch, "30 Quotes from *Friends* You're Still Using Every Week," *Pop Sugar*, April 12, 2018, https://www.popsugar.com/entertainment/Friends-TV-Show-Quotes-41453405; Lesley Messer, Ali Gazan, and Michael Rothman, "'Friends Turns 20: The 20 Most Memorable Quotes from the Series," *ABC*

News, September 22, 2014, https://www.digitalspy.com/tv/ustv/a789050/friends-23-phrases-hit-sitcom-gave-us-we-use-every-day-breezy-friend-zone/; Catriona Wightman, "23 Everyday Phrases Friends Gave Us, From the Friend Zone to Breezy," *Digital Spy*, September 22, 2017, https://www.digitalspy.com/tv/ustv/a789050/friends-23-phrases-hit-sitcom-gave-us-we-use-every-day-breezy-friend-zone/; Erin Faith Wilson, "How You Doin'? 10 'Friends' Catchphrases That Will Never Die," *Elite Daily*, January 21, 2016, https://www.elitedaily.com/entertainment/catchphrases-friends-never-die/1348939.

24. Kaitlin Reilly, "'He's Her Lobster!' A 'Friends' Dictionary to Help You Interpret Ross, Rachel, and the Whole Gang," *Bustle*, May 6, 2014, https://www.bustle.com/articles/23107-hes-her-lobster-a-friends-dictionary-to-help-you-interpret-ross-rachel-and-the-whole-gang.

25. Kirsch, "30 Quotes from *Friends*."

26. Cobb, Ewen, and Hamad, *Friends* Reconsidered," 1.

27. Vanessa Golemewski, "The Surprising Success Rate of 'How YOU Doin'?'" *Refinery 29*, September 14, 2015, https://www.refinery29.com/en-us/2015/09/93481/joey-friends-pick-up-lines.

28. Howard Rudnick, "How My Girlfriend's Love For 'Friends' Made Me Realize She's My Lobster," *Elite Daily*, January 14, 2016, https://www.elitedaily.com/dating/friends-lobster-love-girlfriend/1348403.

29. Ganger, "10 'Friends' Quotes."

30. Kirsch, "30 Quotes from *Friends*."

31. Mallory Schlossberg, "What Were Monica Geller's 7 Erogenous Zones on 'Friends'? Let's Take a Look," *Bustle*, May 5, 2014, https://www.bustle.com/articles/23291-what-were-monica-gellers-7-erogenous-zones-on-friends-lets-take-a-look-video; additional hilarious men's responses, with diagrams, can be seen at Robin Edds, "We Asked Men to Label Women's 7 Erogenous Zones, According to Monica Geller," *BuzzFeed*, June 23, 2015, https://www.buzzfeed.com/robinedds/seven-seven-seven-seven-seven.

32. Shalin Jacob, "Here Are the 7 Erogenous Zones in Women, According to Monica Geller from F.R.I.E.N.D.S," *Scoop Whoop*, February 4, 2016, https://www.scoopwhoop.com/Erogenous-Zones-Women-Monica-Seven-FRIENDS/#.7h27x0f50; this list seems to be the one most agreed with in other sources as well. See "What Was the Basic 7 Erogenious Zones as Explained by Monica," *Quora*, https://www.quora.com/What-was-the-basic-7-erogenious-zones-as-explained-by-Monica.

33. Sali Tagliamonte and Chris Roberts, "So Weird; So Cool; So Innovative: The Use of Intensifiers in the Television Series Friends," *American Speech* 80, no. 3 (Fall 2005): 280–300.

34. Kirsch, "30 Quotes from Friends."

35. Catriona Harvey-Jenner, "So THIS is How Janice from Friends' Signature Laugh and Catchphrase Came About," *Cosmopolitan*, August 23, 2016, https://www.cosmopolitan.com/uk/entertainment/news/a45488/how-janice-friends-signature-laugh-catchphrase-created/.

36. Harvey-Jenner, "So THIS is How Janice."

37. Kirsch, "30 Quotes from *Friends*."

38. Alice Leppert, "*Friends* Forever: Sitcom Celebrity and Its Afterlives," *Television & New Media* (2018): 14.

39. Lily Loofbourow, "The End of the *Friends* Era of Gossip, Fame, and Meta-Spinoffs," *The Week*, August 21, 2017, http://theweek.com/articles/719464/end-friends-era-gossip-fame-metaspinoffs.

40. Loofbourow, "The End of the Friends Era."

41. Loofbourow, "The End of the *Friends* Era."

42. Leppert, "*Friends* Forever," 9.

43. Leppert, "*Friends* Forever," 11.

44. *Episodes*, Episode 1.1, "Episode 1."

45. Leppert, "*Friends* Forever."

46. Studio head and Matt LeBlanc nemesis Merc Lapidus is played by John Pankow, who also played Ira, main character Paul Buchman's cousin and friend, in *Mad about You*.

47. Leppert, "*Friends* Forever," 8.

48. Leppert, "*Friends* Forever," 8.

49. Leppert, "*Friends* Forever," 8.

50. Loofbourow, "The End of the *Friends* Era."

51. Loofbourow, "The End of the *Friends* Era."

52. Leppert, "*Friends* Forever."

53. David Wild, *Friends . . . 'til the End* (Burbank: Warner Brothers Entertainment Inc., 2004): 210.

54. Loofbourow, "The End of the *Friends* Era."

55. Loofbourow, "The End of the *Friends* Era."

56. Laura Bradley, "David Schwimmer's Will & Grace Character Is Not Exactly Ross Geller—But He's Close," *Vanity Fair*, October 5, 2018, https://www.vanityfair.com/hollywood/2018/10/david-schwimmer-will-and-grace-character-ross-geller.

APPENDIX

1. "14 Best 'Friends' Episodes to Binge Watch Right Now," *Huffington Post*, January 1, 2015, https://www.huffingtonpost.com/2014/12/31/best-friends-episodes_n_6397222.html; "Best of 'Friends:' 20 Classic Episodes," CNN, April

14, 2017, https://www.cnn.com/2014/09/22/showbiz/gallery/top-friends-episodes/index.html; Alexandra Martell, "The 17 Very Funniest 'Friends' Episodes You Need to Marathon," *Cosmopolitan*, January 1, 2015, https://www.cosmopolitan.com/entertainment/tv/a34624/best-friends-episodes-you-need-to-marathon/; Louisa Mellor, "Friends: 25 Best Episodes," *Den of Geek*, January 9, 2018, http://www.denofgeek.com/us/270092/friends-the-top-25-episodes; Jarett Wieselman, "The 15 Funniest 'Friends' Episodes," *Buzzfeed*, December 31, 2014, https://www.buzzfeed.com/jarettwieselman/funniest-friends-episodes; Catriona Wightman, "Friends: The 25 Best Episodes EVER, ranked," *Digital Spy*, October 15, 2016, http://www.digitalspy.com/tv/ustv/feature/g24315/friends-the-25-best-episodes-ever-ranked/; David Wild, *Friends . . . 'til the End* (Burbank: Warner Brothers Entertainment Inc., 2004).

2. Also made the list of best bottle episodes of all time according to Jessica M. Cruz and Seija Rankin, "From Stewie's Therapy Session to 'The One where No One's Ready': TV's Best Bottle Episodes," *Entertainment Weekly*, May 19, 2018, http://ew.com/tv/bottle-episodes/that-time-family-guy-jumped-the-shark/#friends-the-one-where-no-ones-ready.

BIBLIOGRAPHY

"10 Unforgettable Lines from Friends." *Channel 24*, November 10, 2016. https://www.channel24.co.za/ShowMax/10-unforgettable-lines-from-friends-20161109.

"14 Best 'Friends' Episodes to Binge Watch Right Now." *Huffington Post*. January 1, 2015. https://www.huffingtonpost.com/2014/12/31/best-friends-episodes_n_6397222.html.

"35 Of the Most Heartbreaking (and Hilarious) Friendzones on Film." *Your Tango*. October 25, 2016. https://www.yourtango.com/2014223890/love-dating-absolute-worst-friendzones-film-and-tv.

"38 Most Memorable 'Friends' Quotes That Will Always Be There for You—Friends Quotes." *Viralscape*. http://viralscape.com/friends-quotes/.

"55 Memorable and Funny Friends TV Show Quotes." *Good Morning Quote*. July 21, 2015. https://www.goodmorningquote.com/funny-friends-tv-show-quotes-sayings/.

Akass, Kim, and Janet McCabe, editors. *Reading Sex and the City*. London: I.B. Tauris, 2003.

Allen, Samantha. "How Matthew Perry Forgot Three Years of 'Friends.'" *Daily Beast*. January 27, 2016. https://www.thedailybeast.com/how-matthew-perry-forgot-three-years-of-friends.

Arthurs, Jane. "*Sex and the City* and Consumer Culture: Remediating Postfeminist Drama." *Feminist Media Studies* 3, no. 1 (2011): 83–98.

Bartleet, Larry. "11 of the Wildest Friends Fan Theories." *NME*. January 3, 2018. http://www.nme.com/blogs/tv-blogs/11-wildest-friends-fan-theories-2202741.

Behrens, Deborah. "Hal Linden and Christina Pickles Summer *On Golden Pond*." *LA Stage Times*. October 3, 2017.

Belz, Karen. "This 'Friends' Fan Sent Out 100 Tweets about Why Joey and Rachel Should Have Ended Up Together." *Hello Giggles*. August 10, 2017. https://hellogiggles.com/reviews-coverage/tv-shows/this-friends-fan-sent-out-100-tweets-about-why-joey-and-rachel-should-have-ended-up-together/.

Bernstein, Jonathan. "Friends at 20: How Ross and Rachel started a TV Revolution." *Telegraph*. September 22, 2014. http://www.telegraph.co.uk/culture/tvandradio/11110627/Friends-at-20-how-Ross-and-Rachel-started-a-TV-revolution.html.

"Best of 'Friends:' 20 Classic Episodes." *CNN*. April 14, 2017. https://www.cnn.com/2014/09/22/showbiz/gallery/top-friends-episodes/index.html.

Blatt, Ben. "Which Friends on *Friends* Were the Closest Friends?" *Slate*. May 4, 2014. http://www.slate.com/articles/arts/culturebox/2014/05/friends_chandler_joey_ross_rachel_monica_phoebe_which_friends_were_closest.html.

Borowitz, Andy. "The Big Pitch: Six Ways to Keep Our Favorite Friends Around." *TV Guide*. October 22, 2002: 24–25.

Bradley, Laura. "David Schwimmer's Will & Grace Character Is Not Exactly Ross Geller—But He's Close." *Vanity Fair*. October 5, 2018. https://www.vanityfair.com/hollywood/2018/10/david-schwimmer-will-and-grace-character-ross-geller.

Burlingame, Jon. *TV's Biggest Hits: The Story of Television Themes from "Dragnet" to "Friends."* New York: Schrimmer Books, 1996.

Busis, Hillary. "'Friends': We Ranked All of Phoebe's Songs." *Entertainment Weekly*. May 7, 2014. https://ew.com/article/2014/05/07/friends-phoebe-songs-ranked/.

Callihan, Kristen. *Game On Series: The Friends Zone*. Seattle, WA: Amazon Digital Services, 2015.

Carter, Bill. "'Friends' Finale's Audience is the Fourth Biggest Ever." *New York Times*. May 8, 2004. https://www.nytimes.com/2004/05/08/arts/friends-finale-s-audience-is-the-fourth-biggest-ever.html

"The Central Perk Orange Sofa in Friends—A History of Culture in 100 Sofas (No. 7)." *Sofa.com*. February 11, 2015. https://www.sofa.com/inspiration-corner/the-central-perk-orange-sofa-in-friends/.

Chitnis, Ketan S., Avinash Thombre, Everett M. Rogers, Arvind Singhal, and Ami Sengupta. "(Dis)similar Readings: Indian and American Audiences' Interpretation of *Friends*." *International Communication Gazette* 68, no. 2 (2006): 131–45.

Chocano, Carina. "A Circle of 'Friends.'" *Los Angeles Times*. April 25, 2004: E1, E28–E29.

Cobb, Shelley. "'I'd Like Y'all to Get a Black Friend': The Politics of Race in Friends." *Television & New Media* (2018): 1–16.

Cobb, Shelley, Neil Ewen, and Hannah Hamad. "*Friends* Reconsidered: Cultural Politics, Intergenerationality, and Afterlives." *Television & New Media* (2018): 1–9.

Coontz, Stephanie. *The Way We Never Were: American Families and the Nostalgia Trap*. New York: Basic Books, 1992.

Corinthios, Aurelie. "Friends Fans Divided Over Theory Explaining Why Monica and Ross Had to Be Siblings." *People*. May 15, 2018. https://people.com/tv/friends-fans-divided-over-ross-monica-theory/.

Crabtree, Erin. "Netflix Reportedly Paid $100 Million to Keep 'Friends' Throughout 2019." *US Weekly*. December 5, 2018. https://www.usmagazine.com/entertainment/news/netflix-paid-how-much-to-keep-friends-throughout-2019/.

Cruz, Jessica M., and Seija Rankin. "From Stewie's Therapy Session to 'The One where No One's Ready': TV's Best Bottle Episodes." *Entertainment Weekly*. May 19, 2018. http://ew.com/tv/bottle-episodes/that-time-family-guy-jumped-the-shark/#friends-the-one-where-no-ones-ready.

Dadds, Kimberley. "Which 'Friends' Character Are You Based on These 'Would You Rather' Questions?" *Buzzfeed*. August 10, 2015. https://www.buzzfeed.com/kimberleydadds/which-friends-character-are-you-would-you-rather?utm_term=.bg6jNpnJK#.ao1PmaBlx.

Daley, Megan. "Friends Fan Theory: Super Dark Interpretation Could Ruin Your Memories." *Entertainment Weekly*. August 27, 2015. http://www.ew.com/article/2015/08/27/friends-fan-theory/.

Daly, Rhian. "This is the Nation's Favourite 'Friends' Character." *NME*. January 31, 2018. https://www.nme.com/news/tv/new-yougov-poll-got-nation-vote-favourite-friends-character-2232879.

Dickson, E. J. "6 Reasons the 'Friends Zone' Needs to Die." *Salon*. October 12, 2013. https://www.salon.com/2013/10/12/6_reasons_the_friend_zone_needs_to_die/.

Dilip, Mangala. "The Tragedy of Matthew Perry: Pornstars, Drugs and the Decline of an Icon." *Media, Entertainment, Arts Worldwide*. June 11, 2018. https://meaww.com/the-sad-tragic-life-of-mathew-perry-you-did-not-know-about.

Docfuture1. "A Semi-Alphabetical Listing of Black Actors with Speaking Roles on *Friends*." *YouTube*. December 16, 2010. https://www.youtube.com/watch?v=oUc0vbSlanM.

Doyle, John. "Is Nostalgia for *Friends* All About White Privilege?" *The Globe and Mail*. May 12, 2018. https://www.theglobeandmail.com/arts/television/is-nostalgia-for-friends-all-about-white-privilege/article21149416/.

Edds, Robin. "If 'Friends' Had Been Set in 2015." *BuzzFeed*. February 18, 2015. https://www. buzzfeed.com/robinedds/if-friends-had-been-set-in-2015?utm_term=.tvbYogLE8#. jrq7NLdJP.

———. "We Asked Men to Label Women's 7 Erogenous Zones, According to Monica Geller." *BuzzFeed*. June 23, 2015. https://www.buzzfeed.com/robinedds/seven-seven-seven-seven-seven.

Ewen, Neil. "If I Don't Input Those Numbers . . . It Doesn't Make Much of a Difference: Insulated Precarity and Gendered Labor in *Friends*." *Television & New Media*, (2018): 1–17.

Fishman, Rob. "*Friends*: Discrimination and Mediated Communication." *Discoveries: John S. Knight Institute for Writing in the Disciplines* 7 (Spring 2006): 107–14.

Fishman, Scott. "Christina Pickles on Winning Her First Emmy at 83, 'St. Elsewhere' & 'Friends' Memories." *TV Insider*. September 14, 2018. https://www.tvinsider.com/716066/christina-pickles-interview-break-a-hip-web-series/.

Fiske, John. "The Cultural Economy of Fandom." In *The Adoring Audience: Fan Culture and Popular Media*, edited by Lisa A. Lewis. New York: Routledge, 1992.

"Friend Zone." *Know Your Meme*. 2012. https://knowyourmeme.com/memes/friend-zone.

"Friends (1994–2004): Awards." *Internet Movie Database*. https://www.imdb.com/title/tt0108778/awards.

"Friendzone." *Urban Dictionary*. https://www.urbandictionary.com/define.php?term=Friendzone.

FunLvnCriminal. "Friend Zone, Truth or Fiction? Ladies?" *Straight Dope*. July 17, 2002. https://boards.straightdope.com/sdmb/showthread.php?t=126060.

Ganger, Candace. "10 'Friends' Quotes That We Now Use in Everyday Conversation." *Hello Giggles*. March 9, 2016. https://hellogiggles.com/reviews-coverage/friends-quotes-we -love/.

George, Kat. "703 Outfits Rachel Wore on 'Friends,' Ranked from Worst to Best (yes, that's every single outfit)." *Bustle*. May 19, 2015. https://www.bustle.com/articles/84388-703-outfits-rachel-wore-on-friends-ranked-from-worst-to-best-yes-thats-every-single-outfit.

Ghahremani, Tanya. "The Central Perk Couch on 'Friends' Was Always Unoccupied for a Reason You Never Noticed." *Bustle*. January 16, 2015. https://www.bustle.com/articles/59138-the-central-perk-couch-on-friends-was-always-unoccupied-for-a-reason-you-never-noticed.

Golemewski, Vanessa. "The Surprising Success Rate of 'How YOU Doin'?'" *Refinery 29*. September 14, 2015. https://www.refinery29.com/en-us/2015/09/93481/joey-friends-pick-up-lines.

Graeber, David. *Bullshit Jobs: A Theory*. New York: Simon & Schuster, 2018.

Gregory, Mathilda. "Fat Monica Was the TV Role Model I Never Expected." *BuzzFeed*. August 16, 2015. https://www.buzzfeed.com/mathildia/why-i-loved-fat-monica.

Greig, Finlay. "50 of the Funniest Friends Quotes and Jokes." *INews.co.uk*. January 5, 2018. https://inews.co.uk/culture/television/friends-quotes-jokes/.

Hale-Stern, Kaila. "Brie Larson's Captain Marvel Has the Same Haircut We All Had in the '90s." *Mary Sue*. January 25, 2018. https://www.themarysue.com/captain-marvel-the-rachel/.

Hall, Jacob. "The Weird Connections between 'Home Alone' and 'Friends.'" *Slash Film*. December 30, 2016. http://www.slashfilm.com/home-alone-friends-connection/.

Hamad, Hannah. "The One with the Feminist Critique: Revisiting Millennial Postfeminism with *Friends*." *Television & New Media* (2018): 1–16.

Hanson, Peter. *The Cinema of Generation X: A Critical Study*. Jefferson, NC: McFarland, 2002.

Harper, Holly. "Fat Monica From 'Friends' Isn't Even Fat." *Odyssey*. April 5, 2016. https://www.theodysseyonline.com/fat-monica-from-friends-isnt-even-fat.

Harrison, Andrew. "The Hunting of the Snark: Friends, 20 Years On." *New Statesman*. September 12, 2014. http://www.newstatesman.com/culture/2014/09/hunting-snark-friends-20-years.

Harvey-Jenner, Catriona. "So THIS Is How Janice from Friends' Signature Laugh and Catchphrase Came About." *Cosmopolitan*. August 23, 2016. https://www.cosmopolitan.com/uk/entertainment/news/a45488/how-janice-friends-signature-laugh-catchphrase-created/.

Hibberd, James. "Friends Is Not Leaving Netflix Jan. 1 after Fandom Panic." *Entertainment Weekly*. December 3, 2018. https://ew.com/tv/2018/12/03/friends-leaving-netflix/.

Hodgson, Claire. "Courteney Cox Reveals She Was REALLY Jealous of the Rachel Haircut." *Cosmopolitan*. September 24, 2014. https://www.cosmopolitan.com/uk/entertainment/news/a29907/courteney-cox-jealous-rachel-haircut-friends/.

Hopkins, David. "How a TV Sitcom Triggered the Downfall of Western Civilization." *Medium*. March 21, 2016. https://medium.com/@thatdavidhopkins/how-a-tv-sitcom-triggered-the-downfall-of-western-civilization-336e8ccf7dd0.

"How YOU Doin'? 20 Friends Quotes that Still Won't Answer the Age Old Question." *Brostrick*. June 9, 2015. https://www.brostrick.com/viral/funny-quotes-from-friends-tv-show/.

Hurley, Laura. "Friends Almost Let Joey and Phoebe Have the Best Sex Joke Ever." *Cinema Blend*. 2015. https://www.cinemablend.com/television/Friends-Almost-Let-Joey-Phoebe-Have-Best-Sex-Joke-Ever-84947.html.

Isley, Camilla. *Friend Zone: A New Adult Romance*. Pink Bloom Press, 2017.

Jacob, Shalin. "Here Are the 7 Erogenous Zones in Women, According to Monica Geller from F.R.I.E.N.D.S." *Scoop Whoop*. February 4, 2016. https://www.scoopwhoop.com/Erogenous-Zones-Women-Monica-Seven-FRIENDS/#.7h27x0f50.

Johnson, Zach. "Courteney Cox and Brian Van Holt Break Up, David Arquette Reveals." *E! News*. October 31, 2013. https://www.eonline.com/news/476095/courteney-cox-and-brian-van-holt-break-up-david-arquette-reveals.

Kane, Jessica. "13 Reasons David Schwimmer Is Ross Geller." *Huffington Post*. December 6, 2017. https://www.huffingtonpost.com/2013/07/22/david-schwimmer-ross-geller_n_3636512.html.

Kheraj, Alim. "This 'Friends' Theory Suggests That the Show Is Actually an Elaborate Set Up for Starbucks, and Huh?" *Hello Giggles*. July 5, 2017. https://hellogiggles.com/lifestyle/food-drink/friends-theory-suggests-show-actually-elaborate-set-starbucks-huh/.

Kinane, Ruth. "Friends: 7 of the Craziest Fan Theories." *Entertainment Weekly*. September 1, 2017. http://ew.com/tv/2017/09/01/friends-craziest-fan-theories/.

King, Eric. "How Much Coffee Did They Drink?" *Entertainment Weekly*. June 28, 2017. https://ew.com/tv/2017/06/28/friends-coffee-breakdown/.

Kirsch, Becky. "30 Quotes from *Friends* You're Still Using Every Week." *Pop Sugar*. April 12, 2018. https://www.popsugar.com/entertainment/Friends-TV-Show-Quotes-41453405.

Kitchener, Shaun. "Friends Writer Reveals Surprising Secret behind Phoebe Buffay Song Smelly Cat." *Express*. March 30, 2016. https://www.express.co.uk/showbiz/tv-radio/656725/Friends-writer-Smelly-Cat.

Lecklider, Aaron S. "The Real Victims of Anti-Intellectualism." *Chronicle of Higher Education*. September 2017. https://www.chronicle.com/article/The-Real-Victims-of/241101.

Lee, Jasmine. "What Did 'Friends' Say about '90s Dating Culture?" *Screen Prism*. December 1, 2015. http://screenprism.com/insights/article/what-did-friends-say-about-90s-dating-culture-what-has-changed-since-then.

Leppert, Alice. "*Friends* Forever: Sitcom Celebrity and Its Afterlives." *Television & New Media* (2018): 1–17.

Lim, Louisa. "'Friends' Will Be There for You at Beijing's Central Perk." *NPR*. January 23, 2013. https://www.npr.org/2013/01/23/170074762/friends-will-be-there-for-you-at-beijings-central-perk.

Loofbourow, Lily. "The End of the *Friends* Era of Gossip, Fame, and Meta-Spinoffs." *Week*. August 21, 2017. http://theweek.com/articles/719464/end-friends-era-gossip-fame-metaspinoffs.

Lyons, Margaret. "*Friends* Invented the Term *Friend Zone*." *Vulture*. December 30, 2014. https://www.vulture.com/2014/12/friend-zone.html.

Mamula, Tijana. "Homophobic Friends." *YouTube*. October 9, 2011. https://www.youtube.com/watch?v=SsQ5za-J6I8.

Mandel, Nora Lee. "Who's Jewish on 'Friends.'" *Lilith*. Summer 1996. https://www.lilith.org/articles/whos-jewish-on-friends/.

Martell, Alexandra. "The 17 Very Funniest 'Friends' Episodes You Need to Marathon." *Cosmopolitan*. January 1, 2015. https://www.cosmopolitan.com/entertainment/tv/a34624/best-friends-episodes-you-need-to-marathon/.

"Matthew Perry: 'My Drug and Alcohol Addiction Was So Public.'" *News.com.au*. August 21, 2015. https://www.news.com.au/entertainment/celebrity-life/matthew-perry-my-drug-and-alcohol-addiction-was-so-public/news-story/f74e61177a59bbdaa119a079c2de8968.

McRobbie, Angela. "Post-Feminism and Popular Culture." *Feminist Media Studies* 4, no. 3 (2004): 255–64.

Mellor, Louisa. "Friends: 25 Best Episodes." *Den of Geek*. January 9, 2018. http://www.denofgeek.com/us/270092/friends-the-top-25-episodes.

Messer, Lesley, Ali Gazan, and Michael Rothman. "'Friends Turns 20: The 20 Most Memorable Quotes from the Series." *ABC News*. September 22, 2014. https://www.digitalspy.com/tv/ustv/a789050/friends-23-phrases-hit-sitcom-gave-us-we-use-every-day-breezy-friend-zone/.

Miller, Claire Cain. "The Divorce Surge Is Over, but the Myth Lives On." *New York Times*. December 2, 2014. https://www.nytimes.com/2014/12/02/upshot/the-divorce-surge-is-over-but-the-myth-lives-on.html.

Mock, Brentin. "What Made Coffeehouse Culture Go Boom?" *CityLab*. January 23, 2017. https://www.citylab.com/life/2017/01/the-cafe-tipping-point/513656/.

Moore, Paul. "Netflix Are Trolling Any New Friends Fans That Find the Show Offensive." *Joe*. https://www.joe.ie/movies-tv/netflix-are-trolling-any-new-friends-fans-that-find-the-show-offensive-614145.

Mottram, James. "Elliott Gould: 'I Didn't Have a Drug Problem. I Had a Problem with Reality.'" *Independent*. July 22, 2012. https://www.independent.co.uk/news/people/profiles/elliott-gould-i-didnt-have-a-drug-problem-i-had-a-problem-with-reality-7956788.html.

Muzellec, Laurent, Christopher Kanitz, and Theodore Lynn. "Fancy a Coffee with Friends in 'Central Perk'?: Reverse Product Placement, Fictional Brands and Purchase Intention." *International Journal of Advertising* 32, no. 3 (2013): 399.

Mychashiw, Marianne. "In Honor of the Friends Reunion, See 13 Celebrities Who Have Also Rocked 'The Rachel' Haircut." *In Style*. https://www.instyle.com/beauty/honor-friends-reunion-13-celebrities-who-have-also-rocked-rachel-haircut.

Nededog, Jethro. "Matthew Perry Says He Can't Remember 3 Years of Shooting 'Friends' Because of Alcohol and Drug Abuse." *Business Insider*. January 25, 2016. https://www.businessinsider.com/matthew-perry-friends-drug-abuse-2016-1.

Nguyen, Hoang. "The One where We Ran a Poll on Friends." *Today*. March 5, 2018. https://today.yougov.com/topics/entertainment/articles-reports/2018/03/05/one-where-we-ran-poll-friends.

Nicholson, Jeremy. "Escape the Friend Zone: From Friend to Girlfriend or Boyfriend." *Psychology Today*. December 15, 2011. https://www.psychologytoday.com/us/blog/the-attraction-doctor/201112/escape-the-friend-zone-friend-girlfriend-or-boyfriend.

———. "Avoiding the Friend Zone: Becoming a Girlfriend or Boyfriend." *Psychology Today*. March 1, 2013. https://www.psychologytoday.com/us/blog/the-attraction-doctor/201302/avoiding-the-friend-zone-becoming-girlfriend-or-boyfriend.

Paajanen, Sean. "The Evolution of the Coffee House." *Spruce Eats*. November 9, 2018. https://www.thespruceeats.com/evolution-of-the-coffee-house-765825.

Prince, Rosa. "Friends Coffee Shop Opens to Mark 20th Anniversary of Hit Sitcom." *Telegraph*. September 17, 2014. https://www.telegraph.co.uk/news/worldnews/northamerica/usa/11102423/Friends-coffee-shop-opens-to-mark-20th-anniversary-of-hit-sitcom.html.

"The Real Life Partners of the Friends Cast." *Go Social*. http://www.gosocial.co/the-real-life-partners-of-the-friends-cast/.

Reilly, Kaitlin. "'He's Her Lobster!' A 'Friends' Dictionary to Help You Interpret Ross, Rachel, and the Whole Gang." *Bustle*. May 6, 2014. https://www.bustle.com/articles/23107-hes-her-lobster-a-friends-dictionary-to-help-you-interpret-ross-rachel-and-the-whole-gang.

Rhiannon, Alexis. "How Phoebe from 'Friends' Comes Up with Her Ridiculous, Hilarious Songs." *Bustle*. May 22, 2015. https://www.bustle.com/articles/83675-how-phoebe-from-friends-comes-up-with-her-ridiculous-hilarious-songs.

Rosa, Christopher. "The *Gilmore Girls* and *Friends* Worlds Combine in This Fan Theory about Paris Geller." *Glamour*. November 5, 2016. https://www.glamour.com/story/gilmore-girls-friends-fan-theory-paris-geller.

Rudnick, Howard. "How My Girlfriend's Love for 'Friends' Made Me Realize She's My Lobster." *Elite Daily*. January 14, 2016. https://www.elitedaily.com/dating/friends-lobster-love-girlfriend/1348403.

Sandell, Jillian. "I'll Be There for You: *Friends* and the Fantasy of Alternative Families." *American Studies* 39, no. 2 (Summer 1998): 141–55.

Schlossberg, Mallory. "What Were Monica Geller's 7 Erogenous Zones on 'Friends'? Let's Take a Look." *Bustle*. May 5, 2014. https://www.bustle.com/articles/23291-what-were-monica-gellers-7-erogenous-zones-on-friends-lets-take-a-look-video.

Schuman, Rebecca. "You've Reached the Winter of Our Discontent." *Longreads*. March 2018. https://longreads.com/2018/03/27/youve-reached-the-winter-of-our-discontent/.

Sender, Katherine, and Margaret Sullivan. "Epidemics of Will, Failures of Self-esteem: Responding to Fat Bodies in *The Biggest Loser* and *What Not to Wear*." *Continuum: Journal of Media and Cultural Studies* 22 (2008): 573–84

Shugart, Helene A. "Isn't It Ironic? The Intersection of Third-Wave Feminism and Generation X." *Women's Studies in Communication* 24, no. 2 (2001): 131–68.

Skladany, Skladany. "Which Famous 'Friends' Episode Defines Your Life?" *Zimbio*. http://www.zimbio.com/quiz/HYRuG8gpOlk/Famous+Friends+Episode+Defines+Life.

So, Andrea. "Why Monica and Chandler Are Secretly the Heroes of 'Friends.'" *Hello Giggles*. October 5, 2015. https://hellogiggles.com/reviews-coverage/monica-and-chandler-relationship-model/.

"Starbucks Company Timeline." *Starbucks*. https://www.starbucks.com/about-us/company-information/starbucks-company-timeline.

Stone, Natalie. "Jennifer Aniston's 'Rachel' Haircut: The Story behind the Iconic Photo of Her Wildly Popular Friends Hairdo." *People*. October 25, 2017. https://people.com/tv/jennifer-aniston-story-behind-friends-rachel-haircut-photo/.

Tagliamonte, Sali, and Chris Roberts. "So Weird; So Cool; So Innovative: The Use of Intensifiers in the Television Series Friends." *American Speech* 80, no. 3 (Fall 2005): 280–300.

Tasker, Yvonne, and Diane Negra. "Introduction: Feminist Politics and Postfeminist Culture." In *Interrogating Postfeminism: Gender and the Politics of Popular Culture*. Durham, NC: Duke University Press, 2007.

Taylor, Ella. *Prime-Time Families: Television Culture in Postwar America*. Berkeley: University of California Press, 1989.

Thompson, Lauren Jade. "'It's Like a Guy Never Lived Here!': Reading the Gendered Domestic Spaces of *Friends*." *Television & New Media* (2018): 1–17.

Thomsom, Molly. "People Are Weirdly Googling 'What Is the Rachel?' Today, and We Feel 10,000 Years Old." *Hello Giggles*. May 4, 2018. https://hellogiggles.com/news/what-is-the-rachel/.

Todd, Anne Marie. "Saying Goodbye to *Friends*: Fan Culture as Lived Experience." *Journal of Popular Culture* 44, no. 4 (2011): 854–71.

Toobin, Jeffrey. "Gawker's Demise and the Trump-Era Threat to the First Amendment." *New Yorker*. December 19 and 26, 2016. https://www.newyorker.com/magazine/2016/12/19/gawkers-demise-and-the-trump-era-threat-to-the-first-amendment.

Trendell, Andrew. "New 'Friends' Conspiracy Fan Theory Links the Show to the Rise of Starbucks." *NME*. July 5, 2017. https://www.nme.com/news/tv/new-friends-conspiracy-fan-theory-links-show-rise-starbucks-2098758.

Van Lulling, Todd. "My Year-Long Quest to Uncover the Identity of 'Ugly Naked Guy.'" *Huffington Post*. June 1, 2016. https://www.huffingtonpost.com/entry/ugly-naked-guy-friends_us_573caa4ae4b0ef86171cef1f.

Velez, Ali. "'Friends' Fans Beware: This 'Would You Rather' Test Is Pretty Brutal." *Buzzfeed.* October 30, 2017. https://www.buzzfeed.com/alivelez/friends-would-you-rather?utm_term= .gx57qnJY6#.nhvgO4yvw.

Webber, Stephanie. "Tate Donovan Was 'Dying Inside' Working with Ex Jennifer Aniston on 'Friends.'" *Us Magazine.* September 5, 2018. https://www.usmagazine.com/celebrity-news/ news/tate-donovan-dying-inside-working-with-ex-jennifer-aniston-on-friends/.

Weber, Lindsey. "Friends Countdown: Is Rachel Green Jewish?" *Vulture.* December 17, 2014. https://www.vulture.com/2014/12/friends-countdown-is-rachel-green-jewish.html.

Weldon, Sarah. "A Definitive Timeline of Jennifer Aniston and Justin Theroux's Relationship." *Cosmopolitan.* February 16, 2018. https://www.cosmopolitan.com/entertainment/ celebs/a18208604/jennifer-aniston-justin-theroux-relationship-timeline/.

"What Was the Basic 7 Erogenious Zones as Explained by Monica." *Quora.* https:// www.quora.com/What-was-the-basic-7-erogenious-zones-as-explained-by-Monica.

Wieselman, Jarett. "The 15 Funniest 'Friends' Episodes." *Buzzfeed.* December 31, 2014. https:/ /www.buzzfeed.com/jarettwieselman/funniest-friends-episodes.

Wightman, Catriona. "Friends: The 25 Best Episodes EVER, Ranked." *Digital Spy.* October 15, 2016. http://www.digitalspy.com/tv/ustv/feature/g24315/friends-the-25-best-episodes-ever-ranked/.

———. "23 Everyday Phrases Friends Gave Us, from the Friend Zone to Breezy." *Digital Spy.* September 22, 2017. https://www.digitalspy.com/tv/ustv/a789050/friends-23-phrases-hit-sitcom-gave-us-we-use-every-day-breezy-friend-zone/.

Wild, David. *Friends . . . 'til the End.* Burbank, CA: Warner Brothers Entertainment Inc., 2004.

Wilson, Erin Faith. "How You Doin'? 10 'Friends' Catchphrases That Will Never Die." *Elite Daily.* January 21, 2016. https://www.elitedaily.com/entertainment/catchphrases-friends-never-die/1348939.

The Wing Girls. *How to Get Out of the Friend Zone: Turn Your Friendship into a Relationship.* San Francisco: Chronicle Books, 2013.

"Words with Friends: The Language of a Sitcom." *Oxford Dictionaries.* September 17, 2013. https://blog.oxforddictionaries.com/2013/09/17/the-language-of-friends/.

Wright, Raven. *How to Get Out of the Friend Zone.* Seattle, WA: Amazon Digital Services, 2015.

Yapalater, Lauren. "A Timeline of Jennifer Aniston's Relationships." *Buzzfeed.* August 13, 2012. https://www.buzzfeed.com/lyapalater/a-timeline-of-jennifer-anistons-relationships.

"The Year 1994 from the People History." *People History.* July 10, 2018. http://www. thepeoplehistory.com/1994.html.

Zalenski, Annie. "The Rembrandts' 'I'll Be There for You' Was a Golden Albatross." *AV Club.* June 11, 2015. https://music.avclub.com/the-rembrandts-i-ll-be-there-for-you-was-a-golden-al-1798280808.

INDEX

ABOUT THE AUTHOR

Jennifer C. Dunn is a professor of rhetoric and public culture. She has been teaching about gender, media, popular culture, and rhetoric at Dominican University since 2009, where she also serves as the Communication Arts and Sciences Department chair. Her research focuses on identities and representations in media, research methods, and cultural history. Her coauthored (with Stephanie L. Young) textbook *Pursuing Popular Culture: Methods for Researching the Everyday* (2016) was recently recognized as the Best Book for Use in the Classroom (2018) by the Midwest Popular Culture Association; and her most recent coauthored (with Jimmie Manning) book, *Transgressing Feminist Theory and Discourse: Advancing Conversations across Disciplines* (2018), was awarded the Innovator Award for Outstanding Edited Collection (2019) from the Sexual Orientation and Gender Identity Caucus of the Central States Communication Association. In her spare time, she enjoys watching television, tasting craft beers with her husband, and playing with her Greyhound, Fiona Gallagher.